MATCHES

IN THE

GAS TANK

Trial By Fire in the Armstrong Cult

A MEMOIR | CARLA POWERS

 **bright sky press**
HOUSTON, TEXAS

2365 Rice Boulevard, Suite 202
Houston, Texas 77005
www.brightskypress.com

10   9   8   7   6   5   4   3   2   1

Library of Congress Cataloging-in-Publication Data

Powers, Carla, 1955-
Matches in the gas tank : trial by fire in the Armstrong cult / by Carla Powers.
p. cm.
ISBN 978-1-933979-53-3 (hardcover)
1. Powers, Carla, 1955—Childhood and youth. 2. Powers, Carla, 1955—Family.
3. Radio Church of God. 4. Armstrong, Herbert W.—Influence.
5. Big Sandy (Tex.)—Religious life and customs. 6. Big Sandy (Tex.)—Biography.
7. Cults—United States—Case studies.
8. Fathers and daughters—United States—Case studies. I. Title.

BX6177.3.T4P69 2009
289.9—dc22   2009028205
[B]

Edited by Nora Shire
Book design by Bright Sky Press
Cover design by Wyn Bomar Design
Printed in the United States of America

MATCHES

IN THE

GAS TANK

···

Trial By Fire in the Armstrong Cult

A MEMOIR | CARLA POWERS

bright sky press
HOUSTON, TEXAS

TABLE OF CONTENTS

DISCLAIMER

This memoir records facts and events as my mother, my brothers, and I remember them. It is possible that some of our recollections are flawed by the passage of time. The lenses through which we view our years in the Armstrong cult indubitably differ from others who shared similar experiences, though many facts, events, and doctrines described in this book are verifiable. I have reconstructed most conversations from actual events; some are composites. Occasionally an event is out of chronological sequence. I have often changed the names and identifying characteristics of the living to protect their identity.

More information about Herbert W. Armstrong and the Radio Church of God may be found through web links at **www.matchesinthegastank.com**.

To my family

CHAPTER ONE

The Betrayer
Feast of Trumpets 1967

I fidgeted in the brown Samsonite chair. I had no padding in my bony twelve-year-old body to cushion the hard metal surface. The morning service had lasted two hours and twenty minutes. After an hour-long lunch break, half of which was spent waiting in line to pay for and fill our plates at the church's buffet lunch, we were back in the cavernous auditorium listening to a sermonette.

Mother sat in an aisle seat, her long skirt covering her legs, with a Bible open in her lap, taking notes in a steno pad. Eight-year-old Steve was positioned between Mother and me, within pinching distance. He was behaving at the moment, drawing cars in a Big Chief tablet with a fat pencil. Dan, who was almost three, was asleep on a tattered quilt folded on the rough concrete under our feet. Who knew where Dad was or what he was doing.

I clipped a ballpoint pen to my spiral notebook and laid them on the empty chair beside me. My middle finger had a blister above the first knuckle, and it hurt to write. Besides, I'd heard this stuff a hundred times. I didn't need to write it down again.

I took in as much of the room as I could by moving only my eyes. If I turned my head or body, a deacon might spank me for failing to pay attention. There were no signs that this was a church. No crosses. No stained glass, altars, candles, or chalices. Ministers didn't wear religious vestments; the choir didn't wear robes. The only seating was row upon row of double-hinged folding chairs. The air wasn't fragrant with incense. It smelled of East Texas sweat and dust and pine.

The building was prefabricated steel: a two-story rectangular box the size of a football field with a gabled roof. Windows set high above the sight line provided filtered light. The interior walls were wavy sheets of metal, mounting bolts exposed, sprayed with gray insulation. Industrial light fixtures hung from the beams. Solid-steel double doors were placed along the perimeter. Large fans circulated the muggy air.

A young preaching elder was speaking on a stage containing a podium, a Steinway concert grand, choir risers, and enormous bouquets of pastel gladiolas. God's message boomed out from massive stereophonic speakers mounted on the walls.

This is the first day of the month of Tishri. We sound a trumpet, just as the Israelites sounded the shofar, to celebrate the time when Jesus Christ will return to fight the followers of Satan and establish the Kingdom of God.

We are God's people — the select handful who will be spared when this earth is annihilated in the great battle between Christ and the Antichrist. Those who call themselves Christians but defile Christ by celebrating pagan holidays like Christmas and Easter will have to choose: follow God's way as taught by his apostle, Herbert W. Armstrong, or die in the Lake of Fire.

The minister looked at the congregation and let his words soak in for a few seconds before he closed his Bible and left the stage.

Mr. Lundgren, our close family friend, sat on the front row. After the announcements, he and three other trumpeters moved to the proscenium to present the special music. Before the sermon, deacons passed the offering bowl for the second time that day. Mother scrounged in her purse and extracted a wrinkled dollar bill that she placed in the dish. I contributed a quarter of my babysitting money.

Herbert W. Armstrong walked to the podium and stood before the mike. He was middle-aged, prosperously rotund, and clothed in a fine wool suit. His full gray hair was combed straight back; his cold stare pierced rimless glasses. His bearing was regal; he radiated authority. His voice exuded charisma: a beautiful baritone with the timbre of a finely-tuned instrument. Each word was delivered with absolute conviction because, as he told us, God had given him extraordinary intelligence and speaking ability so he could serve as His emissary on earth.

"Eight years from today, Jesus Christ will return," Mr. Armstrong thundered, holding his Bible in the air. A sea of heads nodded in assent. "Before that glorious day, God's church and His people will suffer great persecution."

I felt chill bumps rise on my skin. I got queasy every time a minister prophesied about the end times. As excited as I was about fleeing to Petra before the Great Tribulation and being at Christ's return for the Kingdom of God, I was disappointed that I'd never experience a full human life. No husband, no family, no home. Those things didn't exist in God's Kingdom.

God's apostle continued:

We have built fences and gates to keep away unwanted visitors, but fences and gates don't stop talk. Recently the *Dallas Morning News* reported that we were conducting animal sacrifices.

We must be even more vigilant when we speak with outsiders. Do essential business with them, but do not tell them anything about God's Work or His people. They are ignorant. They do not understand.

I have had a vision that there is a Judas among us. Some day in the future, someone who may be sitting in this very room will bring persecution on God's people and His church. He will tell nonbelievers about God's teachings and cast them in a light that will incite hatred against us.

I thought about my friends and neighbors. None of them would ever betray us. Then a thought popped in my head. *What if it's me?*

CHAPTER TWO

The Call
January 2002

It was a rainy, unseasonably hot night. I'd had a tough day at the office, capped off by a meeting with the president of the company.[1]

The elegant forty-something assistant with slightly-curled blonde hair touching her waist motioned me toward the corner office on the 45th floor. It was half again larger than my own corner office on the 48th floor.

I smoothed the skirt of my best suit. Armani — black label. Heaven forbid I'd go into battle without armor.

"Good afternoon, Carla. Come on in," he said in impeccable English with an ever-so-slight European accent. Following custom, we moved to a round glass table placed before a bank of windows. "Why is it that I only see you when there's bad news?"

I grinned. "You never want to talk about the good stuff. You just read the reports. When you're unhappy, you have to grill me."

His eyes twinkled behind stylish glasses, then turned serious. "American litigation still frustrates me. It is so expensive. Discovery. Juries. Plaintiffs' lawyers making tens of millions of dollars. How can we cut these costs?"

I'd tried to deal with that question many times and gave my usual but not entirely satisfying answer. "We constantly evaluate the way we allocate the work, who we pick as counsel, our internal systems, and the vendors but there's only so much we can do. I'm always open to new ideas."

We spent the next hour reviewing budgets, cost estimates, and historical expenditures.

At 8:30, I trudged up the carpeted rear stairway in my home, high-heeled Ferragamos in hand. Reaching the sitting room at the top, I flicked on a PBS program about Mark Twain. The phone rang before I'd shed my suit.

No! I'd been talking all day. The last thing I wanted to do was pick up the blasted phone. But something told me to check Caller ID. My cousin Margie. I had to answer the damn thing.

I don't rate high in Margie's book. Years ago she decided that it was unchristian of me not to make up with "that sweet old man." I have neither the patience nor the inclination to remind her of all the things her convenient memory has expunged. If she wants to believe I'm unforgiving, so be it. She wouldn't have called unless there was major news. We don't share pleasantries.

"I hate to do this to you," she said, stretching *hate* until it broke into two Arkansas syllables, "but your Dad has had a massive heart attack. He's in a coma, on life support."

It took a couple of seconds to tune out Ken Burns. Dad. Coma. Life support. The old terrorist was finally going to croak? My well-worn adrenals kicked in. I felt a surge of hot electricity run down both arms. My heart hammered and my breathing became shallow. "When?"

"Saturday. Took the hospital a while to find any family." The twang faded as she let the accusation register.

"Where is he?"

"Longview. Good Shepherd Hospital."

I remembered the Longview of my childhood. While I had no recollection of the hospital, I imagined a shabby post-war pink brick building with cracks running through it, dingy paint, flickering fluorescent lights, and an uneven asphalt parking lot. A sad place to die.

"What else?" I felt cold and worked to keep my teeth from chattering.

"They think he's brain-dead. You've gotta get up there. Now."

"Why?" I answered with practiced nonchalance.

"They need a family member to take him off the breathing machine. I'm not close enough kin." She couldn't conceal her irritation at not being able to run the show.

"That's too bad."

"Yes, it is."

"All right, Margie. I'll take care of it."

I wrote down the names and phone numbers she gave me.

"Hey," I thought, "this is no big deal." A goofy picture of John Wayne drawling, "Pilgrim, pull the plug and get the hell out of Dodge" kept running through my head. It occurred to me that I should feel at least a little sad. But I didn't. My father was being kept alive by a machine, and I didn't give a damn. I felt like a sorry excuse for a human being.

I called the first number Margie supplied and spoke with the ICU nurse. "My dad, Charles Powers, is in ICU. Can you please tell me what's happening with him?"

"Oh, good. I was hoping you'd get in touch. He's in real bad shape. I'm sorry."

"Thanks for your concern. I don't think it has registered yet." I felt myself take the part of the grieving daughter. *Get a grip. You're just acting that way because you think you're supposed to. This is business.* "Can you give me some details?"

"Pneumonia. Kidney failure. Liver failure. Congestive heart failure. He's not responsive. You don't want welfare to come in here."

"Welfare? Why would they get involved?"

"He's been in the hospital more than forty-eight hours and he's not in any condition to make decisions. If your family doesn't take charge of his care, welfare'll do it. They never discontinue life support, so he'd be hooked up until he died. No telling how long that might be."

So, he could linger for weeks or months? The implications hit me. I'd be back in Dad's world, forced to stare down the demons I'd run away from years before.

"I have to drive from Houston," I said, "and it wouldn't be safe to get on the road now. Is tomorrow morning soon enough?"

"Yeah. I'll tell the doctor."

"Should I give a 'do not resuscitate' order?"

"I would if I was in your shoes. I'll put it in his chart."

I asked the nurse to call if Dad's condition changed and promised to arrive before 10 a.m.

It struck me as odd that he hadn't asked any questions about my relationship with my father. The fact that I have Dad's DNA was enough to place decisions about his life and death in my hands. While my feelings for the man lying in ICU miles away had been cauterized decades ago, the responsibility that had been placed upon me constricted my lungs and made my heart beat faster.

I went downstairs to the octagonal solarium, enclosed in French doors and windows. The shutters were open, but the foggy, wet night had swallowed the backyard. The pool was invisible. A timer had switched on an abstract wood floor lamp, but the room felt dark and gloomy. I clicked on a blue ceramic table lamp. Still not enough light. I flipped the switches on eight recessed cans in the ceiling and, at last, the hobgoblins disappeared.

I dug my toes into the deep-pile area rug and paced its perimeter. I stopped in front of an 8X10-inch photograph in a green faux marble frame. The woman in the picture is young, wearing an emerald-green dress with a bolero jacket and dusty black flats. She leans one elbow against a 1953 cream-colored, ragtop Ford Crestliner with red-ringed white sidewalls. Hitched to the car is a silver trailer with a red door. Mary Ann Holloway Powers is tall, with a Coke bottle figure. Her hair is auburn, lifted slightly off her shoulders by the breeze. The face is pretty, maybe even beautiful, but the tilt of her head makes it impossible to see for sure.

Beside her a crew-cut young man wears a black-and-white plaid shirt, muscles binding the short sleeves. There is a hint of a smile on the heart-shaped face. His eyes seem to disappear as he squints into the sunlight. His forehead is slightly furrowed from the glare. Outstretched hands support a toddler. She's small, fat-cheeked, with wisps of blonde hair. Her dress is red-and-white polka dots, covered by ruffled organza. Red socks, white shoes, and on her wrist, a red satin ribbon that holds a tiny red ring. Mommy and Daddy and I were at the Radio Church of God campus in Big Sandy, Texas. It was October 1956 at the Feast of Tabernacles.

I put the picture down and tugged at the highlighted ash-brown hair on the top on my head, digging my fingernails into my scalp until it bled. <u>Damn him. Damn him to hell.</u> I shook my head. The question that I had asked myself a thousand times screamed into my head. *How could he have thrown us away?* Despite him, Steve, Dan, and I had managed to turn out okay. At least it looked that way from the outside.

Now Dad's life was over. None of those things he could have done to make the past right would happen. I felt a tiny bit of sorrow. Not so much for him but for the life he had wasted. Regret for his choice to miss so much. I knew that the pain and emptiness he had felt over these years — when he was sober enough to feel anything — exceeded the emotional debt he owed to us.

For a minute or two I battled with myself. Should I call my brothers?

At Thanksgiving in 1997, while preparing for our annual ritual of looking at old family slides, Mother reminded us that Dad would turn seventy the next March. It was a topic we had always avoided. This time she wouldn't leave it alone. "I bought a $10,000 burial policy on your dad."

Dan and I gave each other a puzzled look. Steve kept fiddling with the projector, but I could read the same reaction on his face. He finally broke the silence. "Why?"

"The Powers don't have any money. They're going to expect you to pay for the funeral. I don't want that expense dumped on you."

"I'm glad you did something," I replied. "It hadn't occurred to me."

"Will we go?" Dan asked. "I never knew him."

Mother was indignant. "Of course you'll go. We'll all be there. It's the decent thing to do."

It would be odd to be at Dad's funeral, taking our places as family, gathering to pay homage to a man who, aside from being a sperm donor, had done nothing but wreak havoc with our lives. I had fantasized about standing away from the mourners during the service, like an observer happening upon a stranger's burial.

As I paced the solarium in my stocking feet, absently straightening the wooden game board on the coffee table, it struck me that this scenario had never occurred to us: It was one thing to show up as they lowered the casket into the earth, but something entirely different to be at his side when he died. Maybe even to have a role in the decision about when and how he would die. My first thought was to spare my mother and siblings, and just handle it. But then I considered how I would feel if Steve or Dan had gotten the call from Margie and had chosen not to tell me.

I dialed Steve's number. He worked twelve-hour days, six days a week at his company, PowerTech Propellers, overseeing the foundry he'd recently built, along with all the business details from finish work to shipping. He was visibly exhausted at Christmas, and I was worried about his health.

"Hi, Steve, it's me. You okay? Gloria and the kids?"

"We're fine, Sis. What's going on?"

"Margie just called. It's Dad." I recapped what I knew. "If I were him, I wouldn't want us making this decision."

Steve answered quickly and without reservation, "We'll make him comfortable until he dies and then give him a decent burial." I could hear the compassion in his voice.

"I agree that it's the decent thing to do and we'll do it. But I don't understand how you can be so forgiving."

"I'm not sure I do, either, but it's how I feel. He spent his whole life demanding dignity and didn't get it. We'll make sure he gets it now."

Dad had ranted about the Armstrongs taking away his dignity, about Mother and us children failing to give him dignity. I wanted to tell Steve that dignity, like respect, has to be earned, but he knew that. There was no point in making an issue of it now.

"How do you feel about keeping him hooked to a respirator?" I asked, getting back to business.

"If he's brain-dead?"

"You're okay with the DNR order?"

"Absolutely."

"I guess we need to tell Mother."

"Yeah, but she's over in Longview tonight playing cards with Dorothy and James. Let's not bother her till morning."

"What about Dan?"

"We should call him tonight," Steve answered.

Our younger brother surprised me by saying he would be there.

"I'd been thinking about going to see him," he said, "but I couldn't get past the weirdness of introducing myself to my own dad. I don't even know what he looks like. If I don't go, the only memory I'll have is of him lying in a casket."

That settled, I stepped inside my dressing room. Cedar-lined, it was the size of my parents' old bedroom. I flipped through the clothes I wear when I need confidence — perfectly tailored Escada suits, Chanel jackets that purr couture, no-nonsense Akris pantsuits, impeccably cut Bill Blass dresses. When I arrived at the hospital, no one would see the head of litigation for one of the largest companies in the world. I would just be the no-name daughter of an indigent alcoholic. For the first time in three decades, whether I liked it or not, my identity would be linked to my father's.

A thought came into my mind about how Dad would look after fifty years of drinking two six-packs of Old Milwaukee or a bottle of rotgut whiskey a day. For the last three decades, he'd lived one step from the gutter. I knew the doctors and nurses expected me — his child — to show up in a Budweiser T-shirt and dirty, low-slung jeans.

I settled on an Yves Saint Laurent black pinstriped pantsuit and slipped into it. Ridiculous. Only ministers wear suits to the hospital. Besides, it telegraphed that I was trying to make a statement. I needed something that looked effortless. The black Escada jacket and gray Armani slacks didn't work, either. They looked funereal, and I wasn't in mourning. I pulled out a lavender silk jacket, black wool shell, and gray pants. Yes. Pearl and diamond ear studs and a single strand of pearls. With black flats and a classic Chanel purse, I was competent and in control.

I laid out the clothes for the morning, poured a long snifter of cognac, and retreated to a guest bedroom where I could be alone. I lit a candle and picked up a tiny oval frame that held Dad's third-grade picture. I had begun to display the picture in a guest room when the resemblance between that boy and my own son became unmistakable. Looking into the black-and-white photo, now yellowed with age, I saw a little boy in overalls with a mischievous grin and terrible bowl-cut hair, ready to conquer the world. I stared at it to see if I could cry, but there were no tears.

Tomorrow I would make the trip back to East Texas. If I took U.S. 59 north to 259, it would take a little less than four hours. The journey away had taken a lifetime.

CHAPTER THREE

Headin' for Home

I drove north on U.S. 59, whizzing past the southbound rush-hour traffic, dense as a parking lot. I would have happily traded places with the commuters. The goings-on of an ordinary working day felt orderly, safe. What I was doing — fusing a world I had erased with the one I had carefully created — was anything but. It seemed odd that the world wasn't stopping to acknowledge that this wasn't just any day.

Enough. I pulled into the drive-through of a Popeye's and ordered a greasy biscuit and coffee. *I was allowing myself to become melodramatic.* I'd spend the day taking care of family business — the story I told the office to avoid well-intentioned condolences — and be done with it. This didn't have to be an existential experience. I stirred a half-packet of Sweet'N Low and some creamer into the steaming cup and popped a Ridley Pearson mystery into the Jag's tape player. I didn't hear a word. My thoughts bounced like marbles dumped on the floor.

The last time I had seen Dad was in Mount Vernon, Arkansas. It was in 1972, and I was seventeen years old. Mother, my brothers, and I were visiting Mother's family over the Christmas holiday. Dad's brother Vernon asked us to come to his home for a visit. We had no idea that Dad would be there, or we wouldn't have gone within a hundred miles.

The houses where Uncle Vernon and Aunt Lois lived in the 1950s, '60s, and '70s blend into a single picture in my mind: a decrepit farmhouse on a dusty, denuded lot two miles from the remains of a backwoods hamlet. The yard contained car parts and rusted farm equipment. A wringer washer and two hounds — Inky and Blackie — graced the porch. Inside, wiring was strung along the walls and ceiling. Some of the rough cabinets in the kitchen were concealed by muslin curtains; holes in furniture were camouflaged with doilies or towels. It was dark, damp, fetid. But there was one new thing in the house: a big TV that was always on.

Aunt Lois, who apparently suffered from agoraphobia, wasn't one for extending hospitality. We were there to visit and go, not to eat.

We'd been at the house for an hour when Dad showed up. I saw him get out of his car and willed myself to be invisible. My heart raced; my belly spasmed. Uncle

Vernon met Dad outside and handed him something from his wallet. As they walked inside, I could see and smell that Dad was drunk.

"What the hell are you doing here?" he snarled at us, as we huddled together in a corner. "The good Mr. Armstrong wouldn't think much of you celebrating Nimrod's birthday, would he?" He made no effort to come toward us. We responded in kind.

He said nothing more and stormed out of the house with three five-dollar bills crumpled in his hand. Dan was eight, Steve fourteen.

After that encounter, Dad stayed completely out of our lives. And none of us made any effort to contact him. Years passed. I didn't think of myself as having a father. He didn't see me graduate from college or law school or move up in my profession. Steve didn't have a father to celebrate his successes in real estate development, construction, or the propeller business. Dan never had a dad to listen when he was the youngest disc jockey in Texas or see him as a TV sports-caster or watch his award-winning production work. Dad missed the drama of our dysfunctional relationships, marriages, and divorces. He never saw any of his four grandchildren. None of us even told our kids that they had a grandfather.

Dad did call me, once. A few months after I started practicing law. It was at home on a Saturday. I grabbed the brown wall phone in the kitchen on the fourth ring and leaned against a rattan breakfast room chair.

"Carla, it's Daddy," he said. I sucked in air. My hands barely held onto the receiver. *What should I say?*

"I've been thinking that I might want to see you," he continued.

"That would be nice," I responded. My racing thoughts belied my polite reply. *I don't want him to know where I live. I don't want him back in my life, terrorizing me or stealing my car or my money.* Then my more reflective self butted in. *What if he had changed? What if he'd finally realized what he had lost and was trying to make amends?*

"I heard from Sis that you're a lawyer," he went on. *Maybe I had won him back with my achievements. Maybe I had proven that I was too valuable to throw away.*

"Yes, I started practicing in Houston in May."

"You're old enough now to know the truth."

"Pardon?"

"Everything happened because your Mother was a whore," he said. "She was screwing Garner Ted Armstrong — goddamned bastard minister. That's what caused all my troubles."

I felt like he'd punched me in the face. *How many times had I heard the same crock of shit?* "Daddy, I'd like to see you, to have a relationship with you. But we'd have to start fresh. I don't want to think or talk about the past. It's over. We can't change it. I won't listen to…anything bad you have to say about Mother."

"You don't sound like my little girl anymore," he accused.

Before I could pull together my defense, I heard the dial tone in my ear.

Reality set in. He still scared the hell out of me. How did he get my phone number? The listing was in my husband's name, not mine. Did he have my address? Was he going to show up at my home unannounced? I spent the weekend in a dither.

Years later, I wondered whether, after the passage of so much time, I could get to know some of the Powers clan. I called Margie.

"Your dad's doing good," she said.

"When did you see him?" I asked.

"He brought a little travel trailer up to Mom and Daddy's house. He's staying up here for a while," Margie answered

"Still drinking?" I queried.

"Not that I could tell. I could talk to him about seeing you."

"Margie, I know you mean well, but he'd have to prove that he's a different person before I'd want anything to do with him."

"The Bible tells us that we have to forgive and forget." Margie took on the tone of a Sunday school teacher.

"It would be foolish for me to let him turn my life upside down."

"It's your choice whether or not to be Christian," she sniffed. "He's not the man you remember. He's old and sweet."

"If he tells you that he wants to talk to me, I'll talk to him over the phone."

"I'll let you know."

Margie reported back that Dad wasn't interested in talking with me. But she wouldn't let me off the hook. "It's your responsibility to make up with him."

While I wasn't willing to reach out to Dad directly, I found an indirect way to determine whether he was the person Margie described. I sent pictures of my boy to Dad's sister, Hattie, and her husband Jake — knowing that they would display them on top of their television. Since Dad visited them every now and then, he would see the photos of his grandson. I hoped his heart would melt when he saw the round face with chubby cheeks, snaggleteeth, and laughing eyes. A boy who looked like the third grader in the oval-framed picture in my guest room.

It didn't work. Dad didn't pay any attention to the picture. When Uncle Jake asked why he didn't get back in touch with his family, Dad responded, "I have no family. My family is dead." After fifteen years of therapy, I felt the same about him.

I hadn't been back to northeast Texas for years, but by the time I got up past Lufkin, a hard-wired affinity for the place kicked in. It felt like I was coming home. Rolling hills covered in pine, oak, sweet gum, and dogwood were intensely familiar. Thick, humid air smelled of hay and compost and earth, the way it always had. Clear, sandy-bottomed streams ran toward the muddy Sabine. All I needed was a cane pole and worms to snag catfish, bream, and crappie. Herefords and Brangus grazed in wide pastures and drank from ponds stocked by the local Extension Service. Two-lane farm-to-market roads bisected the counties. Pumpjacks looking like oversized grasshoppers still faithfully extracted oil from the ground.

Yet, despite the natural beauty, I felt the poverty creep into my soul the way cold settles in a muscle. I saw things I'd never noticed as a kid. Countryside strewn with trailer parks where corroding aluminum houses, wheels removed, sat permanently atop cinder blocks. Old frame houses in weed-choked yards, littered with broken-down cars. Porches sagging under chrome kitchen chairs and couches with their stuffing poking out. Driveways consisting of dirt ruts made by generations of pick-'em-up trucks. Abandoned taxidermy shops, barbeque or catfish restaurants advertised with hand-lettered signs, bait and tackle shacks, flea markets and stands selling wooden flowers for the yard. Roadkill, from housecats to deer, smeared on the pavement and shoulders of the road.

When this was my home, these signs of despair were life. Because they were unremarkable, I took no notice. Now I watched the scenery with a morbid fascination usually reserved for a kaleidoscope of blue and red lights on the side of the road. Families of nine (or a solitary octogenarian) in a paint-blistered building restored to marginal habitability: cracked walls, patched roof, water-stained ceiling. Little is new other than the Dollar Stores, the Chicken Expresses, and the gas station markets. People thirty-five look fifty-five because they've never been to a dentist. Just trying to survive wears their bodies out, giving them swollen arthritic knuckles at forty and undiagnosed cancers at fifty. Lots of folks are one government check away from homelessness.

There is a place in my heart for these scrappy people who have lived their entire lives as I lived the first eighteen of mine. They remind me that, but for the grace of God, this is where I would be. No amount of success has been able to erase the fear that tells me that if I'm not perfect, this is where I will end up again.

I suddenly realized that I couldn't just drive up to the hospital in Longview to assist my father's death. I needed to see where I'd come from with the eyes of the woman I'd worked so hard to become. I needed to go deep into the woods of Upshur County, Texas, equidistant from the Arkansas border to the northeast, the Oklahoma border to the north, and the Louisiana border to the east.

When my father first saw Big Sandy in 1955, it was his land of opportunity. It took him five years to work up the courage, but in 1960 he pulled up stakes in Arkansas and headed there to live with his brethren in Christ in the Radio Church of God. He brought my mother, my brother Steve and me; Dan hadn't yet been born.

I did have business to attend in Longview first, and I knew I would handle it appropriately. But if I was ever going to understand myself, I realized I had to understand my father's choices. What makes a man destroy his life? I had blocked this life from my memory, but it still came back to me in nightmares. As the cold fingers of the past attempted to close around my soul, I knew I had to unlock their grasp.

I had to go back to Big Sandy.

CHAPTER FOUR

Being Powers

Five years ago, if you'd asked my friends — lawyers, doctors, business executives — about my upbringing, they would have shrugged, "Middle-class. Good family. Comfortably well-off." That's what I wanted them to believe.

When I started college, I slammed the door on the past. Facts about my low-class life had cost me a bid to the sorority of my choice — Phi Mu — when Barb, a girl from my hometown, black-balled me. Being poor and strange had trumped being smart and articulate. From that point, I shed friends from high school because they might share facts that suggested I wasn't who I pretended to be.

The day I moved into the Pearce dorm at Louisiana Tech, I jettisoned everything that no longer suited me. I was a girl who'd been in the Miss Louisiana pageant, attending college on a full academic scholarship. My clothes were nice; no one knew they were secondhand. My parents were divorced and my dad lived in Texas. I attended the Fellowship Baptist Church in Dubberly, Louisiana, though I didn't mention that it was only once a year. I ate whatever I wanted, wore makeup, hiked my skirts to my thighs, and partied on Friday nights.

In law school, few people asked questions about my background. But when I started work at one of Houston's silk-stocking law firms in 1979, I was thrust into the world of Republican power and old money, or at least as old as money gets in Houston. Some of my colleagues were the children of ambassadors, scions of society, and powerful judges. I was clueless how to act like I belonged.

I decided I could most readily figure out how to look the part. I sported a two-carat diamond solitaire on my left ring finger and a Rolex on my wrist. I drove a new white Cadillac Coupe Deville with baby-blue interior. But dressing well was my signature.

It was a firm tradition to hold a coffee in the Petroleum Club to welcome new lawyers, and I was determined to make a good impression. Days before the event, I asked the maitre d' to show me around the club. I imitated nonchalance as I took in the crystal chandeliers, elegant silver, dark-skinned waiters wearing black livery, and gleaming china. I was going to need something special to wear.

At Lord & Taylor, I scoured the racks of Evan-Picone suits. I could have gone to Brooks Brothers for a perfectly appropriate A-line khaki skirt, navy blazer, and buttoned-down oxford shirt with a yellow bow-tie, but I refused to look like a man with long hair. Standing in the receiving line with two other new associates at the coffee, I felt good about my light-taupe suit, dark-taupe blouse, and matching shoes, but had no clue how to juggle a cup and saucer while shaking hands. Another newbie had the same problem and spilled a cup of coffee all over her white suit. At the end of the event, I congratulated myself on handling everything just right. When I got home that night and took off my jacket, I found a tag pinned beneath the right armhole. Every time I'd shaken someone's hand, I'd flashed the tag.

It was much more difficult to act the part from the inside. I felt awkward, socially inept, comparatively uneducated, parochial, afraid that I would do or say something wrong. I knew I wasn't the helpless little girl from Big Sandy anymore, but I had no idea who I was. The idea of self-analysis was too scary to consider. I conjured a picture of success and molded myself to become it. I would try and win big cases. I would become a partner in a big law firm. I would demonstrate my accomplishments through ever-larger W-2s and grander possessions.

I married a handsome, melancholy, insecure man a decade older than me who twisted me in knots with an endless loop of giving and withholding affection. Shortly before we were to marry, I learned that he'd had a relationship with another woman while I was away in law school.

I sat on a rock outside his apartment overlooking Cross Lake in Shreveport, Louisiana, arguing with myself. *He's always unhappy. He'll never change. Is he capable of loving me?* But Mother was pushing. She was ready to start a new life and wanted someone else to be responsible for me. It didn't occur to me that that someone could be me. "You need to forgive him," she said. "You were away in law school, and he was home by himself." I convinced myself that if I could make him happy, he would love me forever.

Three years after graduating from law school, I was already into a one-woman attack on every power structure I could find. I was drawn to environments where I had to ward off lecherous old men, claw for substantive assignments, work impossibly hard to please people who were incapable of being pleased, and do battle with sexism and racism. I infiltrated the neighborhoods, restaurants, and clubs of the wealthy and privileged just to prove I could, while privately disdaining their exclusivity. I became the first female partner in my next firm by working so hard and generating so much revenue that the old guard couldn't deny me entrance to their fraternity. I tried and won cases by eviscerating witnesses, giving tearful, flag-waving closing arguments, and fighting over every inch of ground. Judges called me talented; adversaries called me Bitch.

I graduated to driving a Mercedes, shopping at Neiman's, and living in a house I couldn't afford in one of the most exclusive neighborhoods in Houston. I worked at convincing myself that my husband really was entertaining customers every night until the clubs closed. I gave no thought to the idea that there might be more to life than rising to the top of my profession and acquiring stuff.

When I turned thirty-five, I was in the middle of a divorce, childless, and broke, but kicking butt in my law firm, putting in 2,500 billable hours, and generating $2 million a year in business. I sat in the middle of my king-sized bed in a 15X25-foot master bedroom, sobbing. The furniture was gone, except for the bed, one night table, and a lamp. The double French doors and large windows were uncovered; the oak floors bare. Now my estranged husband wanted to come home after ditching me for another woman for the third time. I wasn't going to be suckered again. But questions kept rolling around in my head. *Had he ever loved me? Was there something wrong with me? Was I too messed up for anyone to love?*

That night I started to talk to God. Well, not exactly talking. More like yelling. *What have I done to deserve this?* I pumped both fists toward the heavens. *Why have I been through so much hell? What do I need to change?* After leeching myself of pain for half an hour, I felt a presence envelop me. It was the embodiment of warmth, softness, and love. I was comforted. This surprised me because the God I met in the Radio Church of God was an angry, vengeful God. I wondered whether there might be a power in the universe very different from the one Herbert W. Armstrong and his son, Garner Ted, described.

This experience left me convinced that something in my life needed to change. I had worn a disguise so long that I didn't know the person behind it and had no clue how to begin to chisel it away. I was terrified at what it might look like. I considered my options.

Organized religion wasn't one. When I thought of religion, it took me back to the Armstrongs and the Radio Church of God. I couldn't accept anything with the same label, even though I'd tried. At the Methodist church in my neighborhood, I sat in the genteel, milquetoast environment with tears streaming down my face. I cried because I envied the people who found comfort in rituals they had performed since childhood. I cried from the irrational fear that I would be singled out from the pulpit for public humiliation. I cried for my inability to share the beliefs that seemed to come so easily to others.

One of my friends was into genealogy. As I bit into my tuna and avocado sandwich, she said, "Knowing something about my ancestors has helped me understand myself a little better." I quietly chewed, and she continued, "Do you know anything about your family?"

"Not really," I answered and took another bite so I wouldn't have to say any more. Having been separated from biological family by the church, I hardly knew any of them and had no sense of family history.

"It's been fun to find the records. Like solving a mystery," she said, dipping her spoon into a bowl of Crumley Cogwheel's heavenly, but sinful, cheese soup.

I perked up. I'd always been a mystery fan. "How'd you get started?"

"I first decided that I'd research my mom's family. I wanted to focus on one family line at a time. Then I got information about where my grandfather was born and started with census records. I'll help you, if you want."

I was curious.

From the time I was a little girl, Dad had told me, "You're special. You're a Powers." I remembered his boozy tales of the family's past prominence. I had lovingly handled the second-edition Webster's dictionary neatly inscribed "Dr. Justice F. Powers" and ancient medical saddlebags stored in the recesses of Mother and Dad's bedroom closet. It seemed impossible that one of my forebears was a doctor, a man with education and standing in the community. If it were true, I couldn't imagine how the family had fallen so far, so fast.

I began spending Saturdays in Houston's Clayton Genealogical Library, a vast repository of census records, cryptic old New England texts, church records, maps, ship's logs. Every week I learned new information that I wanted to share with someone.

"I finally found him." I was giddy as I spoke into the phone. "The first Powers. He was actually named Power. He was fifteen or sixteen when he came to America in the 1650s. Can you believe it?"

"That's great," Mother answered politely.

"His wife was a first-generation American whose family got here not long after the Mayflower. They were Puritans. Her name was Triall. Her Mother was called Thankslord. Pretty amazing, isn't it?" I flipped through the stacks of copies I'd piled on the dining room table, looking for more interesting tidbits.

When I finally stopped prattling on, Mother asked, "Did you find out anything about the Holloways or Matchetts?"

"No. I'll get to your family after I finish with the Powers."

I went to Massachusetts and Vermont to hold in my hands the dirt my ancestors had farmed and touch their gravestones. Perhaps it was wishful thinking, but I concluded that they were tough, clannish, adventurous, and independent.

The most elusive character I found was Dr. Justice Franklin Powers — my dad's great-grandfather — whose saddlebags were stuffed in my parents' closet. I saw his headstone in a cemetery in Mount Vernon, Arkansas, and asked Dad's sister Hattie what she knew about him. "He was a doctor. During the war, he was taken prisoner by the Yankees. His son, who was my grandfather, was a doctor, too." I pressed for more, but that was the extent of her knowledge.

While researching, I learned that after his father's death, Dr. Justice moved from Vermont to Missouri where he attended the Missouri Medical College. I drove to the little town of Hermitage in the Missouri Ozarks looking for clues. After buying a large, round gourd painted as Santa Claus in an old country store, I chatted with the owner.

"I've been working on my family genealogy and think my great-great-grandfather lived here. Do you know where I'd find old records?"

"I don't know about the records, but there is a little museum across the road." She pointed to a frame building three blocks away.

I perked up. "Is it open?"

"No. We don't keep it open anymore. No one seemed interested in visiting."

"I'd love to see it," I said, unable to conceal my disappointment.

"If you like, I can call the man who has the key and see if he'll let you take a look."

Thirty minutes later I was inside a treasure-trove of mid-19ᵗʰ century Americana. On the counter were three copies of a book with an oxblood cover, *History of Hickory County*. Written by F. Marion Wilson in 1907, it had no index but contained information dating back to the 1840s. I bought a copy and had to read each page to find references to Dr. J. F.

"...Northern and Eastern people were not generally welcome in a slave state....A Vermont Yankee doctor came into the neighborhood of Preston before the Civil War, and to make himself agreeable, and a fit man to live in a slave state, bought a crippled 'nigger,' cheap, and went with the Confederacy when the Civil War came up."[2]

I was disgusted.

The doctor must have convinced his neighbors that he was a true believer in slavery because he was elected to the Missouri legislature from 1854–1858. In 1861, he got the townsfolk "greatly excited about the issues of the Civil War."[3] Justice Franklin and several others formed a company of Confederate state guards, where he served as a Regimental Surgeon. The historian unloaded on the feckless Dr. Powers:

It is probably, not out of place, and justice to say, that...Dr. J. F. Powers, a Vermont Yankee, who owned a cripple negro,...were the principal and earnest advocates of secession in and about Preston, and were the cause of the organization of the Mabary company, with John Mabary, as Capt. because he had the nerve and courage while Robertson, Powers et al were purely noise makers and agitators.[4]

I wasn't able to reconcile this man with the one described in the Mount Vernon, Arkansas, newspaper as "loved and respected in Mount Vernon and surrounding communities where he cared for the sick, rich or poor, exalted or lowly, with the same courtesy."[5] It made me wonder about the influence he wielded over his children and grandchildren. Was he a chameleon who changed his views to curry favor from those around him? Did he realize that it was an abomination to own another person and change his ways? Or, did he fill his children with hate and bile? I thought about my grandfather and his coldness, my dad and his vitriol.

Dr. Justice's son, Dr. Justus Tavner Powers — my great-grandfather — was the last person I researched. His story was short. He received his medical degree at St. Louis Medical College in the 1880s and returned to Mount Vernon to practice with his father. But Dr. J. T. died young, leaving his widow Matilda with five children, including young Charley, my grandfather, who was twelve.

I concluded that the combination of Matilda and J. T.'s genes led to a less-than-optimal result in three of their five children. Gertrude and Kate married, had children, and lived comfortable middle-class lives; their grandchildren became lawyers, professors, and a nationally known football coach. In contrast, Ethel and Frank never married or left home. Then there was my grandfather, Charley. After serving in France during World War I, he married Cora Jackson, a mentally ill Louisiana Cajun whom we grandkids called Boggie Cora.

I pieced together from various family members that Charley and Cora moved to Wyoming in the 1920s, barely surviving on money he made as an itinerant butcher. Four babies arrived in ten years: Vernon, Hattie, Jack and, in 1928, my dad, Charles. Granddaddy couldn't keep a job to support them. The destitute family returned to Arkansas during the Depression and moved into the old home-place with Matilda. Granddaddy never held another steady job. Matilda supported the clan by running a store where she sold clothing and women's fancy hats that she had made.

Mother's version of Dad's childhood and young adult years provided me with some perspective for his behavior later in life. She said that Charley and Cora didn't pay any attention to the kids or provide any discipline. Dad was the wildest of the bunch and, as a child, demonstrated a penchant for setting fires. He used pages of the Sears Roebuck catalogue (left in the outhouse for toilet paper) to torch the family privy. Determined to do whatever he wanted whenever the hell he wanted to do it, Dad announced in the fifth grade that he wasn't going to school anymore. No one stopped him.

By 1948, when Dad was twenty-one, he was making a decent living doing auto body work in Conway, the Faulkner County seat.

When I started to piece together my history, I realized that I didn't know anything about my parents' courtship. I asked Mother, "How did you and Dad meet?"

"It was in the fall of 1948. I was fifteen and walking arm in arm on the road with two of my girlfriends, wearing rolled-up jeans, long-tailed shirt, and saddle oxfords." Her eyes focused on the scene playing in her mind and her lips curled in a smile.

I interrupted, "Were you in the ninth or tenth grade?"

"Tenth. I was just about to turn sixteen. Anyway, a Ford roared up behind us. The guy driving had on a brown leather bomber jacket with a fake fur collar. He pulled up beside us and slowed to a crawl." She stared off in the distance.

"Well...?" I urged.

"He was so handsome! He stared in my eyes, and said, 'Hello, Beautiful.'"

CHAPTER FIVE

The Sharecropper's Daughter

Mother met me the minute I stepped off the elevator at the hospital in Longview. I was trying to get my bearings when she grabbed my arm and propelled me away from the worn waiting room with mismatched chairs. We turned down a long, unwelcoming corridor relieved by a handful of solid doors. It was strangely quiet, and I didn't see a soul. The lights were low and my first thought was that we were in the wrong place. It looked like an office suite.

Every time in my adult life when I had seen Mother, even after a brief absence, we hugged. Today she was so focused on getting me to the ICU that we didn't embrace or exchange greetings.

"He's down this way," she said, linking her arm through mine and moving me forward.

"Where're we going?" I felt like a horse in harness.

"The ICU. Just down the hallway."

I came to a stop and faced her. "Mother, I'm not going in there. Forget it."

"You have to see him. He looks good. You won't believe it," she said, starting to drag me down the hall again.

I wondered what was going on with her. We had spoken by phone twice that morning before I arrived, and I knew that she'd been there for more than an hour. Was she there to support us in making decisions about Dad's medical care or was this about something else?

"I came here to take care of what I have to take care of, and leave. I don't want to see him."

"Carla, he's your dad. You're not about to let him die without seeing him."

"He's not conscious, is he?"

"Of course not. It's like he's just asleep….So young-looking."

There are times when it's easier to do what Mother wants than to argue with her. But as we walked, my heart started to thump. We made a right across the threshold of a room with three or four curtained-off beds. I took a deep breath. The only thing I felt was anxiety. In the bed to my right, I saw the top of a gray head and a mound that looked like a bundle of laundry.

"That him?" I was whispering, afraid to look at the man's face.

"No, silly. Does that look like your dad?" She pointed at a bed against the far wall.

I tiptoed across the room and anchored myself six feet away from the foot of the bed. Mother walked right up and grabbed his hand. She stroked his fingers. "See? Isn't he just like I said? He just doesn't have any teeth."

Here was the man who had beaten her, deafened her in one ear, called her a whore, and left her to fend for herself and three children — and she was running her fingers through his hair! They had been divorced for more than thirty years and she was acting like his wife. It was as surreal as a Fellini movie.

I forced myself to look at the figure connected to a bank of tubes and monitors. She was right. I would have known him anywhere. He didn't look like a seventy-four-year-old with a cirrhotic liver and heart failure. He was still a bull of a man. Massive biceps strained the sleeves of his hospital gown. Clean-shaven, with short salt-and-pepper hair and firm jowls, he could have passed for fifty-five.

"Come say something to him."

That familiar feeling came over me again. I feared he would sit up in his bed and roar that we should leave him the hell alone. I couldn't say a word. I couldn't move.

A man about forty dressed in nursing scrubs motioned for me to come to the other side of the room.

I turned away from Dad and felt a wave of relief as I walked back to reality. "How's he doing?"

"The same. They don't think he has any brain activity, but the doctor wants to run some tests. He'll meet with you in an hour or so. I'll come down to the waiting room and find you when it's time."

I thanked the nurse and walked out of ICU with Mother.

"Are you okay?" I asked.

"Yep," she said, nodding affirmatively.

"Maybe you have unfinished business with him?" He didn't show up in court when she filed for divorce. She'd last seen him in Arkansas in 1972 just like Steve, Dan, and I.

"I don't know." She was quiet for a minute. "Seeing him laying in the bed, peaceful and quiet, makes me remember why I loved him."

"Why did you stay with him so long? Was it because the church made women submit to their husbands?"

"No, that didn't have anything to do with it. I loved him and hoped he'd change."

As a kid, I knew that whatever made Dad happy, made Mother happy. "But what about the danger? What it was doing to us?"

"He was my husband. For a long time, he came first."

That didn't surprise me. For most of the years when Mother and Dad were together, I knew he was more important to her than my brothers or me. She made sure we were fed, clothed, taught, and groomed, but her life didn't revolve around us. We weren't allowed to make demands. We were expected to be obedient, self-sufficient, helpful, and unemotional. And we were.

"When did you decide that you had to get away?"

"That last year in Big Sandy when things got so bad, I knew he wasn't going to change. The matches in the gas tank episode finally did it for me."

"But it was bad for years before that. Why did you wait so long?"

"Like I said, I kept thinking he'd change. Then once I decided that he wasn't going to straighten up, I had no idea how I'd support you kids if I left."

I had believed all traces of the wife from Big Sandy were gone. Till now.

My mother, Mary Ann Holloway, was the fourth of five children born to Doyle and Cordie Delia Holloway, sharecroppers in Wooster, Arkansas. While I was on my genealogy kick, we'd gone to see the then-abandoned unpainted house on Horseshoe Mountain where she'd grown up, its wood black from long exposure to the elements. It squatted two feet off the ground on a checkerboard of native stone piers. The inside walls were plastered with newspaper to keep the air from coming through the cracks. Crude planking provided a floor, but the gaps were big enough to allow snakes and varmints to find their way in.

The distance between Mother's childhood circumstances and my current life was incalculable. She had grown up in a house without electricity and plumbing. All of the family's water was hand-carried from the well uphill to the house. A single-hole outhouse stood twenty yards away. Heat came from a wood-burning tin stove in the kitchen. She had reminisced about her dad, my Papaw, stacking wood in its belly, splashing kerosene on the sticks, and throwing a match inside to start the fire. The stove was so lightweight that it danced a jig when the flammables ignited.

Cordie Holloway — my Memow — spent her days working the fields and her garden. In August and September, when breathing the wet-hot air became a chore, she boiled big vats of water to can vegetables, fruit, preserves, and pickles. Most years Papaw slaughtered a hog, and no scrap was wasted. Memow and Papaw rendered the fat into lard, saving the cracklings for cornbread. They cleaned the intestines and used them for sausage casing, adding blood to bits of fat and meat to make the filling. They boiled the head for jellied meat — headcheese — and pickled the feet. They salted the rest, and Papaw smoked it in a shanty barn so it would keep without refrigeration. Memow washed seven people's clothes in a tub with homemade lye soap, rubbing stains against a wooden rub-board, rinsing and threading them through a wringer until her hands were raw. She gathered the garments from the clothesline and smoothed the wrinkles with five-pound irons heated on top of the stove. In the winter she made clothes on an old treadle sewing machine using feed sacks or castoffs for material. Only Papaw's and the boys' overalls were bought at Uncle Will Clements' store down the road.

As an adult, I realize Memow and Papaw's relationship left a lot to be desired. I don't remember seeing them touch. Papaw would sit in his easy chair, watching

TV or reading the *Log Cabin Democrat*, while Memow held court in the kitchen. They didn't share meals. He'd eat at the table, while she'd stand over the stove eating little bits of this and that mixed together in a coffee cup. The only communication I remember was Memow fussing at Papaw and him ignoring her. If she nagged too much, he'd wordlessly get up from his chair with his Red Man chewing tobacco and tomato can spittoon and retire to his bedroom. He never set foot inside her bedroom. She only went into his to clean.

The differences between them were impossible to bridge. Papaw was a gentle soul who liked to tell jokes and tall tales. He worked hard in the fields and later laying bricks, but he had no ambition or intellectual curiosity. Early in their lives, Memow had tried to push Papaw to improve their lot in life, but the harder she pushed, the more he resisted. She knew she was smart and wanted to make something of her life, but at that time in rural Arkansas, a woman could be no more than her husband or father.

Mother has said that by the time she met the handsome guy who called her "Beautiful," she'd had enough of Memow's unfulfilled dreams, acerbic tongue, and black holes of depression. She was desperate to leave home. It didn't hurt that she fell crazy in love. On a warm April night in 1949, Mother and Dad drove across the Faulkner County line and woke up a justice of the peace. Dressed in his nightclothes, his honor married them. Dad was twenty-two. Mother was sixteen.

She quit high school before the end of her sophomore year and moved with Dad into a little silver trailer parked on land next to the old Powers home-place in Mount Vernon. She got a job working with Hattie at Sterling's Drug Store, selling cosmetics and perfume. Her happiness was marred only by Boggie Cora's antics.

Mother was proud of the stylish clothes she was now able to afford. She returned from work one day to find them strewn around the trailer. As she picked up her garments, she felt that they were damp. Looking closer, she saw that they were discolored and smelled of chlorine. When Mother realized that Cora had sprinkled her clothes with bleach, she ran inside the big house and confronted her. "What has happened to my clothes?" she cried. The loony old woman just cackled. Mother said that at the time she couldn't imagine anything worse happening.

In 1952, Dad was drafted. Mother went to see him when he finished basic training at Fort Bragg, but after he shipped out, they didn't see each other until he was discharged in 1954. Dad's stint in the Army tapped a vein of wanderlust. He and Mother hitched a pop-top trailer to the back of their 1949 Ford convertible and hit the road. They explored new places, dreaming of a fresh start, away from Faulkner County, Arkansas, and their families.

In 1955, shortly before I was born, they bought a white dollhouse on Factory Street, in a modest but well-kept new neighborhood near Conway's airport. Mother kept the four tiny rooms — kitchen, living room, bedroom and bath — immaculate. My parents painted, covered the hardwoods with fuzzy rugs, and reveled in a bathtub that ran with hot water. It was all anyone could want.

It had always irritated me that when Mother mentioned Dad it was usually in the context of those halcyon years, filled with images of picnics and passion. He was Saint Charles. It seemed to me that she had chosen to forget everything else.

Mother and Dad didn't grow up with strong ties to any religion, though everybody bowed to social convention and occasionally showed up for Sunday services at the local Baptist church. When Mother's sister Dortha married a Baptist preacher named Shelby Hightower, he gently urged Dad to start going to church. Dad ignored him. Later when Dad talked about Uncle Shelby, he'd say, "He's an ignorant ass. I can't stand his preacher voice."

CHAPTER SIX

Indoctrination in a Cult

In 1998, eight years after my divorce, everything and nothing had changed. I'd made little progress toward confronting the demons in my soul. My personal life was in shambles; my professional life was overwhelming. I'd screwed up again and married a self-centered man-boy. Our son was four, and I never stopped worrying about the out-of-control behaviors and narcissism he was learning. I was caught in a vicious cycle: The harder I worked to pay for the new art and toy trains and collectibles that were delivered every day, the more was ordered. I was emotionally wrung out from sharing a home with someone who was filled with rage one day and over-the-top with happiness the next.

For months, in my unconventional, unreligious way, I had been asking God for direction. One morning I was awakened at 2:00 by an inner voice. "Get up and start writing," it told me. The message was so powerful that I got out of bed and went to the computer. I stayed there until daylight. Words describing people, places, and events I had avoided all of my adult life gushed out. Radio Church of God services, Herbert W. and Garner Ted Armstrong, Imperial School. Dad, fire, fear.

Night after night in the wee hours after my son and husband were asleep, I wrote. Remembering a photo Dad had taken of himself and his descriptions of listening to *The World Tomorrow* broadcast while stationed overseas, I pictured him lying on his bunk in the Army barracks in Verdun, France, hands behind his head, listening to Radio Luxembourg. He heard an introduction I had learned to recite by heart by the time I was three.

"Herbert W. Armstrong brings you the plain truth about today's world news and the prophecies of The World Tomorrow."[6]

Then the strong Midwestern voice would have said something like:

"…We live in a godless, sinful world. Mankind has rejected the laws God gave us for a peaceful, productive world. Jesus Christ will soon return to restore order to this chaos. Only those select few who have the wisdom to heed God's commands will survive and rule in the Kingdom of God."

It was out of character for the Charles Powers I knew to have tuned in a religious radio program. While I'll never know why he stopped moving the dial when he heard Armstrong's voice for the first time — perhaps to a twenty-five-year-old man who had never ventured far from central Arkansas, the familiar accent was a palliative for homesickness — he said that after hearing the broadcast once, he made a point of listening each week. I kept asking myself how and why he made the transition from unspiritual, headstrong rebel to convert in a bizarre radio church. After turning those questions over in my head, it occurred to me that the picture Armstrong presented during the seduction was very different from the reality members lived after the deal was sealed. While I dreaded the prospect, I knew that if I wanted answers, I'd have to try to put myself in Dad's shoes and read what he read, hear what he heard in the 1950s. The truth lay beyond my childhood recollections.

I started with two bibles that we'd taken to church. In one, Mother had taken copious notes. It was there, in her near-perfect cursive, that I found Armstrong's list of the seven laws of success: (1) goal setting, (2) preparation to achieve that goal, (3) good health, (4) drive, (5) resourcefulness, (6) perseverance, and (7) guidance and continuous help of God. Mother also listed in her bible the seven rules on overcoming and the seven proofs that God exists. I was reminded that there were seven points because, Armstrong said, seven is God's number of completion. There were marginal notations of the "correct" translations of passages, cross-references to other scriptures, dates, words underlined in red.

Finding few insights from the notes, I started searching "Herbert W. Armstrong" and "Radio Church of God" on the Internet, following trails into scores of websites. I was overwhelmed with the vast reservoir of information, including articles, booklets, teaching materials, transcriptions of broadcasts, photographs. It was as though every word uttered by Armstrong had made its way into an archive. I printed hundreds of pages of material but didn't have the resolve to read any of it. Instead, I studied the psychology of cults and read Protestant commentary about the Radio Church of God and Armstrong. I became interested in biblical history, seeking understanding about which events were factually supported. I became fascinated with the Gnostics and dipped my toes into deeper water by considering that many events recited in the bible could be symbolic.

One Saturday afternoon, a time of the week when in my first seventeen years I would have been sitting in a Radio Church of God service, I decided that I was ready to tackle the pile of material I'd been avoiding. I crawled onto a white sectional couch in my solarium, switched on a brass table lamp, and started reading. Biographical material on the Armstrong family, postings by those who believed they'd been called to preach the now-dead Armstrong's message to the world, articles by angry former members who believed their lives had been wrecked by the church, co-worker letters from the mid-1950s, books written by Armstrong. I'd read a few minutes, then pace the room to calm myself. Adrenalin washed through me in waves. My heart was pumping at 105 beats per minute, my breaths shallow. My chest heaved from sobs. I went to the powder room and grabbed a wad of toilet tissue to blow my nose. In a few minutes I went to the kitchen and grabbed a whole box of Kleenex. I was furious one minute, sad the next.

Reading Armstrong's words, I began to see how they could have resonated with my father. Back in Arkansas, preachers told people to grind through their miserable lives, follow Jesus' teachings, and dream of the joys that awaited them in heaven. Armstrong's message appeared to be that God's people could have material gratification here and now, in addition to rewards in the Kingdom of God.

I also concluded that Armstrong's speaking and teaching style appealed to my dad's view of himself. He didn't see himself as a man with a fourth-grade education. I believe that in his mind's eye, he viewed himself as an intellectual. He told me that my intelligence came from him. Dad didn't respond to emotion-wringing by a weepy minister. Armstrong was different from Oral Roberts and Roy Hargis, who invoked the plaintive name of *Jeeesuuus* over and over in an effort to hawk prayer cloths or vials of healing oil. With a delivery style more like Chet Huntley, the anchor for NBC News, he came across as a trusted spokesman for the times; almost like a professor. He used statistics, quotes from prominent people, historical texts, and Greek and Hebrew words to convey his message. Herbert W. Armstrong didn't urge people to join the Radio Church of God. He wanted to teach, to share. This man sounded like the father every person wants but too few have.

And, Armstrong told Charles Powers that he — Charles — was special. He could — no, he *would* — be successful if he followed Armstrong's tutelage. It didn't matter that Charles Powers had no education. It didn't matter that he had few skills. It didn't matter that he was poor.

"…What a happy life God has made available! What blessedness — what joy! — I want to share that life with you!

For more information, write to me, Herbert W. Armstrong, at Box 111, Pasadena, California."[7]

I imagine my father sprawled on his bunk and listening, wanting very much to believe he was special. He was, after all, a Powers. Special, and ready to be successful, like Mr. Armstrong promised. So, just as the seductive voice suggested, he wrote in for more information.

Once, during the contrition period following a drunken rant when I was nine, I sat on Dad's knee in our tiny den in Big Sandy and asked why he'd joined the Radio Church of God. "Toddy," he said, using shorthand for one of my nicknames — Toddy Foddy Fink Stink — "I never had any education, and my family didn't teach me anything. I needed to learn how to make something of myself. Mr. Armstrong said he would show me the way."

During the next year I read a lot and wrote little. Mother answered scores of questions, and I quizzed Steve about his recollections of Dad. Dan didn't remember Dad, at all. My memories intruded at all hours. Almost every night I had nightmares about Dad or the church. Being chased by ministers, held captive by the church, in the midst of war on the campus, burning in a fire. As a result of that work, I pieced together what I think it was like in the Radio Church in the early years of Dad's conversion, long before I was old enough to process this part of my world.

One of Armstrong's fundamental tenets was that the world couldn't end and Christ wouldn't return to earth until Armstrong's version of the gospel was preached throughout the world. His mission was not to save souls. It was to get the word out. He claimed that out of the hundreds of millions of people who had access to the message, God called only a select handful to hear and understand it. These were the foot soldiers, the faithful whose labors were required to generate the money to support "the Work," the few who would rule under Armstrong in the Millennium and in the World Tomorrow. Armstrong had a huge personal stake in this outcome. He taught — and I'm convinced that he believed — that when Jesus Christ returned, He would anoint Armstrong to become the twelfth apostle in place of Judas Iscariot who would be resurrected and burned alive in the Lake of Fire.

In the early 1950s, Radio Church of God membership was perhaps a couple thousand. Ambassador College had just been founded in Pasadena, California, to train the church's ministers and their wives. Another property had been purchased in Big Sandy, Texas, and a tabernacle was being built there, a little at a time, as money became available. In 1954, Armstrong told co-workers that *The World Tomorrow* broadcast was heard around the world, except for Australia, South Africa, and South America. The church's magazine, *The Plain Truth*, was offered free to listeners.

In his radio ministry and through *The Plain Truth* magazine, Armstrong didn't invite people to join the church. He offered them an opportunity to write for information. That was because God's laws were difficult to understand and accept. Only the special few who made it through "reeducation" and passed the tests required for baptism were called by God for membership.

Through the free materials, prospective members were slowly and carefully indoctrinated. When Dad returned home from the service in 1954, he received his first Ambassador College Bible Correspondence Course. Online I found complete course materials, the first of which is eight pages long in single-spaced, ten-point type. If I critiqued the writing against the legal writing I routinely see, I'd fire the author. Armstrong's fondness for capitalizing words and sentences he wanted to emphasize is distracting. Peppering the writing with exclamation marks is reminiscent of pulp fiction. Treating adults as though they are children is stultifying.

Armstrong gave students explicit directions on how to study. A student was to write "neatly" and "in his own handwriting" on three-ring notebook paper:

"Bible Correspondence Course
Lesson One
Why Study the Bible?

What is the 'End of the World'?
1.   Was Jesus ever asked about the now-threatening doom of civilization —
the END OF THIS AGE and the signs of His return? Matthew 24:3.

2.   Does this verse refer to the end of the PHYSICAL EARTH? — or does
it refer to the end of the PRESENT AGE of human misrule? How do modern
translations of the Bible properly render Mat. 24:3..."[8]

The first lesson had twenty-nine questions, not including subparts. It even
detailed the kind of binder that students were to use and how materials were to
be organized in it. Every Bible verse was to be written in its entirety. Every word.
Students were told that they should study at least a half hour a day. After each
fourth lesson, there was a test.

The correspondence course was meant to convince students — largely rural,
poor, and uneducated — that they were learning sophisticated truths. The use of
flawed syllogisms is endemic in Armstrong's materials. The first lesson offered an
example of his fractured logic: Jesus Christ will return when times are bad; times
are bad; therefore, Christ's return is imminent. It was supported by the words of
well-known public figures who opined that the world was teetering on the brink
of annihilation, such as President Dwight Eisenhower who said in his inaugural
address: "Science seems ready to confer upon us, as its final gift, the power to erase
human life from this planet," and General MacArthur who warned Congress that
Armageddon was at our door.[9] Armstrong posited that the final days before the
return of Jesus Christ were to be like the days of Noah, corrupt and filled with violence. J. Edgar Hoover affirmed that times were violent and chaotic. Thus, it was
clear, said Armstrong, that these were the end-times and Christ's return to take
over the kingdoms of this world was imminent.

In sermons, radio broadcasts, and written materials, Armstrong challenged
conventional religious doctrines with scriptures that he directed students to read
from their own Bibles. He pulled part of a scripture from one place in the Bible and
tied it to another unrelated scripture elsewhere, creating his own unique version
of truth. He launched into long explanations about how the Greek and Hebrew
words in the original books of the Bible were mistranslated. I repeatedly heard him
say, "Don't believe me — believe your Bible." Once a person lost trust in a few key
societal concepts, he was prepared to reject all conventional knowledge and look
to Armstrong as the fountain of all knowledge.

In the Bible Correspondence Courses, Armstrong reinforced his building blocks
of belief; those inclined to believe no longer questioned after a lesson or two. By
the fifth installment, those destined for membership knew that everything they

had learned in their lives was false education — "miseducation" — and accepted their need to be reeducated. The Bible was the reeducation rulebook, but only a teacher called by God could interpret and enforce the rulebook. That teacher, of course, was Armstrong. The student's reeducation would produce a Utopia — The World Tomorrow.

By the seventh lesson, converts were primed for the *coup de grace:* forking over their money. Many already believed that ten percent of their total pre-tax income was supposed to go to God's church, which they now accepted was the Radio Church of God. But, instead of stopping where other churches drew the tithing line, Armstrong cited Levitical law. He decreed that believers must set aside a second ten percent of earnings for use as God commanded. Since God's commands were issued only through Armstrong, he decided how members would use this money. And every three years a third ten percent should be sent to the church for the care of widows, orphans and "Levites." The "Spiritual Levites" — with the God-given right to spend that money on themselves — were Armstrong and his ministers. On holy days, Armstrong decreed mandatory "freewill offerings." Members were supposed to joyously give in excess of their tithes on these occasions. When money was needed for something extraordinary, there were "special offerings." These were called opportunities for church members to be blessed. Opportunities abounded.

I've thought about how financially burdensome this was for my family in the 1950s. Dad made no more than $200 a month as an auto body repairman at Beatty's garage. After joining the church, he and Mother had to set aside $40 a month for two years, and an additional $20 a month during the third year. On top of that, they had to save for holy day and special offerings. I understand now why most everything we ate came from the backyard garden and the chicken house next to it. The financial deprivation was nothing compared to the consequence of not adhering to this law, which, according to Armstrong, was being wiped off the face of the earth.

People who sent money received Armstrong's "co-worker" letters. He was prolific.

> "...December 18, 1952:
> We're on the air OVER ALL EUROPE! At last! This Gospel of the Kingdom of God IS now starting to go out with a tremendous LOUD VOICE to all the world for a witness to ALL NATIONS...
> What a responsibility this places on you and me! But we need not fear, or falter. It is GOD'S doing. We are merely the instruments He has chosen."[10]

He wrote at least twenty-one letters to everyone on his coworker list in 1955 and eighteen in 1956. All were penned with over-the-top excitement, as though the reader were a vital part of the cause. All contained requests for money. Sometimes coworkers were told that if $10,000 weren't received in a week, the whole operation would be shut down and Christ's return would be delayed. Armstrong's followers always came through.

For years Dad worked through the lessons of the Bible Correspondence Course. I remember seeing him at the kitchen table with his Bible, the current lesson, and his bulging study binder before him. Pen tightly gripped in his right hand, he would be hunched over a sheath of loose-leaf notebook paper, scribbling prose fraught with spelling and punctuation errors.

CHAPTER SEVEN

The First Visit

In the fall of 1955, Dad visited the Radio Church of God campus in Big Sandy to attend the Feast of Tabernacles and Last Great Day. I was three months old.

According to Mother, after listening to *The World Tomorrow* broadcasts for two years, receiving *The Plain Truth*, and working through several lessons of The Bible Correspondence Course, Dad wanted to hear Mr. Armstrong in person. But that wasn't as simple as calling for directions, though having detailed instructions to the campus in Big Sandy was essential. The place was in the middle of nowhere, unmarked, and indistinguishable from the farms and ranches around it. The skeleton of the unfinished meeting building was set a third of mile from the road down a winding path in a copse of pine and oak.

The biggest obstacle to attending a service was getting an invitation. Anyone who showed up without permission was asked to leave. In order to gain admission, Dad had to complete enough "reeducation" to believe that Armstrong's teachings provided the path to eternal life, pay his tithes, and pass a screening interview with a minister.

The Radio Church of God was initially premised on the idea that instead of convening in a house of worship, members would listen to the radio broadcasts, work through the written materials at home, and congregate with other like-minded souls to celebrate the holy days. These seven holy convocations were celebrated in place of pagan holidays like Christmas and Easter.[11]

Passover teaches that Jesus Christ gave His life so that the sins of humanity could be forgiven and the death penalty for sin removed.

Days of Unleavened Bread teaches us to repent of our sins. Because leavening symbolizes sin, it is removed from our homes for seven days.

Feast of Pentecost pictures the coming of the Holy Spirit and the establishment of the Church.

Feast of Trumpets celebrates the time when Jesus Christ will return to the earth, resurrect the dead saints, and instantly change those saints who are still alive to immortal spirit beings.

Day of Atonement is a day of fasting that teaches us that Jesus Christ gave His life to atone for the sins of all mankind. It also points to the time when Satan will be bound for 1,000 years.

Feast of Tabernacles teaches us that when Jesus Christ returns, a new world order will be established with Christ as King of Kings and Lord of Lords, assisted by the resurrected saints, who will set up His government on the earth for 1,000 years.

Last Great Day teaches us that Jesus Christ will raise from the dead all people who died without being given a full opportunity for salvation. They will be given the chance to accept or reject God's teachings.

In the fifties, these holy-day gatherings provided prospective members like Dad the chance to meet with ministers to demonstrate their readiness for baptism. I can imagine I know what it was like for Mother and Dad when they first visited Big Sandy because the scene repeated itself many times over the years with little variation.

Dad drove a cream-colored 1953 Ford Crestliner convertible with a black rag-top, pulling a tiny silver trailer. He made a left onto Highway 80 East and started looking for a dirt road on the left side of the highway. During the Feast, a small sign was posted: "Radio Church of God Tabernacle."

Dad violated church rules by bringing Mother before she was converted. Armstrong had strict rules about bringing non-members to church services:

"...First, DO NOT bring visitors whom you HOPE to get interested. This is NOT an evangelistic service preaching the Gospel to THE WORLD — it is a Festival God commands for HIS PEOPLE, — already converted, and already HIS people — to GO AWAY from the world..."[12]

But when Dad checked in, Mother wasn't turned away. They drove through a campground divided into a checkerboard of sandy unpaved streets and camp-sites that became a quagmire when it rained. Dad backed the trailer into a space, unhitched it from the car, and placed blocks around the trailer's tires to keep it in place. After breakfast, Dad and Mother, pushing my stroller, joined the people walking to church along a path beaten in the sparse native grass.

I never knew a time when the people didn't look poor, poor. Most men wore threadbare suits and shirts their wives had labored to starch and iron. They carried briefcases or tucked Bibles and notebooks under their arms. The women covered themselves in the long skirts and modest blouses the church required. Most had that old-before-their-time look seen in country women who worked too hard car-ing for too many children who had come too close together. Since Satan used makeup to take women away from God's light, none wore cosmetics, and they wore their tresses hanging down their backs or piled atop their heads.

I know what we wore that day in 1955, because Dad used a timer to take a picture of the three of us. I had on what Mother had made: a red and white dress layered with ruffles, with matching socks and tiny red-stoned jewelry. Mother was dressed in an aqua sweater dress, high heels, red lipstick, and mascara. We fit in like cardinals in a covey of quail.

When I was little and we made the walk from the campgrounds to the church building, we dodged bull nettles and cockleburs bristling with stickers. The bull nettle was particularly nasty. If you brushed one, its barbs would leave painful, itchy welts. An occasional gust of wind and scores of moving feet stirred up the dust, which covered our shoes and ankles. The grit filled our mouths and burned our eyes. Big Sandy was aptly named.

There was no horseplay among the children who walked with their parents. They wore hand-me-downs, with too-short sleeves and pant legs, patched knees and worn shoes. But all were neat, clean and pressed. Adults didn't engage in animated conversation as they walked. You didn't hear laughter. They plodded together, eyes forward, heads slightly bowed. Like ants, laden with a burden that could barely be borne.

The hot trail ended in a forest where a path snaked through pine, oak, dogwood, and redbud. An unfinished domed shell that looked like a huge Quonset hut faced in redwood stood in a clearing beside a sandy-bottomed natural stream.

I can envision what it was like when Mother and Dad reached the tabernacle for the first time. The inside of the building looked like an unfinished high school gymnasium set up with row after row of brown folding chairs. A stage at the front held a lectern, a piano, and a spray of orange and yellow flowers. Nothing suggested it was a sanctuary. But there were lots of friendly faces, including the deacon who greeted them. As they looked for empty seats, half a dozen strangers warmly welcomed Mother and Dad. They sat near the back so Mother could slip out if I started crying.

Mother has told me that she had no idea what the church taught. Neither the radio broadcasts nor Dad had disclosed much about the church's doctrines. She said she expected it to be like a Baptist revival. It didn't unfold that way. By the time the 10:00 a.m. service began, everyone was quietly seated. A pianist walked across the stage and took her place at the instrument; a song leader went to the microphone and raised his hands. The congregation rose, opening their gray, rag-paper hymnals. Most of the songs were psalms set to music by Armstrong's brother, Dwight. Without the passion of old-time gospel music, the music was didactic and flat. "Deeeeepart from eeeeviiiiil, do what is good, seeeeeek peace, pursue it eaaarnestly."[13]

The morning service was supposed to last two hours. It began with a twenty-minute homily called a sermonette, given by a lower-ranking minister. Mother was stunned when she heard the message repeated so often in Armstrong's writings:

"…The so-called Christian holiday of Christmas came to us from the ancient heathen celebration of the birthday of the sun god, Sol, which took place on December 25. It has nothing to do with the birth of Jesus Christ which occurred in the spring. Shepherds would not have been out tending the flocks in the month of December. The Bible condemns this practice and all others associated with the worship of Baal, an idol. Christmas can't be seen as anything other than an abomination in the eyes of God."[14]

She looked at Dad. He didn't acknowledge her and kept his eyes on the preacher. Christmas was her favorite holiday. Surely he didn't expect them to give up Christmas? Mother was confident that this information was news to him, too, and that they would pack up and head back to Arkansas after the service. She carried me outside while the congregation sang two songs, followed by more music, announcements and offerings. She returned to her seat just as the sermon of the anointed one — Herbert W. Armstrong — began.

"…We live in a Sunday-observing world. We take for granted the observance of Sunday as the Sabbath. But we will be judged by Almighty God on whether we adhere to every word in the Bible, not whether we sincerely tried to do the right thing but were in error. Sunday is the first day of the week. Jesus kept the Sabbath. The Sabbath he kept was the seventh day. Any person who does not keep Saturday as the Sabbath will burn in the Lake of Fire.[15]

Mother tuned out. Dad listened with rapt attention. He heard and saw something very different. Armstrong presented himself as a person with culture and blue-blooded breeding, expert in classical music, architecture, history, geography, and urbanity. His success spoke for itself.

At noon, Mother started to squirm. But Mr. Armstrong was wound up and preached for another twenty-five minutes. After the sermon, more singing, more prayer.

Following the service, many from the congregation scrambled to get in line for lunch — called dinner in that part of the world. While walking, Mother tugged at Dad's arm.

"Charles, did you know that they don't celebrate Christmas? That is the most ridiculous thing I've ever heard."

"Not exactly," he answered, avoiding her eyes.

"Church on Saturday?" she demanded.

"Sorta," Dad mumbled and kept shuffling ahead in the line.

"Are we going back home today?" Mother asked.

"No," said Dad, this time looking directly at her. "I want to hear more."

Mother shook her head in disgust, "This place gives me the creeps."

"Such nice people," replied Dad.

The afternoon service followed the same format. Mother heard about the importance of fasting; she learned that the "eating of filthy swine's flesh has been a major cause of cancer."[16] The evangelist droned about the churches of the world worshipping Satan and manifestations of that evil, such as modern music.

After the service, Mother packed up my things and was ready to go back to the trailer. But the crowd didn't disperse. The couple sitting behind my parents introduced themselves and mentioned that most people stayed after church for fellowship.

Dad turned to Mother. "Let's head to the front. I'd like to shake Mr. Armstrong's hand."

They moved slowly, stopped again and again by greeters. It took a half hour to reach the area in front of the stage. By then, Armstrong was gone.

Instead of heading toward the campground, some of the crowd were exiting out the east side of the building. Mother and Dad walked outside to see where they were going. Two hundred yards from the tabernacle, people stood around a waterhole. A man in thigh-high waders had his hands on the head of a man who had emerged from the pond, his suit dripping.

"Baptisms," Mother said. "I'm worn out."

"You want to take Toddy back to the trailer?"

"Yeah."

"I'll be there in a few minutes."

When Dad returned to the trailer an hour later, he was full of stories about the warm, friendly people he'd met and how he had enjoyed their company. It was clear that he wasn't ready to return home to Arkansas.

Later in the week, my father was finally able to meet Herbert W. Armstrong. I don't know the words that were exchanged between them, but I can visualize that encounter.

"Hello," Dad mumbled. He shyly extended his hand.

"Greetings," boomed Armstrong, tightly grasping Dad's hand and flashing a wide smile. "What is your name, son?"

"Charles. Charles Powers from Conway, Arkansas."

"It's good to have you here."

"Thank you, sir. I like your sermons."

"Not my words. They're God's."

"I believe that, sir."

"Keep working and you'll be ready for baptism soon."

"Thank you," Dad said.

Armstrong pressed his hand. "God be with you."

I believe that Dad was captivated by Armstrong and caught up in the feeling of belonging. He was in his late twenties, uneducated, and in a dead-end blue-collar job. He had never known unconditional love from anyone other than his wife and baby. No one had cared enough to make him follow any rules. Then, miraculously, God, though the Radio Church of God, had chosen him. He was special. He was somebody. He understood what the rich and the educated could not comprehend.

He was called to the extraordinary work of the Radio Church of God and Herbert W. Armstrong. He was welcomed like family by scores of people. He was home.

Mother and Dad stayed all eight days of the Feast of Tabernacles. Mother has said that by the time they were ready to go, she had a pretty good idea of what the church taught and wanted no part of it. But she made no attempt to dissuade Dad. She was twenty-three years old and cared about making a home. She has told me that she thought the church was a fancy of Dad's that would pass. She was willing to accept isolation from the rest of the world and to follow rules that were contrary to her beliefs so Dad could do what he wanted. At the same time, Mother knew that once he'd made up his mind about something, there wasn't any changing it. Had she battled him, it would have undermined their relationship, and he would have still gotten his way.

When Mother and Dad returned home to Arkansas, she put her lipstick and mascara in the trash.

CHAPTER EIGHT

Rules of the Game

When Mother and I returned to the waiting room after visiting Dad in the ICU, I noticed a stout woman with cropped gray hair and no makeup sitting on the far wall, reading *USA Today*. I recognized her immediately, though it took a couple of beats to put a name with the face. She was one of the church ladies. Wanda Moore's son Leon was Dad's friend and sometime-employer, though Leon was only two years older than I. Wanda stood when she saw me enter and took two long, firm strides in my direction.

She wrapped her muscular arms around me in a bear hug. "I knew it was you when I saw you get off the elevator and walk back to see your daddy. I don't know that I would've recognized you after all these years, though, if I hadn't known you were coming. I knew your momma right away. She's just as pretty as always. You, too, but now you're all grown up. Even though he's in bad shape, your daddy looks real good…"

"I'm glad to see you, too," I answered when she finally paused for a breath. "How've you been?"

"For an old woman I can still do most everything I want. It must've been all that wheat germ." Wanda smiled and winked at me as she lowered herself into an orange molded plastic chair.

"And blackstrap molasses," I said, remembering the tarry goo that I used to add to my glass of milk. Armstrong taught that processed food was sinful, and he encouraged his followers to supplement their diets with wheat germ and blackstrap molasses.

"How's the family?" I asked.

"Getting by. More than our share of troubles."

"I'm sorry."

"The church messed up my kids," she said, vigorously shaking her head from side to side. "Can't seem to stay married. I don't guess you'd know about that."

"Umm-hmm," I answered noncommittally, while straightening the pile of magazines on the chipped particle board table beside my chair. I didn't want to tell Wanda about my marriage fiascos. I do a lot of things well, but picking men isn't one of them. Anxious to move on before Wanda zeroed in on my discomfort, I changed the subject. "See Dad much?"

"Not in years. He did some work for Leon but didn't come around the house. I didn't want him there."

"I understand."

"When he drank, your daddy got mean. He'd go off on the church every time."

"How'd he support himself?" I asked, wondering how he'd made enough money to pay for booze, food, and shelter.

"Up until a week ago, he was working on an old car at Leon's shop swinging a sledgehammer."

I leaned toward Wanda and whispered, "Do you know the guy in the corner with the ponytail? He keeps looking over here, like he knows me."

"He was sittin' there talking to Leon when I got here. I'd never met him before. Said his name is Billy."

"I guess he's one of Dad's friends," I said. "Just wanted to make sure it wasn't somebody I was supposed to remember."

"Nah, he didn't have anything to do with the church. Leon said he's the boy your dad treated like a son."

The words had the sting of an angry red wasp. Like a son? That lowlife stranger in a stained T-shirt and a greasy hat? What about us? I looked away from the man and took a sip of cold, bitter hospital coffee. I said, "Is there a church left in Big Sandy?"

"Not sure," answered Wanda tersely.

"You left?" I answered with surprise.

"Honey, I may be dumb but I'm not stupid. I let those sons of bitches ruin twenty-five years of my life. That's enough." Her eyes flashed in fury but she kept her voice steady.

I wanted to give her a high-five and shout, "You go, girl."

Wanda wasn't comfortable with silence and quickly moved on. "You know Herbert W. split the sheets with Garner Ted?"

"I read that." I'd been interested in Garner Ted when I started my research because his son David was my elementary school friend.

"Must've been fifteen years ago."

"They never got along that well. What finally brought it to a head?"

"Garner Ted couldn't keep his pants zipped," Wanda answered without changing inflection.

I gave her a knowing nod. "That's no big surprise. What'd he do after he left the church?"

"Started his own in Tyler." She picked up her purse and started fishing. "Don't mind me. I'm looking for a pen and something to write on so I can get your address and phone number before I leave."

"You ever go to Garner Ted's church?" I asked.

"Naw. I wouldn't walk across the street to see that bastard. Heard he had a pretty good-sized church but got in trouble for forcing himself on some woman."

"That even made the Houston paper." I remembered laughing out loud when I'd read the short article.

"He said it was a lie made up by the Devil, trying to silence God's work." Wanda shook her head. "His flock actually believed him."

I rolled my eyes and shifted in the molded plastic seat. "What happened to the campus in Big Sandy?"

"Shut down. They're trying to sell it but haven't gotten any takers."

"It needs to be exorcised before anyone uses it."

"Amen," said Wanda.

I wrote my address and phone number on the back of an electric bill Wanda had found in her purse. She said she'd stay in touch and, after another hug, headed for the elevator.

I pulled the *Houston Chronicle* I'd brought from home out of its plastic wrapper and perused the front page. I couldn't stay focused. I recalled Mother telling me five years earlier that when she and Dad returned to Arkansas after attending the Feast in 1955, they built a life around the church's teachings. As I grew in years and awareness, it was all I knew. From sunset on Friday night until sunset on Saturday night, we kept the Sabbath: no radio other than *The World Tomorrow*, no housework, no chores. Mother didn't wear makeup. Her skirts and her hair were long. We followed Old Testament dietary laws: no pork, no unclean meats, no seafood without scales and fins. We didn't celebrate the pagan holidays of Christmas or Easter or Halloween. Even though polio had paralyzed my cousin Donna's legs, I wasn't allowed to receive a shot or visit a doctor or take any medicine. Birthdays were ignored. Each day Mother and Dad spent a minimum of thirty minutes inside an empty closet, designated as the prayer closet, praying aloud. In the evenings, Mother and Dad listened to *The World Tomorrow* broadcasts, worked lessons in the Bible Correspondence Course, and read the Bible. And, because the Bible taught that a little wine is good for your health, they started drinking.

I don't profess to know the whole story of Herbert W. Armstrong and the Radio Church of God. There are many versions of history, and now that the Worldwide Church of God (its name since 1968) has more or less adopted mainstream Protestant views, most traces of the daily realities of my childhood have been wiped away. I know that the yarn I grew up hearing that Herbert W. abandoned life as a wealthy and successful advertising man to follow God's call is bullshit; the truth is elusive. I've read a number of accounts that say he was a high-school dropout who sold advertising space in the Des Moines *Daily Capital* newspaper before his career collapsed in 1922. Armstrong moved to Oregon and pursued newspaper advertising there, again without success. A foray into the laundry business also failed, and he and his wife Loma spent the next seven years in poverty.

I heard the elder Armstrong say a dozen times in sermons that Loma challenged him to prove from the scriptures that Saturday was not still the Sabbath.

He spent six months studying, trying to prove her wrong and affirm his Quaker faith. He concluded that Loma was right and that major world churches had distorted other biblical teachings, especially the abolition of Mosaic laws. He took to the radio in 1933 in Eugene, Oregon, and the next year began the publication of *The Plain Truth*. In 1946, he moved to Pasadena, California, to lead his own church incorporated as the Radio Church of God.

It didn't take research for me to remember the basic doctrines I learned from Armstrong. The Radio Church of God was the One True Church, the only religious organization that followed God's laws. Anyone who wasn't a member of our church was going to die in the Great Tribulation or the Lake of Fire. My goal as a child was unequivocal: Survive the Great Tribulation in the Place of Safety and gain entry to the utopian Kingdom of God that would take place when the Tribulation ended.

My desire to follow the path Armstrong showed us was motivated by terrifying descriptions of the Tribulation. In case our imaginations weren't sufficiently vivid, Basil Wolverton, a former *Mad Magazine* illustrator who was one of Armstrong's closest confidants, drew pictures for *The Plain Truth* that were meant to scare the hell out of us. Mountains of dead bodies with empty eye sockets. People running from a nuclear explosion. A tsunami with floating skyscrapers. Emaciated parents holding dead children. Bodies covered with boils. Death by fire.

We were told that the Place of Safety was to be the ancient red-rock city of Petra in the Jordanian desert. Countless times I heard the ministers preach about the need to be prepared to go on an hour's notice. It wasn't entirely clear how we were going to get halfway around the world, until one of the evangelists told us that God was going to test our faith by requiring us to travel on planes that weren't airworthy. Since there was no food or water in Petra, God would provide us with water and manna, like he had for the Israelites after Moses led them out of Egypt. I never thought through — and the church never said — how we were supposed to live in barren rock caves without bedding or clothing or sanitary provisions. I just knew that I'd do anything to get there.

While we were holed up in Petra, Armstrong was going to teach us how to be leaders in the Kingdom of God. When the Tribulation ended, Jesus Christ would return to earth, and for a thousand years Armstrong would be in charge of educating the whole world. The faithful members of the Radio Church of God would help him. Satan was supposed to be imprisoned during that time so he wouldn't get in Herbert W. and Jesus' way.

As a young person, I knew with absolute certainty that the world as I knew it would end before I became an adult. The emergence of the Beast — the Antichrist described in Revelation — was the sign that the Tribulation was about to begin. We spent hours discussing who the Beast might be. I read that when Armstrong started his ministry in the 1930s, he prophesied that it was the Italian dictator Mussolini. In the late 1930s he modified that view, saying that Mussolini, Stalin, and the Pope would team up. When Hitler emerged, Armstrong declared him the

Beast, though the Pope remained a contender. When these prophecies weren't fulfilled and World War II ended, Armstrong insisted that Hitler was alive in South America, regrouping for his next assault on the world. Why the failure of these prophecies didn't cause folks to snap to the fact that Herbert W.'s visions weren't coming from God is a mystery to me.

By the time I was old enough to get the gist of the discussion about the Beast, Herbert W. was still preaching about the possibility that Hitler was alive in Argentina. When it became apparent that Hitler wasn't going to resurface to take over the world, Armstrong announced that God hadn't yet revealed the identity of the Beast but had given him the key to determining the date when Jesus Christ was to return. It had to do with nineteen-year time cycles that never made any sense to me. All I needed to know was that the big day would occur on the Feast of Trumpets in 1975. All of my future plans centered on that date.

CHAPTER NINE
Kinfolk

I walked out of the dingy waiting room towards the elevator and noticed the ponytailed man again, the one my father supposedly treated "like a son." I moved toward the soda machine so I could eye him from head to toe without being too obvious. The crevices in his face bespoke years of hard living, though I guessed he was in his thirties. His eyes had the dejected look of a whipped dog. Grease smeared his Snap-On Tools cap, and he fidgeted like a person desperate for a smoke. My Powers arrogance kicked in. Bet he's a lowlife. Dad's drinking buddy. Like a son? Never.

He was kneeling on one knee, speaking to a blonde child of ten who was crying. He put his arms around the little girl and stroked her hair. "Honey, it'll be okay. Grandpa'll be okay."

As much as I wanted to, I couldn't despise him. This man was brushing away the tears of a little girl crying over my father. I was his flesh and blood and I couldn't shed a tear. I wished I could have felt a little of what they felt, to have known the man they loved. Somewhere in a distant lobe of my brain, the germ of a thought began. Perhaps love requires accepting people for who they are without regard for their clothes and job descriptions.

The man was looking my way and it would have been rude to ignore his silent introduction. I walked a couple of steps toward the pair and extended my hand. "I'm Carla. Carla Powers."

"I'm Billy." He was so nervous that his hands shook.

"Nice to meet you, Billy. Thanks for being here."

"Weren't nothin'."

"Who's this?" I gestured toward the little girl.

"Molly. She's mine," he said proudly. "Purdy, ain't she?"

I looked at the tall thin child, hair pulled into a ponytail like the one I'd worn at that age. "She sure is, Billy."

After an awkward moment when neither of us could think of anything else to say, I took a step toward the elevator. "See you later."

Dad had learned early in his days with the church to transform friends into family. I guessed that it wasn't a stretch for him to see Billy as a son and Molly as a granddaughter. The Radio Church of God required congregants to make a complete break with their biological families and all nonmember friends. After Dad joined the church and we moved to Little Rock in 1958, we had little contact with our relatives, though Mother and Dad never followed the letter of the dictate and made occasional visits. Granddaddy Powers had moved to a town two hours away, and he seemed as uninterested in us as we were in him. Aunts, uncles, and cousins were strangers.

Dad remained closest to his sister Hattie, a Southern Baptist who went to church every time the doors opened. Whenever the two of them got together, Aunt Hattie gave Dad hell over the church. She felt it was her Christian duty to save his soul from the bonds of Satan.

At Aunt Hattie and Uncle Jake's house on a two hundred-acre hay farm that pastured a hundred head of cattle, the big meal of the day was dinner, usually served between noon and one. Aunt Hattie was a great southern cook. Fried chicken, mashed potatoes, cream gravy, sliced tomatoes and onions out of the garden, home-grown corn cut from the cob, tender fried okra that had been on the stem two hours earlier, homemade biscuits, coconut cake, sweet tea (though she made unsweetened for us).

The food was arranged on a round oak table in the dining room. I sat in a big-girl chair on three thick books. After Uncle Jake finished the blessing, we dove in. Halfway through the meal, Aunt Hattie started in on Dad.

"Charles, I declare. Devil's work. It's the Devil's work."

Dad ignored her, but Aunt Hattie kept on, pointing the tines of her fork in his face. "I cain't sit here and watch you wreck your life."

Then she turned to Mother. "I know you did it."

"What?" Mother said.

"Talked him into joining that outfit."

"That's not true," Mother answered, the hurt obvious in her voice.

"Now, Sis," Dad said without taking his eyes off his plate, "let's not ruin this good dinner."

"I'd rather spoil your appetite than see you burn in hell," my aunt continued.

"Hattie," Uncle Jake said in a firm voice, "it's not the time."

"The very idey of going to church on Saturday is the silliest thing I ever heard," Aunt Hattie continued. "Sounds like you're one of them Jews."

Dad's face got red. Mother patted his hand and gave him the look that meant *please keep quiet*. It didn't work. "I'm warning you," my father said to Hattie, "Shut up, or we're leaving."

"I'm just trying to save your eternal life." She stopped long enough to take a swig of sweet tea. "It's her fault," she continued, turning to look at Mother. "I always knew she was trouble."

"Hattie," Uncle Jake said, cutting her off, "Enough. Mary, don't pay any attention."

"You're crazy," Dad said to his sister. "Just like Mama. You miserable old bag. You're jealous of Mary Ann. You've been that way since the first day you met her. She's pretty, and you're so homely that no man would have you until you were thirty." Dad pulled out his chair and lifted me up in his arms. "Jake, you're a good man but I can't stand to be in the same house with her."

Mother's eyes teared up. She picked up my doll before following Dad out the front door.

The Holloway clan was more tolerant but became almost as distant as the Powers. It was miserable to visit Memow and Papaw because of their constant feuding, though it kept them too distracted to worry about my parents' religious inclinations. Aunt Dortha lived in Louisiana where Uncle Shelby pastored a tiny Baptist church. There was no money for long-distance calls and, while we lived in Arkansas, we never made the long drive to visit. Uncle Dee lived far away in Kansas. Uncle Bob and his wife were too busy amassing an Arkansas-sized fortune in antiques to socialize, and Uncle Pat, who had just left home, was relishing his freedom.

The families who replaced our relatives were members of the Radio Church of God. Most Sabbaths we either went to the home of another member or they came to ours to fellowship (a church word that meant to visit with other members), study the Bible, and pray. I remember one family in particular, the Watleys. They lived with their three children in a water-stained hovel with a holey roof and ragged furniture. A couple from Malvern, Arkansas, whose names are lost to me, had a home I thought grand, with brick above the siding and dining room chairs covered in a silky stripe. Then, there were the two men from Morrilton who shared a stone house. One — a muscular, crew-cut man named Wesley who worked on cars and did carpentry — was Dad's closest friend. Wesley's housemate, a skinny, sickly man named Ed, fixed radios, kept house, cooked, and cared for their hyperactive Chihuahua.

Dad knew he'd found his real family in the summer of 1958 when we took a road trip to California to visit the Ambassador College campus in Pasadena, California. Armstrong had promised that the church would show the way to a better, more prosperous life. If he followed Armstrong's instruction, Dad believed that he was sure to achieve success and rise above his beginnings. When he set foot on the church property, he no longer had to take Armstrong's promises on faith. This place made him certain. The Ambassador College campus provided instant reinforcement that he'd made the right decision. It represented what he could have: who he could become.

Dad took black-and-white pictures with a good Kodak camera outfitted with German lenses that he'd bought overseas. The photos show a series of widely-spaced mansions with vast manicured lawns. Stately cedars of Lebanon and Norfolk pines so tall that you had to crane your neck to see the tops. Banks of flowers, palm trees, and hedges created vistas from every vantage point. Armstrong's Mediterranean-style mansion, encircled with friezes and roofed in red tile, built atop a hill, provided the centerpiece of the college grounds. All of this was made possible by the tithes and offerings of a few thousand Charles Powerses.

Members were expected to sacrifice for "the Work." And they did. People sent up to a third of their incomes to pay for this opulence instead of buying shoes for their children or stew meat for dinner. Armstrong explained that he could gain the credibility he needed to preach the gospel to world leaders only by having wealth and power behind him. From his point of view, the college both trained future ministers and their wives and showed the outside world that there was scholarship and research behind his dogma.

Looking through the prism of a half-century, I know that the church gave Dad ownership in something grander than he had ever seen or imagined. It reinforced his belief in his superiority. After all, he was Charles Powers. This place represented who he really was. The reasons for Dad's attractions to the church weren't everyone's reasons. Some wanted to be told how to live every minute of every day. Some knew they could use the experience to gain money and power over the weak. Some were like Mother — the frog placed in a pan of cold water over a low flame. The temperature had gone up so slowly that she didn't realize she was being cooked. When it became apparent that the Radio Church of God was going to dictate her and Dad's lives, she adapted. While she didn't believe the church's teachings at first, she found it easier to go along than to protest. Conformity led to acceptance which led to conversion.

When we returned home to Little Rock in August 1958 and Dad went back to his job teaching auto body repair at the Arkansas School for the Deaf, his resolve to keep the letter of Armstrong's laws deepened. Each Friday, he checked the paper for the exact time of sunset. At that moment, our Sabbath observance began. Mother would have prepared all of the food we were to eat for the next twenty-four hours. Tuna casserole, hamburger and noodles, a pot roast or fried chicken on special occasions, deviled eggs, purple-hulled peas, squash and onions, tomatoes, radishes, carrots. The table was set for supper and the kitchen was clean. After eating, we scraped away the remains of our meals, rinsed the plates and left them in the sink so they could be washed Saturday night. The radio was silent, except when *The World Tomorrow* came on. Dad didn't go to the garage or pay bills. He believed Armstrong when he told members that Sabbath-keeping was the test command on which members' salvation and eternity depended.

I learned to play church, sitting quietly and looking at my books. I wasn't allowed to run or make loud noises or ride my pedal car. Mother and Dad studied their Bibles, read *The Plain Truth* and *Good News* magazines, worked on lessons in the Bible Correspondence Course. On Sabbath morning, we ate Uncle Sam Raisin Bran for breakfast and dressed in our best clothes to receive or visit church members. In nice weather we gathered on quilts spread under a shade tree. When it was more comfortable inside, we jammed into some believer's living room. Children sat with their parents during the prayer, singing, Bible reading, and discussions that passed for our church service.

Afterwards, everyone ate a potluck meal the women had brought. We children weren't allowed to play tag or hide-and-go-seek. After more visiting, my family piled in the car for the drive home. Once there, we napped and read until the sun went down.

When Mother became pregnant with Steve, she prepared for natural childbirth by reading and doing the exercises recommended in Dr. Grantley Dick Read's book *Childbirth Without Fear*. She also studied the old Jacobsen book *You Must Relax*. I can still retrieve mental snapshots of Mother lying on the oval hooked rug on the living room floor, panting breaths and building her abs. On the October day in 1958 when Steve was born, she and Dad left in the car and returned five hours later with a baby.

Herbert W. Armstrong was the god of my little-girl world. When *The World Tomorrow* broadcast came on the radio, my family became reverentially quiet. We read Old Testament stories that reinforced what we were told about the God whose name is always capitalized. Yahweh or I AM THAT I AM was a white man who sat on a golden throne in the heavens. Because human nature is evil, He gave us many laws to live by. Love was conditional — follow the rules and He will love you. Ignore the rules and He'll wipe you off the face of the earth.

There was no gray in this world. I knew that one day, if I were good, I would go to the Place of Safety. If I were bad, I would either die in the Tribulation or burn in the Lake of Fire. It wasn't okay to make mistakes because God expected perfection. Every word that Mr. Armstrong said was God's word. If I didn't follow every rule, my life would end before the Kingdom of God.

I had no clue that there was a world in which people celebrated Christmas and Easter and birthdays. That there were doctors and medicines that made you feel better when you were sick. That if you mentioned the names of the holy days to people outside the church, they'd look at you like you'd lost your mind. That women wore paint on their faces. That ministers didn't arrive at most people's houses unannounced and rifle through drawers, closets, and cabinets to see if they were clean. That most people weren't audited by their churches for tithing compliance.

I knew that it was a sin to eat pork or fat. Every vegetable we ate came from our backyard garden, grown without pesticides, fertilized with cow manure. Our eggs were collected from the chicken house and our milk came from the dairy down the road. I didn't eat candy or drink sodas because they were made with white sugar. If I acted up, I got whipped. If I squirmed in church, a deacon would take me out for a spanking. I looked forward to the Feast and knew that before the Days of Unleavened Bread, we would have to clean the house from top to bottom to get rid of every bread and cracker crumb. I knew that the Tribulation would come before I was an adult.

Unlike my parents, I didn't have to be indoctrinated into the Radio Church of God. It was my life.

CHAPTER TEN

Big Sandy

In 1960, when I was five years old, Mother, Dad, Steve and I were still living in the country outside of Little Rock, but change was on the horizon. The grounds in Big Sandy were becoming more than a meeting place for holy days. The church had decided to build a second Ambassador College campus there. It would draw members who could live and work in the nearby town (population 848 in the 1960 census), eventually buying out the nonbelievers and establishing an extension of the church's property. God's laws were difficult to keep, and His chosen people needed to live together so they could keep each other strong in the faith. In 1960, there wasn't much at the campus, other than the tabernacle, campgrounds, and scores of little white metal huts that looked like oversized, gable-roofed phone booths, originally built to house attendees at the Feast of Tabernacles.

During this time, my parents began discussing whether the time was right to make the move.

"I can make a go of it," Dad said to Mother, as they sat at the kitchen table sharing after-dinner coffee.

"You've always wanted your own business," Mother answered, "and you've done real well selling wrecks you've fixed." While teaching at the Arkansas School for the Deaf, Dad also had been working part-time for himself in the ramshackle garage beside our house.

"The church people'll bring their cars to me because there isn't another auto body repairman in the church there now," Dad replied.

"Think there'd be enough work to support us?" Mother asked.

"If there isn't now, there will be soon. I want to get my business going before someone else does." He pulled a piece of notebook paper from his Bible Correspondence Course ring binder and picked up a pencil.

"We can live real close until your business gets built up. You have tools already."

"I'll need a wrecker, a good air compressor, a better torch…" He began to write on the paper.

"How'll we get the money?" Mother asked.

"Don't know yet, but God will provide."

Dad made two trips to Big Sandy to find a place for his business and for us to live. Later in 1960, Dad and Mother sold our house in Little Rock and used the equity to buy a well-worn singlewide, two-bedroom trailer. It was blue and white, but the paint had oxidized so it looked like it was covered in chalk dust. Dad hitched it to the back of a green 1958 Chevrolet wrecker he'd bought, rigged brake lights, and we headed for Texas.

The long, slow drive took us through Prescott, Emmett, Hope, and Texarkana. We entertained ourselves reading Burma-Shave signs. "He lit a match…to check his tank…now they call him…skinless Frank…Burma-Shave." We laughed at the hapless Frank.

In Upshur County, Dad took Highway 155 south from Gilmer, the county seat. Before I-20 was built, Highway 80 was the main artery connecting Dallas with points east. Big Sandy had one light — at the intersection of Highway 80 and Highway 155, which was also called Gilmer Road. There we turned east; two blocks later, Dad pulled in behind the Texaco station at the southwest corner of Highway 80 and South Pearl Street.

He waved at a beanpole-thin man standing in front of the station's garage. "Y'all get out so I can park the trailer."

I crawled over Mother and Steve, reaching for the door handle.

"Whoa! Slow down," Mother said. "There's a lot of traffic."

"I have to go to the bathroom," I answered. "Now!" I squirmed to reinforce the urgency of my situation.

"You're just going to have to wait another minute." Mother opened the door and fumbled to find Steve's shoes, which had rolled under the seat.

The ground rumbled as the big freight-haulers roared through the train overpass just east of the station. The noise of eighteen-wheelers shifting gears, revving engines, and screeching brakes was constant.

Mother lifted two-year-old Steve onto the ground and tightly held his hand. When she put her feet down, they slid out from under her. She pulled herself up and looked at her black hands. Then, for the first time, she took in the empty lot that was our new home.

Gasoline, paint, oil, transmission fluid, and solvents had been poured into the ground. The asphalt was broken into chunks. The soil, an oily black, stank of petroleum. A few weeds had the fortitude to poke through the mess. Discarded buckets, car parts, and cans littered the lot.

Mother bit her lip.

"Mommy, *I have to go.*"

Silently, she took my hand and the three of us walked to the restroom.

Dad backed the trailer into place. He was all smiles, joshing with the skinny man as they took it off the hitch and piled cinderblocks around the trailer's tires so it wouldn't move. When they were done, Dad pulled the wrecker into the shade of the station's canopy, where we waited. Mother had a pained look on her face.

"I'm hungry. Let's get some hamburgers," Dad said jovially, oblivious to Mother's unhappiness.

We crawled back into the truck and sat four abreast on the bench seat.

Dad drove west on Highway 80 past a pond with the grand name of Big Sandy Lake. A couple of weathered picnic tables sat under a tree not far from the bank. Kids thrashed in the brown water. An old wooden skating rink stood on the back of the property. A little farther down the road, there were two hamburger joints.

"I'll get us some food." Dad turned into the second drive-in. "We'll drive around and eat." He didn't ask us what we wanted.

Dad didn't notice Mother's silence as he gave us a guided tour of our new hometown.

"Seven miles that way is a Negro school. Jarvis Christian College. In Hawkins," he said, aiming his index finger toward the west.

At the red light, he turned right, toward downtown. Pearl Street and Gilmer Road were the main north-south drags, running parallel to each other until they crossed Highway 80 and converged two blocks later. The downtown buildings and dilapidated red brick storefronts extended for about a quarter-mile on both sides of the street. Most of the stores were vacant. The only ones left were a fabric store, a five-and-dime, a drugstore, and the post office.

"This used to be a railroad town." Dad pointed to rickety frame houses along the railroad tracks. "That's where the trainmen stayed. Houses must be fifty, sixty years old."

The downtown arc ended at the Texaco station. We re-crossed Highway 80 and drove into the residential part of Pearl Street, a three-block ghetto of tumble-down houses and a couple of trailers. On our right, a quarter-mile of paved road turned to dirt past a tank farm.

"This is a shortcut that goes to the back entrance of the campus. It's the Old Big Sandy Highway." Dad turned the truck down the road and the dust started flying.

From the first time we drove on this road, it gave me the creeps. For reasons I can't explain, big tanks have always bothered me, and these were surrounded with weeds and stickers. I imagined snakes and wildcats lived in the woods off the road. The area always gave me a sense of foreboding.

About a mile out of Big Sandy, we crossed a creaky, wooden one-lane bridge over Big Sandy Creek. The bridge jumped up and down when we drove over it, sounding like a dozen basketballs being dribbled.

"Noooo." Steve hid his eyes.

Dad laughed. "Son, we're going to be just fine."

"Charles, let's go back to the trailer and get settled in. I'm tired of driving," Mother said. It was the first thing she had said since we left the station.

Back at the trailer, Dad connected the electricity and the sewer line while I helped Mother clean up the lot. She hauled a burn barrel from the side of the station to the front of the trailer. We picked up every bit of junk that would move and Mother hosed down the asphalt. It didn't do any good.

"Mommy, my feet are black." The gooey tar stuck to the soles of my feet and wouldn't come off.

Mother looked at me, slowly lowered her eyelids and shook her head in resignation.

"Come sit on the step," she said. "Stay there, don't come in the house. You'll get that mess all over the floor."

I picked at the muck and succeeded in spreading it to my hands.

Mother returned with a bottle of alcohol and a washcloth. I giggled and squirmed as she rubbed my feet.

"Pumpkin, you and Steve are going to have to wear shoes when you go outside," she said. "You might step on something and get cut."

Mother made a home for us in the trailer, sewing curtains to cover the louvered windows over the banquette seating in the living area, putting rugs on the hard linoleum floor, and decorating the bathroom in pink. The bedrooms were too small to hold anything other than beds, which were covered in knobby chenille spreads that left indentations on my skin if I laid on them for long. We drank whole milk poured from wide-mouth gallon jars with three inches of cream on top delivered by Mrs. Wimberley, a dairy farmer who also sold eggs. We picked pecans after they fell on Mrs. Hammock's lawn across the road. We bought produce from a farm in Betty, Texas. We discovered breakfast beef and all-beef hot dogs made for church members at a packing plant in Gladewater.

Dad opened Powers' Auto Body Repair in the Texaco garage. Male laughter echoed across the lot as he visited with his co-workers in Christ in the shop. At home he smiled a lot, showing the space behind his upper right eye tooth where a molar had been extracted and not replaced. Every day I heard him pounding his sledgehammer, banging away at a dent. When he painted a car, he'd pull down the garage door. When you looked inside, all you saw was a white fog, but you heard the roar of the air compressor. The garage smelled of paint and lacquer thinner, mixed with the intense sweetness of Bondo dent filler. Before he walked across the asphalt lot to come home, Dad scrubbed his hands with Go-Jo and wiped them clean with a red shop towel. Some days his khaki work clothes were covered with a fine, misty residue. The same must have been true of his lungs; he didn't use a breathing filter. I thought his work shoes looked like they belonged to an artist, covered in a rainbow of paint spatters.

CHAPTER ELEVEN

American Idyll

I wandered down to the hospital cafeteria, looking for my brothers. The place looked and smelled like the cafeteria of my junior high school. Dan was loading a tray with food. I wasn't hungry, but the grease and sugar were calling my name. At home I don't touch fried chicken or mashed potatoes with cream gravy or lemon meringue pie. In East Texas, that's all I want.

"This is so weird." Dan put his lunch on the table and pulled out a chair.

I unloaded my tray.

"Have you been in to see him?" I asked.

"Yeah," he shook his head and reached for a plastic fork. "I walked in that room and had no clue who I was looking at. You know, Mother could have shown me a perfect stranger and I wouldn't have known the difference. My own father, and I had no memory of ever seeing him before."

"You were too little," I answered, trying to put myself in Dan's place. If I were in his shoes, I'd be a lot more pissed off than he seemed to be.

"I can't imagine a father walking away from his children. How could he do that?" I heard bewilderment and hurt rather than anger in his voice.

I chose to take his question as a rhetorical one and busied myself nibbling a cardboard-tasting tomato wedge slathered with bright orange, gelatinous Thousand Island. "You think he's brain-dead?"

"He doesn't look it. I didn't expect him to look so young and strong. Damn, he's even got hair."

I smiled. "But men get the hair gene from their mothers. Don't worry. You're okay there, too. Papaw had a full head of hair when he died."

Dan put down his hamburger and turned to face me, serious again. "I feel bad that I didn't try to get to know him."

"By the time you were old enough, it was too late. He was ruined." Dan needed to hear again that Dad hadn't been a saint and that he had rejected us because of his own shortcomings, not because we weren't worthy of love.

"When did he change?" Dan asked, though we'd explored this territory before.

"I was in the third grade," I said, "a year before you were born…" I didn't know where the sentence was going.

"The liquor?" Dan asked.

"More complicated than that." I picked at the powdered potatoes and dry, stringy chicken. "Before you were born, he was mean most of the time. But he'd still be sorry after he'd gone on a rampage. After you were born, he was a nasty son of a bitch all the time."

"There must have been a time when he was okay, or Mother wouldn't be upstairs holding his hand," Dan said.

"She says that the six years before I was born were wonderful. When I was little, he hugged and loved on me. A lot more than Mother."

Dan looked away.

"If you had the good memories, you'd have the bad ones, too. I wouldn't wish that on anyone." I put my hand over his and squeezed.

"It didn't hit me until today that I went to high school half-an-hour away from him," Dan said. "And I never saw him. Never thought about finding him." His voice sounded strained.

"You would've just gotten hurt." I remembered the phone call back in 1978 and later how he ignored my son's pictures.

"At least you tried."

"Not after I realized that he would ruin my life if he got close." I wadded up my paper napkin, hard. "I don't know if you've heard this, but about the time I graduated from high school, Granddaddy Powers tried to help Dad, even though he didn't have two nickels to rub together. Do you know what Dad did?"

Dan stared at me.

"He used a gun to rob Granddaddy and steal his car. He robbed his own eighty-year-old father. Is that someone you want knowing where you live?"

Silently we collected the remains of our meal, now congealed in grease, and threw them into the trash.

The world that Dan never knew revolved around two places — home and the Radio Church of God/Ambassador College campus. Dad's business in the Texaco station garage prospered, and within a year he was able to borrow $7,000 from Mr. Dingler at the First State Bank to buy a house at 310 North Pearl Street. Our new house was three-quarters of a mile from Highway 80 in a neighborhood with small, comfortable frame homes. We didn't have sidewalks or curbs, but ditches in front of the houses held the rainwater. In the spring, they were a great place to catch tadpoles.

After living in the trailer on a stinky, noisy, ugly lot, the little yellow house was like a castle. When we first moved in, it was a place of comfort and safety. I pretended that I was a rich woman, dressed in an evening gown and wearing jewels, showing a friend her new home. *Stephanie, here is the living room, I said with a flourish of my right arm. Don't you love the new cream-colored Naugahyde couch with matching chair? And the console hi-fi? Our records sound so good. It's like you're there with the musicians. And right back here is a new mahogany wood dining room table with six chairs.*

We had two bedrooms, a bathroom, a living room large enough to hold a small dining table and chairs in addition to the couch and recliner, a kitchen and a room adjacent to the kitchen that became a den. If you fudged a little with the tape, it would have measured a thousand square feet.

Brown and white awnings shaded the living room and the kitchen windows. The house had no air conditioning; the only relief from the 105-degree summers came from an attic fan that stirred the hot air. Dad was determined to be comfortable and, since he couldn't afford a window unit air conditioner, he got the next best thing — a swamp cooler. This was a big, heavy metal box wedged into the bedroom window and propped outside with boards. The noisy contraption circulated water from a reservoir in front of a blowing fan. It cooled Mother and Dad's bedroom from ninety-five to ninety.

Attached to the house was a one-car garage and, at its back, a storage and laundry room. This area was built on a slab instead of pier and beam like the house, so it was eighteen inches lower. You had to take three steps down to get from the kitchen to the garage. Its floor was flush with the ground in the backyard and made a fine, damp place for copperheads to curl up when it got too hot outside.

I loved the yard. The previous owner, Mr. Gorman, had lavished time and money on it. In front, he'd put two large rose beds filled with fragrant red, pink, and yellow flowers. Mother decided they were too much trouble, so we tore them out and grassed the beds with St. Augustine. A cone-shaped tulip tree bloomed at the edge of Pearl Street on one side of our driveway, dropping blossoms of pinkish purple so sturdy that they felt like plastic. Each time the power company came to trim the tree, Mother stood guard, making sure they didn't ruin the shape. A black wrought-iron pot hanging from an iron tripod also occupied the front yard. It once contained flowers, but by the time we moved in, there was nothing left but dirt. The neighborhood kids imagined that cannibals used it to cook people.

On one side of the house was a silver leaf maple, perfect for climbing. Along the fence that divided our place from the Schmidts', there was a tangle of bushes and shrubs where we kids could hide and pretend that we were deep in an African jungle. The other side of the house was a riot of cannas, irises, gladiolas, and daffodils.

A backyard fig tree produced more figs than we could eat or make into preserves, and a row of four plums in front of the clothesline made sweet and juicy fruit. But since church law forbade the use of insecticides, we had to be careful to avoid the worms that invaded every piece. Every spring, green, yellow, and black caterpillars covered a catalpa tree on the fence line. Mother froze handfuls of them to use as fishing bait, telling us that she'd learned that from Papaw when he used the same kind of worms to fish; the Cadron in Arkansas.

We stayed true to our country roots by tilling the back third of our yard and sowing seeds for vegetables of all kinds. I developed a love for the earth and things that grow in it. It was never a chore to till the soil or weed or plant. I greedily ate strawberries still warm from the sun's heat as soon as they ripened. I pulled carrots and radishes from the soil, rinsed them with the garden hose and had a snack. There was something magical about the smell of the earth, particularly in the spring when it was freshly turned. I liked to lie in the garden and see how much life I could find in a square foot of ground: tiny purple flowers that I called violets, blooming clover that sometimes hid a leaf with four petals, armies of ants and roly-poly worms. Occasionally I'd find a granddaddy longlegs or a walking stick.

We had a spotted rat terrier named Tiny. Dad removed enough of the under-pinning from the back of the house to make the crawl space accessible, and Tiny slept on rags there. I had the job of feeding her from cans of smelly Strongheart dog food. The smell gagged me every time I opened one. For a while we kept rab-bits in a hutch. The big one was named Nibbles, and he bit our fingers when we tried to feed him carrots. Terry the terrapin wandered around the backyard living on bits of hamburger meat and dead flies. For a while there was a guppy tank in the kitchen. We couldn't afford fancy fish or an aerator, so the water stank and slimed after a week. I hated cleaning the fish bowl because a fish or two always jumped out of the water and died because they were invisible on the multi-colored linoleum floor.

A herd of white-faced Herefords grazed in the big pasture behind our back fence. Farther back was a pear orchard. About a half-mile beyond the orchard, almost hidden by dense pines, lay the railroad tracks. There lurked the bogeymen my parents warned us about. Hobos. We kids were to run home as fast as our legs would carry us if we saw one. It's odd that given my fears of everything else, those poor men never concerned me. The few sad souls who came around were polite and just wanted food.

Two miles beyond the railroad tracks, a white wooden fence marked the perim-eter of the Radio Church of God campus. Here the overgrown roadside and forest gave way to an irrigated expanse of Bermuda grass. For years, an old ranch-style house set in a grove of pine trees and a white frame house graced the front of the property.

A runway long enough to accommodate private passenger jets ran parallel to the Old Big Sandy Highway; it was added in the early sixties. We were told that King Hussein of Jordan landed there when he came for a secret visit with Herbert W. We didn't know he had been at the campus until Mr. Armstrong told us about it later. It seemed strange to me that no one I knew had seen King Hussein or his jet, but everyone believed he'd been there. If Mr. Armstrong said it, it must have been true.

Groundskeepers groomed flowers in the esplanade and in beds around the main buildings. They cleared the stream of leaves and branches, cut the grass, edged the roads and walkways, trimmed the trees, limed the track, swept the parking lots. Maintenance men kept every painted surface looking fresh. The pavement was free of cracks. All the lights worked.

The college students always smiled. You never heard cross words or raised voices. Every adult was addressed as "Sir" or "Ma'am." We saw them sitting on blankets under the trees, Bibles spread before them, drinking in the Word. They sprinkled their conversations with church acronyms — HWA (Herbert W. Armstrong), GTA (Garner Ted Armstrong) — and shorthand references like The Kingdom, The Feast, The Work. The young men sported dress pants, starched shirts, and crew cuts. Young women, their long hair coiled into buns or tied into ponytails, wore skirts hemmed to mid-calf and high-collared plain blouses with flat shoes. The girls scrubbed their faces; the men shaved every day. If a student got a little heavy, a college physical education instructor prepared an exercise plan and the student sweated off the extra pounds. The female students spoke with soft voices and looked adoringly at the men. But no one held hands or kissed. Nobody drove too fast. The music — always classical or orchestral or church-approved soft pop — was never too loud. No rock 'n' roll or that awful din black people made. Littering was unthinkable. Tobacco was prohibited.

I thought Big Sandy was perfect. Just as God intended.

CHAPTER TWELVE
Faith Healing

It was early afternoon by the time the ICU nurse asked us to convene in a conference room. Mother and I walked down an endless, antiseptic corridor, passing rooms in which patients bearing the gray pallor of impending death lay quiet and motionless.

I caught sight of a Walgreen's bag. Armstrong's words tumbled into my consciousness. "Pharmakeus," he had often said, "was Greek for 'sorcerer.'" I could almost hear his voice: "Satan," he had repeatedly sermonized, "founded modern medicine. If you rely on doctors, you are telling God that you don't believe he will heal you. You have chosen to rely on Satan's agents instead. If you go to a doctor, you will burn in the LAKE OF FIRE! When you are sick, call one of God's ministers to lay hands on you and anoint you with oil. That is all you need."

"Mother," I asked, "did you buy into all that stuff we were taught? About medicine?"

She looked at me like she'd been thinking the same thing.

"I know it's stupid," I continued, "really stupid, but I'm still uncomfortable with doctors and hospitals."

"I found out later that the preachers, the important ones, went to doctors when they needed one," Mother said. "But they wouldn't let me get my eardrum fixed. Mary Prociw told me to do it anyway, but I was too afraid to break the rule." Mrs. Prociw had been Mother's best friend in Big Sandy.

"Thank goodness the Campho-Phenique worked."

"That was my cure for everything." A wry grin creased her face. "A few drops in my ear every day for four months and the air stopped whistling through."

"Remember that woman with pneumonia? She came to the house, and you did something for her." I pursed my lips as I tried to recall her name.

"Mrs. Flint. I'd forgotten about that," Mother answered.

"What was it you gave her?" I asked.

"I'd read about mustard plasters, so I covered her chest with pieces of a sheet I wrung out in hot water and covered that with dry mustard paste."

"And she got well." I remembered the pride I'd felt at her ability to help people.

Mother turned away and continued in a softer voice, "I helped other people, then almost died having Dan."

"I remember coming to the house right after he was born," I said. "The blood . . ."

We were quiet. I'd replayed that day in my mind scores of times. I was only nine years old but the events profoundly impacted me. Until I was thirty I couldn't have blood drawn without passing out for extraordinary periods of time; the longest was forty-five minutes when I was being tested for my marriage license. And, I had no interest in having children until becoming pregnant and miscarrying at thirty-seven caused my maternal instincts to overwhelm the fear. For me, childbirth equaled blood equaled death.

"Did you have any idea before the delivery that something was wrong?"

"Yeah." She stared at the wall. "I could tell he was breech. I kept waiting for him to turn, but he didn't."

"But you still had the delivery table set up in the bedroom of the house. Didn't it occur to you that things might go wrong?" A part of me was still angry with her for making that decision.

"I went to see a doctor — Dr. Kolker — and he said he'd come to the house to assist in the delivery. That made me feel better," she answered, her voice emotionless.

"But wasn't that just as much a sin as going to the hospital?" I asked. I had trouble getting my head around the idea that she would choose death over breaking a rule; that she would follow Armstrong instead of staying alive to take care of us.

"He agreed not to give me medicine or blood or do any surgery. He was just going to assist with natural childbirth."

Big deal, I wanted to say. With his hands tied, Dr. Kolker wouldn't have been much more help than a minister with a vial of oil. "And the ministers said that was okay?"

"Everyone knew that ministers' wives had doctors help them deliver. This time I didn't ask."

On that late November morning in 1964 when I left for school, Mother had been in labor all night. That afternoon, Mrs. Prociw met Steve and me when we got off the bus and took us to her house. The baby still hadn't arrived. I could sense that she was worried. She gave us a snack, and we finished our homework. By suppertime there was still no baby, so we ate with the Prociw family. About seven o'clock, the phone rang. A minute later, Mrs. Prociw came into the den where we were watching TV.

"You have a new baby brother," she said.

I let out a sigh of relief.

"Let's walk to your house so you can see your Mother."

We put on our coats and walked the block and a half home.

No one had prepared me for the scene. We came in the back door and into the kitchen, where the first thing that hit me was the metallic, pungent smell. We walked through the bedroom that Steve and I shared, and started down the hall by the bathroom. Blood was everywhere. It looked like a murder scene. Bloody towels were piled in the bathtub. Blood was spattered on the walls. Blood smeared the floor. I was scared out of my wits, but I didn't let on.

We stepped into the master bedroom, where Mother was lying on the bed, her face a purplish blue. Though she was barely conscious, she was nursing Dan. There was blood on the bed and the delivery table, though efforts had been made to clean them. I knew something was dreadfully wrong. I kissed Mother and Mrs. Prociw took me out of the room. I have forgotten everything else about that night. I have no memory of anyone explaining anything. All I remember is that Mother survived.

I turned to Mother who was lost in her own thoughts. "I've never been clear about why you bled so much."

"Dan was breech with the umbilical cord wrapped around his arm. Since I had to have a vaginal birth, the force of the delivery ripped out part of my uterus."

"Oh, God." I winced. "How did you handle the pain?"

"I didn't feel anything by then. And it wasn't the blackberry brandy I drank while I was in labor. I remember the sensation of leaving my body and looking down on the room. I knew I was dying, but I fought it because you kids needed me. I couldn't bear to leave you alone with your dad." Now there was a steely edge to her voice.

"What stopped the bleeding?"

"I remembered that breast feeding a new baby causes the uterus to contract and stops bleeding, so I found the strength to tell them to put Dan up to nurse. After a few minutes, it stopped."

We got quiet when my brothers, my sister-in-law Gloria, Billy and his daughter Molly joined us in the conference room. We took seats around a large table. After we had waited long enough to appreciate the doctor's importance and his busy schedule, he walked in and stood at the head of the table. Younger than me and not much taller, he carried himself with confidence that comes from having and using authority. "Dr. J. Ulney" was stitched across the breast of his lab coat. Dr. Ulney took control of the proceedings much like a federal judge would take charge of a pretrial conference.

"Good afternoon. I know y'all are here to find out about Charles Powers' condition. It's grave. He doesn't have long to live. If he's kept on a respirator, it's possible that he could live for a month or so, provided he doesn't have another heart attack. He won't survive another heart attack."

"What about the other problems?" I asked.

"He has no liver function as the result of advanced cirrhosis. Congestive heart failure. Severe pneumonia. His kidneys are failing, and his feet are turning dark from lack of circulation. It's remarkable that he's lived so long in such condition."

"Is there any brain activity?" I pressed on.

"We're fairly confident that there's none, but I want to run some more tests." The doctor paused, tilted his chin toward his chest, and gave me a withering look. "I'm most disturbed," he said, "that you're eager to discontinue life support."

I stared back at him, surprised at the hostility.

"As I understand it, you've not seen your father for many years?" he continued.

"That's right," I answered, struggling not to sound defensive. *Was I going to have to tell this jackass my life's story?*

"Yet you seem ready to make a quick decision."

My eyes bore into his. "I was told by the ICU nurse last night that he's in a coma and probably brain-dead." I took a deep breath to keep my voice from quivering with anger. "He told me that the family needed to discontinue life support or the state would keep him hooked up to the respirator. If there's brain activity and you believe he'll have some quality of life, I'm opposed to discontinuing life support. If he's brain-dead, then I think it's wrong to keep his body alive."

"I highly doubt that the nurse said that to you."

I drew in my breath audibly. *Holy shit. He's calling me a liar.* "Why would you doubt it?"

"It would've been against our policy."

"Policy or not, it's what happened." I wasn't about to give up ground.

"Do you have any idea what kind of condition your father was in when he arrived?" he parried.

"I assume it wasn't good. Years of alcoholism had to have taken their toll."

"He looked like a street person. I don't think he'd bathed in six months. He had matted hair that hadn't been cut in a year. A beard out to here," he said, holding his right hand four inches from his chin. "His clothes were filthy. He'd probably worn the same underwear for weeks. We cleaned him up so he'd look presentable." The doctor's words made it clear that he thought it was my fault that Dad was in such pathetic shape.

I drew on years in the courtroom to keep my cool. Caught up in the give-and-take, I had been oblivious to everyone else in the room. I was startled when Steve's voice interrupted. "It's true, we're estranged from Dad, but we're here to do the right thing. We don't want him to become a ward of the state. We want him to get the best care. We want him to be comfortable. If and when you advise us that the time is right, we'll make the decision to discontinue life support." He was playing his usual role of conciliator, just as I had played mine as the out-in-front, argumentative, emotional type who gets things on the table.

Now that he was talking with a man of reason, Dr. Ulney softened. "There was a brief time shortly after he was brought in when Mr. Powers regained consciousness. He told me to do everything I could to save his life. I intend to do that. I'll leave him on the respirator for the next forty-eight hours and observe his condition. If he shows no improvement and the tests all indicate that there's no brain activity, I'll present you with a decision then." He stood up.

Pompous ass, I thought. *He'll tell us what the decision is.*

Steve thanked him. "I live in Shreveport. We're available on short notice if needed. I'd like to be able to speak with you regularly to get an update."

"Fine. You can get my information from the nurse." The doctor walked out of the room. I sat for a moment, trying to avoid going into a rant about Dr. Ulney's performance, and followed the family to the waiting room.

An Episcopal lay minister whom Mother had called to administer last rites was looking for us. It wasn't something that would have occurred to me to arrange, but I wasn't opposed. Mother had been an Episcopalian for several years, as had Steve since he and Gloria married in 1994. For fifteen years I'd been working with an Episcopal priest who had become a Jungian therapist and was more or less comfortable with what I knew about the Episcopalian approach to religion. And Dan, who was not nearly as conflicted about such things, was okay with whatever the rest of us wanted.

"Powers family?" asked the man in a black suit and white shirt as he saw us enter the waiting area.

Mother stepped up and extended her hand. "Yes, thanks for coming. He's this way." We introduced ourselves as we walked.

I couldn't help thinking of the irony of the five of us being together to pray and listen to words spoken from the Bible. I smiled. Imagine Dad knowing that some "damned preacher" was praying over him. If he had any conscious life in him, we'd know about it the instant the first "Father in heaven" was uttered.

Mother, Steve and Gloria, Dan and I stood beside Dad's bed, holding hands. I stood on the end, as far away from the bed as possible. The minister's sacred ritual felt impersonal. He might have been intoning God's words on behalf of a stranger. Then he asked us to repeat the Lord's Prayer in unison: "Forgive us our trespasses as we forgive those who trespass against us." *Dear God,* I prayed, *if there is something after death, please give him another chance.*

We went downstairs and stood in the hospital foyer. Steve and Gloria were going back to Shreveport to be with their children and tend to the propeller business. Dan had to get back to his family and his post-production studio in Austin. Mother was ready to go home to her place on Cross Lake in Shreveport.

I was glad that they were returning to their lives. While I yearned to run back to the comfortable and familiar, there were things I had to do. Places I had to see. Memories I had to face. For once, work would take a backseat. My son would be fine with his dad and in school for another day.

I'd worked for years to understand how and why I had survived the scars inflicted by Dad and the Radio Church of God. I was satisfied that I knew that answer. It was a combination of intelligence, luck, self-discipline, drive, and if I engaged in a little hubris, the sense that I had been spared for a reason. What I didn't know was how to use this knowledge to find my true self and the happiness that had eluded me for forty-six years. There in the midst of the pines and poverty was a place to start.

CHAPTER THIRTEEN

The Oil Patch

I drove out of the hospital parking lot and turned onto Highway 80 for the twenty-five miles to Big Sandy.

West of Longview, I drove through the villages of Greggton and White Oak for the first time in thirty years. When I was a kid, I had no appreciation for the fact that this was the heart of oil country, though I saw the evidence every day. Back then drilling rigs, pumpjacks, and tanker trucks were ubiquitous; oil company signs announced ownership of pipelines, roads, and buildings.

It wasn't until law school that I learned the story of East Texas oil. Gregg, Upshur, Rusk, and Smith counties were ground zero. Just a few miles away in Kilgore, there had been a strike so rich that oil derricks were built on top of each other; unscrupulous operators perfected slant-hole drilling. With a cruel randomness, one property owner would become rich from a Cretaceous-age pool 3,000 feet below the surface of his farm while his neighbor wound up with nothing but cement plugs in a borehole.

At Dad's shop, I'd seen leather-skinned old men in faded overalls and heard them griping about how this oil company or that one had torn up their pasture or let a few head of cattle get out when they opened the gates for the danged tank trucks. These guys drove beat-up pickups with dried cow patties stuck to their tires. Half their teeth were missing. They didn't look like they could afford a cup of coffee. It always shocked me when Dad would mention an old codger and say he was worth millions.

The scenery I now saw along Highway 80 left no doubt that the East Texas oil rush was over. There were no signs of new drilling activity. The pipe yards, equipment storage, and crude tanks that had been the hallmarks of the East Texas landscape were mostly gone. I knew that most fields had watered out — the oil giving way to salt water. Others contained oil reservoirs, but the pressure had become too low for it to be economical to extract. Some old wells were still producing enough to keep the pumps running, but the glory days were gone. Johnson grass had grown over the oil-stained earth and shiny petroleum pools that I remembered. Run-down frame houses and trailer parks remained eyesores behind trees that had grown fatter and taller.

This was the outside world that had terrified me as a girl. Satan's world. I remember being in the Piggly Wiggly Grocery in Longview, warily eying the worldly people around me, fearful that being in their presence might endanger my eternal life. I knew that these wretched sinners were going to be tortured during The Tribulation and burned alive in the Lake of Fire. I was just as sure that, if given a chance, they would persecute members of God's One True Church just as we were told the Jews had persecuted Jesus. I learned never to make eye contact or speak with anyone outside the church. Better that they think me rude or stupid than to say or do something that might put the church in harm's way.

The ministers taught us that the heathen way of life was wrapped in beautiful raiment by the Devil to ensnare people who weren't smart enough to find God's way. It was he who made their unclean food taste good, their women look and act like whores, their sexually stimulating music enticing to young people. Their riches weren't the result of hard work but a trap that kept them from hearing and acknowledging the truth taught by the Radio Church of God. When these people laughed or looked like they were having fun, it was the handiwork of Lucifer, the fallen angel. God's people weren't meant to be happy until the Kingdom of God. We were meant to fight against the evil that would turn us from God's true teachings and labor every minute of every day for God's Work. Joy would come later.

Though I could never confess it, there was one part of the outside world that I loved. The food. On the ugly stretch of pavement between Greggton and Gladewater, I looked for Red Brown's Barbeque and U-turned where I thought it had been, just to make sure I hadn't missed it. The barbeque by which I judge all others was nowhere to be found. There was no finer dining in East Texas than a sliced beef sandwich from Red Brown's. Slabs of brisket blackened from twenty-four hours of hickory smoke yielded moist red-edged meat that was piled on a bun and slathered in a sauce redolent of molasses, pepper, mustard and tomato. Topped with onions, pickles and jalapenos, chased with Fritos, it was a sumptuous experience. If no one from the church was there, Mother and Dad would even let me have a Grapette. I guess they figured that if the church let adults mix their whiskey with 7-Up or Coca-Cola, it wasn't that big a deal for a kid to have a semiannual white sugar fix. And I savored every sinful sip.

As I drove, random memories came back. I looked for the radio station in a red-brick house with its tall antenna that used to sit deep on a lot surrounded by pine trees, but it was gone, too. Once when I was ten, while we were buying groceries in Gladewater, a teenage boy who worked for the station approached me, saying I'd won some records. Mother drove me to the station, and I claimed a stack of 45's by artists I'd never heard of. Which wasn't surprising since my knowledge of music was limited to classical, sacred, and a few pop tunes played by an orchestra or pianists. We tossed the whole lot when we got home.

In Gladewater, I found that the white stucco motel that always reminded me of California was standing. It still looked to me like a decent representation of 1940s California architecture. On the right were the fairgrounds where we'd gone to the

Gladewater Round-up Rodeo. Downtown, the Cozy Theater I'd been inside once — to see Gerry and the Pacemakers in the movie *Ferry Cross the Mersey* — had succumbed to the Longview cineplexes. Somewhere in this faded downtown, I got my first store-bought dress. It was for Passover in 1965, the springtime holy day when everyone wanted to wear something new. Garner Ted's wife, Shirley, was in the store when we picked out my dress: bright yellow with an empire yoke and pleated skirt. I beamed with pride when she told me how pretty I'd look wearing it.

At the edge of town, a quarter-mile from the county line, were the vine-covered remains of the Shamrock Café. In the sixties the Shamrock made the best chili cheese enchiladas and chicken-fried steak in the county. We ate there a couple of times a year. Each booth had its own jukebox. Once Dad gave me a nickel so I could hear "Unchained Melody."

I think we occasionally ate at the Shamrock because there was a liquor store next door. It sat on the Gregg County side of the Upshur-Gregg county line. Texas was and is a patchwork of wet and dry counties. If the Baptists constituted a majority of the voting public, the county would be dry. If the Methodists or Catholics predominated, chances were that it was wet. Even though Radio Church of God members must have drunk more than the Methodists, Catholics, and heathens put together, Upshur County didn't become wet until the seventies.

While we were finishing our last bites at the restaurant, Dad bought booze at the liquor store. He placed a sack of vodka and Seagram's 7 onto the floorboard of the wrecker and then went back inside for a couple of cases of Old Milwaukee. He wedged them between the bag of liquor and Mother's feet. Steve and I sat between our parents on the bench seat.

Outside of Gladewater, Highway 80 West narrowed to two lanes. Courtesy required slow-moving vehicles to pull onto the shoulder so faster vehicles could pass. Those who liked a more leisurely pace drove on the shoulder. Dad pulled over and put the truck in low gear.

"Toddy," he said, "reach into the glove compartment and get the can opener."

I rummaged until I found the church key.

"Open one of those beers and pass it to me." At eight years old, I could poke perfect triangular holes opposite each other on the top of the can.

Dad drank it in three gulps. When he was finished, he belched, rolled down his window and tossed the can over the top of the cab into the bar ditch.

"Charles," Mother said, "that sets a bad example."

Steve chimed in. "That's right, Dad. Remember the signs that say 'Don't Be a Litterbug'?"

"Hand me another beer," he said, burping loudly again. He sipped this one more slowly, but the empty can again went sailing out the window.

Mother glared, but didn't say anything.

Dad looked at Steve and me grinning.

It made me feel bad that Dad littered and even worse that he thought it was funny. The drinking and driving part never entered my head.

CHAPTER FOURTEEN

Somebody's Watching You

I pulled off the highway where Ma Tucker's Café and Powers' Auto Body Repair once did business. Dad had prospered at the Texaco garage, and in 1961 moved his repair shop onto the land next to the campus entrance where his business would be more convenient to the church. With their fleets of Chryslers, trucks and school buses, he had plenty of work. Members couldn't miss his corrugated metal shop as they entered and exited the campus.

On day when I was seven and Steve was four, Dad rushed into the house. Mother was coming from the backyard with a load of clean clothes she had taken off the line.

"I came to get the kids. We're going to the shop," he called in a state of high excitement.

"The shop?" she asked, trying to open the screen door without dropping the basket. "Why?"

"A photographer. He takes cowboy pictures."

"They need baths," she protested.

"Naw, they're fine. The guy has stuff to put on them. Just grab clean pants." Dad picked Steve up from the bed where he was napping. "Son, wake up. Want to ride a pony?"

Steve yawned and rubbed his eyes, then laid his sleepy head on Dad's shoulder.

In that black-and-white picture, taken in the dusty lot in front of Dad's shop, Steve is sitting on a mottled pony, grinning, in a cowboy hat and fringed shirt. They must not have bought my picture, because I don't remember ever seeing it.

A few times I persuaded Dad to take me out of school for lunch at Ma Tucker's. A grilled cheese sandwich and fries or a cup of hot chicken noodle soup was a vast improvement over my favorite homemade sandwich of cheddar cheese, mustard, and sliced green olives on coarse brown bread. We'd sit in a booth with shiny red seats and watch the locals drink coffee and jawbone with each other. The unmistakable proprietor with unnaturally red hair, bright coral lipstick, and cat-eyed glasses on a chain around her neck would give me a pat on the head.

I don't think Mother ever went to Ma Tucker's. My half-dozen trips were with

Dad, and I loved having that time alone with him. He was in his element and bantered with the patrons. I, on the other hand, was completely outside my comfort zone. Smoking was taboo in our world, and the restaurant reeked of tobacco. Most of its patrons weren't church members and I feared non-members. They were loud and used words I'd never heard. I was also afraid that I might swallow something unclean.

The Radio Church of God adhered to many Jewish dietary laws and others that Armstrong developed. The rules were so complicated that the church eventually published a guide that listed clean and unclean foods. I memorized them. We could eat meat from animals with hooves that parted if they chewed a cud. Beef, lamb, and deer were okay, but pigs weren't. Seafood had to possess both fins and scales. Crustaceans, bivalve and univalve mollusks, cephalopods, catfish, swordfish, and sturgeon were off-limits. As for poultry, Armstrong named six characteristics of fowl that were clean, such as having gizzards, craws and elongated middle front, and hind toes.

Animal fat and blood were prohibited. All fat had to be trimmed from meat before it was eaten. Cheap hamburger equaled sin. Mother says that when I was three and was asked to recite the Ten Commandments for the Whitleys at a Sabbath gathering in Little Rock, I replied: "Don't eat pork. Don't eat fat. Don't eat seeds." The food police directed members to use whole-wheat flour and brown sugar, molasses or honey and organically grown fresh vegetables, if available. Foods containing chemicals or preservatives, even pasteurized milk, were to be avoided.

It wasn't a spiritual sin to accidentally eat biblically unclean foods, but if you did it on purpose, it constituted lust, which violated the Tenth Commandment. Confronted with Ma Tucker's superbly grilled cheese sandwich, was I taking a chance on winding up in the Lake of Fire?

The food about which I was most conflicted was bacon — crispy, greasy, salty, glorious bacon. Not the breakfast beef we ate, but the real thing from pork bellies. Memow and Papaw's house always smelled like fried pig. Papaw loved salt pork that had been soaked to get rid of some of the salt, then fried. Memow loved plain old bacon. My mouth would water and I'd have to beat back Satan to keep from diving in.

On the rare occasion when we ate dinner at a restaurant, I was riddled with confusion and peppered waitresses with politely asked questions.

"Ma'am, can you please tell me if the green beans are seasoned with pork?"

"I think they are."

"Then I don't want 'em. Do you have any vegetables that aren't cooked with pork?"

"The corn or the squash….You're probably okay with the broccoli or mashed potatoes."

"Are the biscuits made with lard?"

"I'll have to ask the cook."

"If they have lard, I'll have the Texas toast, if it isn't put on the griddle with any pork. Can you ask the cook to make the chicken-fried steak with vegetable oil?"

"Anything else?"

"I'd like the cream gravy if it doesn't have bacon grease in it."

And when the waitress would valiantly attempt to take my dessert order, I had more questions. "Oh, by the way, I saw some pecan pie when I came in. Was the crust made with lard? Is there white sugar in it?"

It was much easier to eat at home.

During our first two years in Big Sandy, Dad was what was known back then as a hale fellow, well met. Visitors streamed to our house. Dad regaled them with stories, and the kitchen was often filled with laughter. He'd grill chicken or steak on an outdoor cooker he'd fabricated himself and serve our friends. Other times he'd sit at the kitchen table sharing beer, salted herring, and hot jalapeno peppers with the guys. He slapped the men on the back and warmly shook their hands. Whenever we went to his shop, people were always standing around, talking, as Dad did his work. He enfolded Steve and me in bear hugs. I remember him and Mother getting dressed up for dinner and dancing in Longview on their anniversary. Mother wore a lavender party dress with a net overlay on the skirt that she'd made. On her left shoulder Dad pinned the corsage he'd bought for her.

That man started to fade away by the time I was eight. I've concluded that there were two reasons. The first was the rigid strictures of the church and the church community. While no one ever characterized Charles Powers as a conformist, he tried to follow the dictates of the church. But the claustrophobia induced by 24-hour surveillance from scores of petty martinets who were lying in wait to catch a member breaking a rule was too much for him.

On an early spring night, Dad was sitting in an ancient green vinyl recliner in the den reading *The Plain Truth* while Mother and I cleared the supper dishes. We heard tires roll into the graveled driveway.

"Who is it?" Dad asked.

"Can't tell. Too dark," said Mother. She dried her hands and walked to the back door to see who was calling. None of our friends used the front door. "Nobody here."

The front screen door rattled. Dad tossed the magazine aside and muttered, "Not tonight." He opened the wooden front door and extended the screen to admit two men in suits. Ministers.

I went to the bedroom and left the door cracked so I could snoop. Children were expected to disappear whenever there was an adult conversation.

"Hello, Mr. Powers," said one of the men.

"How are you, Mr. Knight?" Dad answered, offering his hand. He was careful to firmly grip the guest's hand as Mr. Armstrong taught. "Mr. Lassiter," he said to second man. He showed them to the living room couch and took a seat.

"We're here to make sure you're tithing enough."

Dad nodded.

My stomach knotted. *Had my parents sinned?*

"We need to see your income tax return for last year and your bank records for the past two years," said Mr. Knight.

"Yes, sir."

"Do you ever get paid in cash?"

"Not very often," Dad answered.

"How do you keep track of the money?"

"I use it to buy groceries."

"Do you write down how much you get?" asked Mr. Lassiter, slowly enunciating his words, as if speaking to an imbecile.

"No, sir."

"Do you tithe on the cash you get?"

"Yes, sir."

"How do you know how much to tithe if you don't keep records?"

"I estimate that I get $50 a month in cash and pay tithes on that amount."

"Mr. Powers, that just isn't good enough," Mr. Lassiter said. "You must keep a written record of each dollar you receive and each dollar you pay in tithes to prove you are giving God every dollar that is His."

"I'm sorry. I didn't know that was necessary." I could tell from the quiver in Dad's voice that he was working to control his anger.

"If you'll get those records, we'll be on our way."

"Just a minute."

Dad walked from the living room into the kitchen where Mother had stayed out of sight. She, too, was expected to leave the talking to the men unless invited to join. Dad motioned to Mother. "Mary, get the stuff they need." He knew she'd heard the conversation.

Mother pulled two shoeboxes from the hall closet and rummaged for the papers.

Dad returned to the living room five minutes later and handed a stack of records to Lassiter.

"We commend you for having these documents organized. We'll be back in two weeks with the results."

After they left, Mother and Dad sat at the kitchen table with tall drinks of whiskey and soda.

"They'll decide we owe something," Mother said. "They always do."

"How much?" Dad asked.

"$35–$50 is my guess," Mother answered, shaking her head.

"Probably right."

Mother stared at the wall in front of her and tapped the fingers of her left hand on her cheek deep in thought. "I can cut $5 a week from the grocery bill if we only have meat for dinner three times a week."

"Won't be enough," Dad replied quickly. "Besides, I can't work all day and not have any meat for supper."

"Maybe you can work some accidents."

"I won't demean myself chasing wrecks." Dad raised the volume two notches.

"Just an idea, Charles. I'll think of something."

Everyone in Big Sandy knew each other. Everyone knew where everyone else lived and the vehicles they drove. People dropped by others' houses without advance warning, usually just to be friendly, but sometimes to scope out what you were wearing or to see whether the house was a wreck. You ran into church people in the liquor store, in Brookshire's, at the post office, at the five-and-dime. They knew what you bought and whether you used money that could go to The Work to buy Jim Beam instead of Four Roses. If your family splurged for a Sabbath-night dinner at El Chico's, someone would be there to report that you ate the tacos in puffy shells and had two glasses of beer. Or, heaven forbid, ate refried beans seasoned with lard. If your car pulled into the driveway after sunset on a Friday night, the next day a minister would ask you why. Much of what went on in Big Sandy was typical of small towns. But the active spying was something more. The church exhorted members to report straying brethren to the ministers so the weak ones would get help. Most members responded enthusiastically.

The second reason for Dad's embitterment was his failure to become a minister. That was the ticket to success in the Radio Church of God. "Ministers give speeches," he said, "so I'll learn how to speak." He knew he had to excel in the Spokesman's Club, a mandatory weekly meeting of church men, patterned on the Toastmasters. He worked hard at learning grammar so he sounded intelligent and educated. He read the dictionary and built his vocabulary.

His big speech in 1962 was about his wartime experiences in Europe. Dad outlined his main points. He gathered slides, photographs, and mementos. He delivered his speech to Mother again and again, and he practiced his gestures in front of a mirror. "These are the white cliffs of Dover where the D-Day invasion was launched," he said. "I first saw them in 1952 on a foggy day…" He laughed and said to Mother, "Hey! Aren't I great?"

The night of the presentation, Dad took extra care getting ready. I watched as he put a fresh blade in his razor and put plenty of shaving cream on his face so he wouldn't nick himself. After he finished shaving, he poured Old Spice into his hands and slapped it on his cheeks.

"Toddy," he said, "should I wear the yellow tie or the red one?"

"Yellow, Daddy," I answered, happy to be asked about such a big decision.

As he left the house, I thought he looked very handsome in his dark blue suit. As handsome as Garner Ted.

But the night didn't go as planned. Dad got nervous. He couldn't remember what he had planned to say. The words didn't come easily. Dad came home despondent. I was awakened by his angry voice. It upset me because it was unusual for him to yell. I lay in my bed straining to hear, so I slipped out of bed and cracked the kitchen door.

"Goddamn smart-asses," he ranted. "Just because they've been to Ambassador College, they think they're better than the rest of us." He filled a juice glass with whiskey and drank it straight.

"I'm sure it wasn't that bad." Mother put her hand on his shoulder. Dad pushed it away.

"They were smirking. Like who was I to try to be something better than a grease monkey?" He avoided eye contact with Mother and focused on the wall.

"Charles. God's ministers wouldn't act like that."

"The hell they wouldn't." He poured another glass of Seagram's.

Mother couldn't say anything that would help.

"I'll never be anything more but a plain member," he said. "Sons of bitches." It was the first time he'd ever made derogatory comments about the ministers — an act of blasphemy in the Radio Church of God.

"To hell with it," he said. He poured himself another drink.

"Charles!"

Dad didn't answer. When the whiskey was gone, he got up and went to bed.

CHAPTER FIFTEEN
....
Imperial School

I was hungry — discovering that Red Brown's Barbeque had gone was a big disappointment. But as I drove past the entrance to the church and saw the white prefabricated buildings that had once been Imperial School, my appetite vanished.

I started Imperial School in the fall of 1961, in the first grade, which I think was the first year the school existed. I loved to learn, but the things that happened at school kept me in a state of high anxiety. Day after day as I waited for the school bus, my stomach had roiled. Eating seemed disgusting, but Mother insisted. She'd present me with a bowl of cracked wheat cereal or scrambled meat and eggs. I'd choke down as little as I could get away with, walk to the end of the driveway, and throw up. At first it upset Mother, and she would bring me water and a washcloth. Later, she decided that I was just high-strung and needed to get over it. Over time, I stopped losing my breakfast, but my fear became more profound.

Children were at the bottom of the church's pecking order. We were required to do the bidding of any adult who ordered us around, though children of ministers were above the children of regular members. Infractions were punished by spankings that any church member could administer. But, a spanking didn't mean a swat with a hand. The custom was to give kids repeated licks with an eighteen-inch-long, one-inch-thick wooden paddle. Every family was expected to buy one, though I can't remember whether the church sold them. The victim was required to bend over and grab his ankles to await the blows. Forty swats were not uncommon; ministers pointed out the symmetry of the biblical 40 lashes. Failure to hold the position during the duration of the whipping was grounds for starting it over. Lots of folks got carried away and missed the kids' rears. "Youngsters should be spanked every day," I'd heard Armstrong say from the pulpit, "whether they need it or not, so they learn to submit to authority." He held in high esteem those members who adhered to this line of thought.

My first-grade teacher, Miss Beason, had a cool turquoise and white Nash Metropolitan but a mean arm when it came to wielding the paddle. One of my classmates was Eleanor Tolson. She lived on my street with her parents and brother, Roger. Eleanor was a little slow and had kidney disease.

"Since when is 'I didn't feel like doing my homework' a good reason?" Miss Beason shouted, shaking her index finger so hard that it engaged her upper torso.

"I was sick." Eleanor cowered in her desk.

"I hear that from you all the time," Miss Beason continued. I watched, enthralled, as her lacquered updo threatened to flop over into her face. "It's just an excuse."

"I really was sick." Tears welled in Eleanor's eyes.

"Young lady, it's time you learn to do what you're told." Miss Beason yanked the paddle off her desk. "Get up here."

Eleanor's eyes widened. She stared straight ahead, lids unblinking, frozen in her chair.

Miss Beason's black flats clop-clopped on the concrete floor as she stomped to Eleanor's desk, grabbed her arm, and yanked her out of the seat. "Take the position." Eleanor bent over and grabbed her knees. "Lower." Miss Beason stood perpendicular to Eleanor's backside and held the paddle in her right hand. She paused for a few seconds, letting Eleanor think about how much it was going to hurt. Then, she extended her arm as far as it would go behind her hip and fired. Miss Beason's taciturn face was broken by an almost imperceptible rise in the corners of her lips.

The first blow hit Eleanor's lower back. She cried in pain. Miss Beason reloaded. The next swat landed on her buttocks; the one after on her legs. Tears rolled down Eleanor's blotched face. Miss Beason settled into a rhythm and hit Eleanor another seven times. When the punishment was over, Miss Beason stood erect, shoulders back, with a look of satisfaction. The conqueror stood over the still-bent conquered. "You may stand now."

Miss Beason turned to face Eleanor, waiting.

"Thank you, Miss Beason," Eleanor sobbed out the mandatory response.

Later, in the bathroom, Eleanor showed me the marks on her body. Red welts striped her back and the tops of her legs. Deep purple patches showed where blood vessels had broken. A spectrum of maroon, violet and yellow represented punishment administered at earlier times.

"And I'm going to get the same thing when I get home," Eleanor moaned. Eleanor's mother took delight in following the church's direction that if children were corrected at school, parents were to give the same punishment or more at home. I knew it was true because I heard Eleanor's screams from her Mother's beatings through the open windows.

School policy was to punish the entire class for one person's misbehavior if the perpetrator couldn't be identified. I tried hard to do everything just right so the teachers wouldn't hit me, but I couldn't control my classmates. If one person in the class talked in line, we were all whipped. The principal and other teachers watched for violations. The moment they caught someone breaking even the smallest rule, they meted out the punishment.

When school started in my first-grade year, the principal, Mr. Wilmer, instructed us, "Girls, no talking in the restroom while you change into shorts for P.E." A couple of weeks later, we were in the restroom stripped down to our panties when Natalie Jefferson whispered, "I hope we get to play dodgeball today."

The door of one of the bathroom stalls flew open. Mr. Wilmer jumped out. "Line up. All of you. When I said 'quiet,' I meant it!"

We did as we were told.

"Sir," I asked, "may we put on our clothes?"

"No. Stand the way you are until I get back." All of us wordlessly looked at each other, knowing what was coming.

Two minutes later he returned with the paddle.

"You first." He pointed to me. "Bend over."

I bent over, wearing only a pair of thin cotton panties. He hit me three times with the big paddle. It hurt so much that I bit my lip.

"Thank you, sir."

The process continued until all ten of us had been whipped.

Punishment bounced off some. With me, it resonated. Deep inside. I had failed to meet God's expectations. I knew that during the Great Tribulation only those who had followed all of God's rules would be taken to Petra — the Place of Safety. How many mistakes would I be permitted before my name was marked off the list? As my fear grew, so did my drive for perfection.

I had just started practicing law in 1978 when more than 900 of Jim Jones' followers drank cyanide-laced Kool-Aid and died. My friends expressed incredulity that anyone could be brainwashed to the point of suicide. I didn't have the courage to tell them that if Armstrong or any minister had told us that the way we were going to get to Petra was to drink poison Kool-Aid, every damn one of us would have lined up for our cup.

To terrorize us into submission, we routinely heard graphic descriptions about the horrors of the Tribulation. Even as children, first-graders, we learned all the gory details. There would be floods in which the children drowned first. Nuclear weapons would be dropped on the U.S., and those who weren't immediately incinerated would suffer a slow, agonizing death from radiation poisoning. Hordes of insects would obliterate all plant life. The ensuing famine would strike those who didn't die some other way. The stomachs of the unfaithful would become engorged from malnutrition as they slowly starved. If you were lucky enough to survive all of this, then the Beast would make you pledge allegiance to him. If you did, he put the numbers 666 on your forehead. This meant you were doomed to the Lake of Fire. But, if you refused the mark of the Beast, you would be killed.

Basil Wolverton, the former *Mad* magazine illustrator, created more images of the Great Tribulation that we were forced to see. People being swallowed by earthquakes while volcanoes poured molten lava on them. Hundred-pound hailstones crushed screaming, bloodied victims. The mass burial site of one-third of mankind, killed by fire, smoke, and sulfur. Faces of people enduring the plagues of heat, famine, and boils. To keep us from becoming complacent with the idea of death and destruction, new pictures came out all the time. This was what awaited, they said, if you failed in your devotion to the One True Church.

Of course, Armstrong and God's ministers assured us in sermons that we could be spared all of this and make it to the Place of Safety if we obeyed every rule imposed by the church. But average performance wasn't good enough for God. One screw-up could be all it took to separate you from your family and the faithful when the order came to flee. Punishment coupled with admonitions about being left behind became a fact of life. Whack!...Do you want to be — whack — left here — whack — when your family — whack — goes to Petra?

Before Armstrong settled on the date of Feast of Trumpets 1975 for Christ's return, we had no idea when the call to flee might come. It scared the bejesus out of me. What would happen if I weren't at home when the call came? What if I was out on a long bike ride when my family was told to flee? Members were ordered to leave everything and immediately get to the campus when the moment arrived. My parents might wait a few minutes for me, but if I had decided to look in the woods for huckleberries instead of coming right home, I would be toast. I never ventured too far from home and made sure Mother knew where I was at all times.

There was no reason to develop a personal sense of morality or ethics because the church had a rule for everything. You did what you were told without thought or question. We were not allowed to listen to music performed by anyone with long hair or a gyrating torso. We were required to pray out loud on our knees for thirty minutes a day in our family's prayer closet. We committed scores of Bible passages to memory. If you talked or passed notes in church, a deacon hauled you out for a whipping. It was a sin for a boy to kiss you, even a peck on the cheek, until you were married. When young males and females were together, a chaperone was required. If a girl wore a skirt that wasn't long enough, she was a hussy and would be sent home from church or school. Masturbation was a sin and could make you go blind. Sex was terrible, awful, nasty — until your wedding night, when it became bliss. Every adult had to be addressed as Mr., Mrs. or Miss. It was wrong to say simply yes or no. It had to be yes, ma'am or no, sir.

Parents were vigilant in observing their children for signs of demon possession. As Armstrong told us, this world is "under subjection of fallen angels. The demons, and the devil who is their head, rule this present earth and sway its inhabitants." Satan was constantly broadcasting evil like a radio station. All you had to do was tune into his frequency, mess up once and you'd be his forever.

Since the conduct that transformed Lucifer into the Devil was the failure to carry out God's commands and acknowledge His government, disobedience or insubordination was *prima facie* evidence of a child's demonic tendencies. Any youngster who expressed anger, questioned an adult or the church, asked whether Bible stories were actual events, or wondered whether God really existed might be Satan's instrument. Parents were told that a child could be taken over by the Devil in the blink of an eye.

Good children were compliant, obedient, quiet. I tried to be perfect, but sometimes I screwed up. Like the time company came to our house in the morning and wouldn't leave. By 2:00 p.m. they were still there and we hadn't had lunch. I was starving and mouthed to Mother that I wanted to eat. She ignored me. Hell-bent on getting rid of the unwelcome visitors, I made a sign that said, "I'm hungry and want to eat" and pinned it to my blouse before parading through the living room. Mother tanned my butt.

I tied myself in knots, worrying that I belonged to the Devil. What else would possess me to smoke purple hull pea shells behind Lynn Mansfield's house or touch myself under my panties? Sometimes I'd find Coke bottles and cash them in for pennies that I used to buy candy made from white sugar. I once ate a piece of bacon at Memow's, knowing it was a sin, just because it smelled so good.

I didn't confide my fears to anyone; that would have shown a lack of trust in God. I had friends, but our conversations were about school or music or our after-school interests. I was closest to a girl named Peggy. Her family was very poor and lived in a ragtag rent house near Gladewater, I always felt bad that she didn't have nice clothes. We helped each other through tough times without directly expressing our worries, like Peggy's mother almost dying after wrecking their sardine-can Toyota and my life inside the little yellow house on Pearl Street.

When I was in my twenties, I decided to find Peggy. I assumed that she'd left the church and had made a life for herself as I had. Mary Prociw supplied Mother with a phone number in Las Vegas. When I called Peggy, telling her that I was going to be in town and would like to get together, she gave me directions to her home.

I eased the rental car into the trailer park and began searching for her place. Though different from East Texas poverty, there was a familiar sense of despair that infected the neighborhood. In the more affluent parts of the city, residents worked hard to defy nature and create an oasis in the desert. This place was brown. Dust covered the trailers whose paint had baked off in the heat. The makeshift porches were decorated with sagging awnings and portable aluminum lawn chairs.

I rapped on the metal door and stepped back so she could open it. Peggy gave me a wan smile.

"It's so good to see you." I gave her a hug that wasn't returned.

"Come on in." She motioned me toward a couch in the dimly lighted room. "I've made tea. Want some?"

I watched as she moved around the claustrophobic kitchen.

"It's not supposed to feel as hot as Texas because there's no humidity, but I don't believe it," I said. It was hotter than the Lake of Fire outside. At least it was air-conditioned inside.

"Me, either," she said, handing me a glass filled with ice and freshly brewed Lipton.

I took a long drink and tried not to stare. My childhood friend looked old, used up. Her skin was lifeless; her face prematurely lined. Her hair was limp, needing a decent cut; her eyes, care-filled.

"So, you're a lawyer," she said. "Like it?"

"Most of the time." I didn't think she wanted to know and I should have kept my mouth shut. But, I couldn't help myself. I had to show off. "I've been working on the Howard Hughes Estate litigation out here. What've you been doing?"

"Making a home for my family, like God intended."

I squirmed on the uncomfortable sofa. "After everything Mother went through . . ." I began. "I wanted to make sure I could always support myself."

"When you have faith and follow God's laws, He provides," Peggy said, parroting words I knew she'd heard from the pulpit.

"My theory is that God helps those who help themselves," I responded, trying to insert some reason into the dialogue. Peggy's lips were pursed and her eyes were cold now. "Do you still go to church?" I asked, having already figured out the answer.

"Of course. There's a nice congregation here. I like the minister and the people."

"I'm glad for you. I want to hear all about your family. How's your Mom? And Rhonda?" I knew that in Peggy's mind I was one of "them," a nonbeliever, someone who could steal her eternal life.

We made uncomfortable small talk for a few more minutes. After she glanced at the kitchen clock for the second time, I said my good-byes. As I drove away, tears stung my eyes. I had been looking for catharsis, for an old friend to laugh with me over the insanity that was our childhood, to recall names, and tell stories. I hadn't thought about the possibility that some of my contemporaries had stayed in the church. That but for fate's intervention, I could be sitting in a trailer on a dusty lot still believing Armstrong. I vowed never to look up another one of my friends from Imperial School.

CHAPTER SIXTEEN
Not Like Everyone Else

In the Radio Church of God, being ordinary was essential to survival. If you weren't on track to becoming a minister or at least a deacon, the secret to avoiding abuse was to be invisible. Those who stood out — whether by spending too much money or by wearing skirts an inch too short or by having acquaintances outside the church — were subjected to ministerial scrutiny. The only people who could get away with being different were those whose background or ethnicity made them exotic. Like the Andos, who had survived the nuclear attack on Hiroshima, or the Shrock family, who kept their Mennonite roots by eschewing motor transportation and came to the Feast in a horse-drawn wagon, wearing black and white clothing.

Dad hated ordinary. He loved characters. He adored eccentricity. He'd make an outrageous statement just to get a rise out of people. Sitting with two men at the kitchen table, he'd come out with something like: "Your chin says a lot about you." His friends looked puzzled. "It's true. If you have a receding chin, it shows that you're from a degenerate bloodline." The men still didn't get it. "Think about the Lowells. They're the most degenerate people in the church, right?" They agreed. "Next time you see them, look at their chins." As long as Dad toed the line on the church's teachings and didn't publicly violate any rules, his behavior was tolerated because he was an entertaining character.

When Dad invited Indian and black professors from Jarvis Christian College in Hawkins over to our house, it would have been only a point of gossip had they been church members. Nonwhites were permitted to join the church as long as they stayed in their place and paid the price of admission. What turned heads was that our dark-skinned guests weren't church members. Dad was breaking the rules by associating with heathens.

For a long time, no one cared if he drank like a fish. Drinking was a fact of life in Big Sandy. Quoting many instances in the Bible when the patriarchs imbibed strong drink, Armstrong taught that God's people could drink as much as they wanted, as long as they didn't get drunk. The definition of drunk seemed to be just short of comatose. Dad's drinking became an issue with the church only when he started making drunken public scenes. What mattered was not the harm the alcohol could do to him, but the effect the scene could have on the church's image.

Dad had an immense appetite for life. He was bright and talented, charming and ambitious. He yearned to travel and experience new people and places. He was fascinated with planes and thumbed through copies of *Flying* magazine until they fell apart. One day we drove to Dallas and parked on the highway by a Love Field runway just to watch the planes take off and land. But with no education or guidance to channel his natural abilities, he was at a dead end. He wanted to satisfy his wanderlust without destroying himself as his Dad had. At the same time, he was proud and arrogant. He couldn't bring himself to follow traditional channels of getting an education and working his way up. It affronted his dignity to admit that he had no education. He had thought the church offered a way to get ahead without doing any more than believing. But it was becoming clear that the rewards the church was promising him were in the Kingdom of God, not on earth. That wasn't good enough for Dad.

In the summer of 1962, he announced, "We're going on a long trip." He'd bought a little green and white travel trailer earlier that year and had put a hitch on our white 1959 Buick Invicta — with cat eyes and fins — to tow it.

Steve and I squealed, "Yippee!"

"We'll go until we get ready to come home," Dad replied with enthusiasm.

"Carla, we've got a lot to do," Mother said with a wide smile. "We have to clean and stock the trailer, pack our things, find someone to take care of Tiny and Nibbles."

"Don't forget the fish," I added.

Dad shut down the shop and locked our house. In Michigan we visited Dad's brother Jack, his wife Vernie, and their four kids. I was a little Miss Priss who hated being around heathens who ate unclean food, smoked cigarettes, and watched television on the Sabbath. I knew we were breaking the rules. But soon enough I was saying "you guys" instead of "y'all," like we did in the great State of Texas. What was happening to my immortal soul? Was I losing my place in Petra?

"Sissy, it's okay," Dad said, pouring himself and Uncle Jack another drink.

I breathed easier when we made our way to the home of the Foxes, members of the One True Church. They lived deep in Wisconsin's Great Woods in a Bavarian-style house. Mr. Fox was a short, roly-poly man in his sixties with a head full of white hair. He let Steve and me feed and milk his goats, and he took us to pick blueberries. "Watch out for bears," he warned soberly, with a mischievous twinkle in his eyes. At night, after much beer and sausage (all-beef, of course), Mr. Fox played his concertina, sang German songs, and told stories of his days as a vaudeville performer. Though I had just turned seven, I was enchanted. Mrs. Fox, like Mother, lived in the shadow of a man who was larger than life, who filled up all of the space. I don't remember her at all.

Outside of Winnipeg, we visited the family of one of my parents' best friends — Mrs. Lundgren, the wife of a physical education instructor at Imperial School and Ambassador College. We trekked up mountains, crossed rivers, and almost lost the trailer on a hill when it popped loose from the hitch. We visited the Olympia Brewery and had a 1,000-mile succession of picnics before arriving at the 1962 World's Fair in Seattle. Even though we drove near Pasadena on our way to Mexico, Dad by-passed Ambassador College.

When we returned, Mr. Lassiter made a call on Dad. He wore a black suit, a narrow blue tie, and starched white shirt. His lace-up dress shoes were polished to a high sheen. Dad was dressed in blue khaki work pants and a matching shirt with "Powers Auto Body Shop" written in script on an oval patch. His black brogans were scuffed and smudged with paint.

"Where'd you go?" Mr. Lassiter demanded, looking over the top of his old-fashioned glasses with heavy black frames on top and wires around the bottom of the lenses.

Dad told him.

"Why didn't you ask permission first?" he asked, standing nose to nose with Dad.

"I didn't see the need," Dad answered, looking into Mr. Lassiter's eyes.

"Cost a lot of money?" he quizzed.

"Not too much," said Dad. "Gas, food, park fees, souvenirs."

"None of us got to take a trip like that."

Dad didn't answer.

"You know, Mr. Powers," the minister said, his beady eyes narrowing to slits, "what you make is God's money."

Dad stared back at the man. His mouth tightened.

"You can keep what you have to have to provide food, clothing, and shelter for your family," Mr. Lassiter said, "but the rest should go to God's work."

"I tithe," answered Dad, his hands balling into fists.

"If you make more than you need for the basics, the extra should go to the church."

Dad exhaled audibly. Again, he said nothing.

"You'd better keep that in mind," the preacher said coldly, as he left the garage.

CHAPTER SEVENTEEN
The Pecking Order

In 1989, when I was going through my first divorce, I started seeing a counselor. As my story unfolded, he told me that he didn't think I'd ever be able to experience joy. It had been wrung out of me. Extinguished by an army of dark-suited demagogues.

The Radio Church of God was a windowless house illuminated with 20-watt bulbs. There was just enough light to function. Those responsible for turning the switches on and off were the ministers. The hierarchy in the Radio Church of God was patterned after the pyramidal structure that Armstrong said would exist during the World Tomorrow. Herbert W. Armstrong, God's apostle, was at the top. He often said that he didn't ask to be called an apostle, that others gave him this title, despite his protestations that he wasn't worthy. Beneath Herbert W. were the evangelists, followed by pastors, then preaching elders, local elders, deacons, and, at the bottom, the members. Financial rewards increased with every step up the pyramid.

Armstrong governed with a dictator's ruthlessness. Over and over he told us that his words were not subject to second-guessing. They were God's words. Period. Only those who forsook intellectual honesty and promised fealty to every burp, wheeze, or fart that came from Armstrong were considered for ordination. With such an ego, Armstrong was subject to manipulation by obsequious ass-kissers. They told him what he wanted to hear and were rewarded with power and money.

Armstrong taught that because it was important to be seen by nonbelievers as men of wealth, he and the evangelists at the top of the church's hierarchy were to be richly blessed with material possessions in this world, in addition to receiving the promise of treasures in the next. Living in Big Sandy, the dichotomy between the wealth of the ministers and the poverty of rank-and-file coworkers was obvious every day. You couldn't help but see the fleets of new Chryslers, half of which were replaced every year. The ministers' beautiful new brick homes on Faculty Row at the campus. The nice clothes, the vacations, the kids' new Schwinns. Even as a child, I understood the gradations of power and money among positions within the church.

Local elder — a non-salaried position — was the lowest position on the ministerial pecking order. It was all a member could aspire to if he didn't attend Ambassador College or somehow catch the eye of an evangelist. These ministers were entrusted with the church's dirty work, so the higher-ranking ministers could keep their hands clean and deny accountability if their subordinates stepped over the line. This meant delivering rebukes for minor rules infractions, checking homes for compliance with dietary laws, ordering people not to get medical help even if they faced certain death without it, marking (excommunicating) people who broke the Sabbath. The church held out a carrot to the local elders: if they did well enough, they might be invited to attend Ambassador College. While this rarely happened, the possibility led many local elders to terrorize members in their jurisdictions in hopes of currying favor. It was a career-builder to verbally abuse members who violated even the most mundane rules. Instilling fear was a useful tool for keeping people in line.

I learned through casual conversations with other children and my parents' discussions that, by and large, these local ministers were not educated. Some lacked high school diplomas. I heard Armstrong rant from the pulpit that a person with a college degree, other than from Ambassador College, was less educated that someone without a degree because he'd been "miseducated." If a man could also yell and pound the podium, spy on his brethren, demand absolute adherence to every church law, beat his children and dominate his wife, he might make it to Ambassador and become a preaching elder.

The next level ministers — preaching elders and pastors — received five-figure checks and new Chryslers. For a regular member, being ordained as a preaching elder was like winning the lottery. Homes, multiple cars, fine food and wine, and travel were perks of the position. But even more important was the clout. Once a person was ordained, he could do no wrong. In God's divine order, the minister was always right. It was essential to have this authority to keep members in line. Whenever a member became a minister, his old friends became subordinates. While the church required members to address each other as "Mr." or "Mrs.," close friends of the same gender often called each other by their first names. This changed when someone was ordained. The rule on honorifics became inviolate.

Local elders often made their unannounced home visits when the man of the house was at work. A shiny black Chrysler would roll to a stop on the street outside the house, and the panic would begin.

Mother was on her hands and knees, brush in hand, scrubbing the bathroom floor with Comet. I was washing dishes at the kitchen sink when the men in dark suits descended.

"Mother, ministers are here," I ran toward the back of the house.

"Ohhh…" She groaned a little under her breath, then jumped from the floor, grabbed a washcloth to wipe her hands and knees and examined her reflection in the mirror. She swept hair away from her forehead. "Pick up anything that's out of place, Carla. Throw it in the hamper. Run!"

Mother scurried to the bedroom where she kept a wraparound skirt hooked to the back of the closet door. She secured it around her waist, covering her shorts. Any woman who answered the door in shorts would receive a rebuke and possibly excommunication.

I threw stray shoes and Steve's dump truck under a pile of dirty towels in the bathroom, then ran to the family room to open the Bible and display it on the table, along with the current issue of *The Plain Truth*.

By this time the ministers were knocking. The front screen door rattled. Mother took a breath and opened it, the picture of serenity. It was important not to project fear.

Mother ushered the two men inside. They looked stern. Smiles never crossed their faces. Their business was serious.

"Hello, Mrs. Powers," said the one with thin strands of greasy hair glued to his scalp. Mother grasped his extended hand and pumped it twice. Mr. Armstrong taught that a confident person with nothing to hide always looked a visitor in the eyes and strongly gripped his hand.

"Mr. Fisher. Mr. Posey. Please come in. May I offer you something to drink?"

"A beer'd be good."

"I'll get it."

"No need. We'll go to the kitchen with you."

I slipped back into the kitchen and had my hands in dishwater when they came into the room. The ministers followed Mother to the refrigerator, peering over her shoulder to see what was inside when she opened the door. Mr. Posey walked toward the bedroom and confirmed that the bed was made and things were organized.

I reached inside the silverware drawer and extracted the opener. The men popped holes in their Budweiser cans and made themselves comfortable at the kitchen table. They said nothing; their eyes took in the kitchen and family room. Floor clean. Check. Counters clear. Check. Dishes washed. Check. Bible visible. Check.

But I knew Mr. Fisher. A holier-than-thou sneer was planted on his lips. More than anything, he wanted to catch a transgression. In the cabinet, perhaps a can of pinto beans that contained a sliver of salt pork. A bank statement that indicated a short payment of tithes. Dust on top of the refrigerator.

"Mrs. Powers..."

I held my breath.

"Why don't you get your Bible and sit with us?"

We had passed! I closed my eyes and exhaled. I took a deep breath. "Mother, may I please go outside and play?"

"Of course, dear," she said sweetly.

I was careful not to slam the backdoor.

In the Radio Church of God, women had a special place: under their husbands' thumbs. The Apostle Paul's directive that wives should submit to their husbands was followed in the extreme. The proper response to a question from a husband was "Yes, sir." A wife who didn't do everything her husband told her to do was "stiff-necked." A slap or two was appropriate for a stiff-necked woman. Afterwards, the wife was supposed to thank her husband for caring enough about her eternal life to deliver loving correction.

Married women couldn't work outside the home. Females weren't permitted to have church leadership roles, other than deaconess, and there were few who attained that position. The most a woman could aspire to be was the wife of a minister, though the minister's wives I remember didn't hold themselves out as being special. I think they must have been so beaten down that they didn't feel more important than anyone else.

In Big Sandy, the church favored paid ministers and important college faculty with homes in a subdivision on the north side of the campus. When the houses were being built in the early '60s, we'd drive down Old Big Sandy Highway to the development's entrance and gape at their grandeur. All of the houses seemed extraordinarily large, set on landscaped lots sitting back from asphalt-paved roads. The sizes of the homes and lots varied, based on rank. The more important the minister, the larger the home. The choicest sites faced a man-made mud hole named Lake Loma in honor of Herbert W.'s wife. A diving tower and pier were built over the water.

I once went inside one of the houses. My principal, Mr. Wilmer, and his family lived there. Mother did sewing for Mrs. Wilmer and delivered it to her home.

Mother knocked on the door.

"Thanks so much for bringing these over. Come in."

"Thank you, Mrs. Wilmer," said Mother and we walked inside the entryway. "I'd feel better if you'd try on this suit one more time. I'm a little concerned about the length of the skirt."

"Okay," said Mrs. Wilmer, taking the clothing from Mother. "Y'all have a seat, and I'll be right back." She gestured toward the living room.

I sat on the edge of the couch, afraid for my skin to touch the fine fabric. The ceilings felt as though they went on forever, and there were big windows that let the sun shine through. The paint was fresh and bright. If I did well in school and went to Ambassador College, I might marry a minister and have a home like this.

When I think about the women in the church, it is almost uniformly with affection. Most were generous with what little they had. I loved Grace Scudder, my piano teacher. An elderly eccentric with an Eleanor Roosevelt voice, she wore old-fashioned brooches and plaited yellow hair coiled against her head.

Mrs. Scudder escorted us into her parlor, furnished with Victorian furniture, elaborate glass pieces, and a tall upright piano. A copy of Walt Whitman's *Leaves of Grass* sat on top of a coffee table.

"So you want to play the piano?" she said, as she poured tea into a china cup and handed it to Mother.

"Oh, yes, ma'am, I do. Can you teach me?" I ignored the glass of thick juice she passed to me. "Please."

"We'll see, my dear," she answered.

"Mrs. Scudder, I know Carla wants to play, and she can do anything if she sets her mind to it. Problem is, we can't afford a piano."

She turned to me. "How badly do you want to learn?"

"More than anything!" I answered too loudly for the refined room.

She smiled at me. "Will you practice?"

"Yes, ma'am. I'll find a way."

"Let's have a couple of lessons before I make up my mind."

I jumped from the couch, pulled out the piano bench and plopped down.

"She's anxious, isn't she?" Her smile deepened the creases in her face. She reached for a dog-eared book on a table beside the piano and held it for Mother to see. "This is the book you'll need to buy. It's called *Michael Aaron Piano Course Grade One*.

"Expensive?" Mother asked.

"Not too bad. $1.25. There's a music store in Gladewater where you can pick up a copy. I'll write down the information for you.

"Carla, have you ever heard of middle C?"

"Yes, ma'am," I answered proudly. "I know where it is."

"Play it for me, please."

After the first lesson, Mrs. Scudder turned to Mother, "Would you mind having her come here after school three days a week to practice?"

"That would be wonderful. She can get off the bus in front of your home."

After two weeks of lessons and practice, Mother arrived at the Scudders' home. Mr. Scudder, a retired banker who always dressed in a three-piece suit with a watch in his vest pocket, invited her inside.

"Thanks, but I just came to pick up Carla. I'm not appropriately dressed. Please send her to the car when she's finished."

"Don't worry about your clothing, there's something Grace wants to show you."

He escorted Mother through the parlor, down a hallway, then into a room decorated with white wrought-iron furniture and plants. I was seated at a round table, and Mrs. Scudder stood over me.

"Mother, look at what Mrs. Scudder made for me." My fingers touched a long piece of poster board on which a scale replica of a piano keyboard had been drawn. "I can practice at home. We just won't hear anything."

"Look at that," Mother said as she ran her fingers over notes that had been colored with black ink.

"We'll make do until you can get her a piano."

"See you next week, Mrs. Scudder. Thanks again!" I folded the keyboard and tucked it under my arm.

"Aren't you forgetting something, young lady?" asked Mrs. Scudder.

I rolled my eyes. "Yes, ma'am," I said with resignation and picked up a glass of nasty-looking orange liquid.

"A glass of carrot juice every day helps your eyes. Don't forget."

"I won't," I said, as I put down the empty glass and tried to keep from upchucking.

Over the years, Mrs. Scudder taught several of the girls in the church. We learned to appreciate classical music and to perform in public. She took our group to Tyler to see an obscure pianist with an Eastern European name. Starting with living-room recitals, we advanced to performances in the auditorium with a hundred people in attendance. Because I couldn't afford to buy music, she hand-copied pieces onto blank sheets. When the church bought a Xerox machine, she cajoled them into letting her use it to copy music. I never remember Mrs. Scudder doing anything more affectionate than putting her arm around my shoulder and giving it a squeeze. But I knew she loved me.

Mrs. Harrington, the voice teacher, taught me about breathing from the diaphragm and "putting my tongue on the cord" to sing. It didn't help: I'm tone-deaf. Mrs. Starley across the street slipped little bits of candy with the money she gave me for cleaning her house. On my birthday she gave me presents, saying that they weren't for my birthday but just for fun. Mary Prociw helped me earn enough money to buy a record player and records by letting me work as her housekeeper.

But this was a world in which women were completely dominated by men, by church, by dogma. As a child, I thought these soft-spoken, submissive women were wonderful. I see them in a different way now. When Warren Jeffs' Latter-day Saints compound in West Texas came into the public view in 2008, the women so reminded me of the women of the Radio Church of God that I cried whenever I saw or heard them. Old-fashioned, modest clothes. Downcast eyes. Just like my church women, after being told for years that they were inferior to men, that God expected them to do whatever they were told by their husbands and the ministers, that all outsiders were evil, that it was God's law to beat and abuse children, they were hollow vessels. But perfect hollow vessels, who kept their children well-groomed, grew nice vegetables, put low-cost, nutritious meals on the table, and knew how to live on pennies so dollars could be given to the church. To these women, anyone outside the church was an enemy. The worst enemies were representatives of the government of man. I can't envision a scenario in which these women would have spoken against a child molester or a murderer or a bigamist within church membership, unless a minister told them to do so.

There were a few women who couldn't keep their bearings in that world. In Big Sandy I knew two girls who were a little older than I was. Their mother had an arm that was severed below the elbow. When I asked about it, Mother said that she had her hand torn off in a washing machine. Years later she confessed that the story wasn't true. The poor woman had taken literally the admonition in the Bible that if a part of your body offends, it should be cut off.

Some women drank themselves into oblivion. One of my classmates was

Natalie Jefferson. Our competitiveness made for an uneasy friendship. Natalie was a good student. She excelled in field events and at running long distances, while I was a sprinter. I was a better pianist, but her singing voice was lovely. When we played each other in basketball or tetherball, it was war. I was never invited to Natalie's home, nor was she to mine. She didn't share personal insights and buried herself in doing well. I never met her mother. She didn't go outside the home and didn't attend church. When I asked, Mother told me that Mrs. Jefferson was an alcoholic, but I was never to say a word about it.

CHAPTER EIGHTEEN

The Virtuous Woman

After we returned from our trip in the summer of 1962, Dad started to spend more than we could afford on booze. There were times when Mother didn't have money to buy food or pay the house note. She started supporting us by "doing" for the church ladies. Mrs. Ellsworth or any one of a dozen other women sat in a kitchen chair while Mother did her hair. Mrs. Garner Ted Armstrong — Shirley — had cut her hair like Jackie Kennedy's, signaling that it was okay to give up the long Pentecostal tresses. Many wanted to follow her lead. Mother measured each strand to the pin on the barber scissors, secured it with her fingers, and clipped. Afterwards, she coated each section with Dippity-Do and wrapped it around a brush curler. A plastic pin that pierced the curler nailed it against the victim's scalp and the lady baked under a portable dryer. Mother's comb-outs usually required ratting the hair, now known as teasing. The women who kept their long tresses wanted them swept into French twists. When the "do" was completed, it was lacquered with half a can of Aqua Net spray. Since this work of art was expected to last a week, the ladies slept in spongy helmets.

Mother was also a seamstress. Dacron knit, new in the sixties, was a gift from heaven because it didn't have to be ironed. Just throw it in the washer, let it drip-dry, and it was as good as new. Women delivered fabric, notions and Butterick patterns to the house. Mother was always busy as the holy days approached and everyone wanted something new to wear. Her blue Alden sewing machine hummed into the wee hours of the morning. The sound of the machine told me whether she was basting a seam, creating a buttonhole, or putting in a zipper.

Mother made almost everything I wore. She went to children's stores in Longview and Tyler and sketched the latest styles. Using hand-drawn patterns and look-alike fabrics, she fashioned clothes for me that would have cost a fortune if we'd bought them. They made me feel like hot stuff, someone special. I hoped they conveyed that I had it all together, even when everything around me was falling apart.

Mother enlisted my help with garage sales. We sold the neighbors' junk for a ten percent commission. My job was labeling each item with a paper price tag held by a straight pin. We used stacks of dime tags. At a profit of a penny an item, it didn't seem worth the effort, even as badly as we needed money. We stopped the rummage sales after a skunk got inside our garage and sprayed the sale's leftovers.

Despite the prohibition on having contact with nonmembers, Mother tried to stay in touch with Aunt Dortha and Uncle Shelby. It wasn't a close relationship, but it provided me with some family connection. Aunt Dortha owned plaster of paris molds that she used to create wall-hangings. Twice Mother took orders from the church ladies for artwork made with Aunt Dortha's molds, and we made the two-hour drive to Louisiana to pick up the greenware. We loaded the trunk with grape clusters, fish, mermaids, cornucopia, and four seasons plaques. Back home, Mother painted the pieces, sold them, and remitted a small amount to Aunt Dortha.

And like her grandmother, Mother was a midwife. She learned and taught natural childbirth techniques using the books she'd found when she was pregnant with Steve. They explained breathing, muscle control, and proper positioning during labor. She'd get late-night calls and head out to assist at a birth. Those hardy women endured labor without anesthesia or an M.D., trusting God and Mother to preserve their lives and bring a healthy child into the world. No one I remember — other than Mother — had serious complications.

The ladies prepared food that they delivered to the homes of the sick and bereaved. Churchwomen brought covered dishes to share at socials. They borrowed eggs and cups of flour from each other and traded ideas about how to get rid of the crumbs without tearing the house apart before the Days of Unleavened Bread. They exchanged hand-me-downs, held morning coffees to study the Bible, and prepared music for the Sabbath service.

Mother filled her recipe box with note cards on which she wrote scriptures that she committed to memory.

One was special — she carried it on a slip of paper in her billfold. Proverbs 31:10-31:

Who can find a virtuous woman? For her price is far above rubies.
The heart of her husband doth safely trust in her, so that he shall have no need of spoil.
. . .
She shall rejoice in time to come.
. . .
Her children arise up, and call her blessed; her husband also, and he praiseth her.

Favour is deceitful, and beauty is vain: but a woman that feareth the Lord, she shall be praised.

There were no references to love, joy, laughter. "She shall rejoice" but only "in time to come." Life was doing. And she did it well.

Mother and I spent many summer days in the kitchen, the Texas heat held at bay only by the attic fan, canning homegrown vegetables. We layered peeled tomatoes in wide-mouth Kerr quart jars, placed a lid on top, and arranged the jars in a cooker on the stove to heat. When done, we used big tongs to set the hot containers on towels to cool. As the seals locked into place, they popped — a sign that the food could be safely put away. Some vegetables, like peas, were blanched in a hot water bath and put into plastic bags for freezing. We chopped tomatoes, onions, and jalapeno peppers for salsa and covered whole peppers with salt and vinegar for pepper sauce. We made pickles with vinegar brine, alum, garlic, and fresh dill.

After the first frost, we drove into the country to collect fallen pecans and walnuts. Back home we cracked them — gently — with a hammer and picked out the meats for freezing. In the spring, we scoured the back roads for poke salat (we called it poke salad), a wild, pungent, leafy green that was boiled before being scrambled with eggs. The ditches yielded blackberries for cobbler. Wild plum trees provided tart fruit that made good jelly.

Mother tortured us with herbal remedies that she learned from books and from other church women. She foraged for weeds that could be made into tonic that was supposed to rid us of worms or whatever ailed us. She loved the health food store in Gladewater because it stocked unusual things we were supposed to eat, like cracked wheat, wheat germ, Tiger's Milk, blackstrap molasses, and soybeans. We drank carrot juice, ate carob instead of chocolate, and filled our tummies with the nastiest raisin bran that anyone ever put in a box. She made our bread with whole-wheat flour and yeast, and sweetened our tea with brown sugar.

When times were good, Mother bought lean hamburger, liver, tongue, soup bones and a little bit of round steak, sirloin, and roast in bulk from the packing plant in Gladewater. Mrs. Wimberley continued to supply yard eggs and whole milk. We used the cream to make butter. Since we had no churn, we put the cream in a quart jar and shook it until the butterfat separated from the milk. It didn't taste like much, but the price was right.

A calf we named Pet was given to us by a rancher who said that her mama had been killed by a wolf. For months, we fed Pet with a bottle. She lived up to her name. When she licked my hand, her tongue felt like sandpaper. Mother swears now that she told us all along that we were raising Pet to be dinner, but I don't remember that. When the calf got too big for the backyard, she moved into the pasture behind the house. Then one day she disappeared. It didn't occur to me that the meat filling the freezer shortly thereafter was Pet.

When the material on the couch and chair in the living room became worn, Mother bought coarse, deep green fabric and recovered both. She did the same with the dining room chairs. When Dan was old enough to move into a big bed, she bought an old iron bunk bedstead from a junk store and stripped the paint with lye, leaving pockmarks on her hands. She painted the bed black, highlighting the detailing with rubbed gold. Her handsewn red and black spreads topped the beds.

Perhaps to save money on the beer Dad was consuming, Mother decided to brew her own. In addition to all of the ingredients, she bought brown quart glass bottles, caps, and a capping machine. She mixed the brew, filled and capped the bottles, then moved them by the case into the garage.

When Steve and I came home from school one day, we walked through the garage. Mother was at the dining room table, sewing.

"Phheww," I said, holding my nose. "What's that *smell?*"

"One of the bottles of beer broke."

"That's not the way real beer smells."

"It hasn't finished fermenting."

I lost interest, threw my books on the table and sauntered to the piano Dad had bought six months after I started taking lessons.

"Before you start practicing," Mother said, "run out to the garage and get some stew meat out of the freezer. Leave it on the sink to thaw."

I pulled the big lid up on the freezer and rummaged through the packages. As I walked back into the house, I heard a "POW!" like a gunshot. A split-second later, glass began raining in the garage. Home brew flowed out of the garage into the driveway.

"Mother!" I yelled. "Another bottle exploded!"

For a week, every time we went to the freezer in the garage, we had to cover ourselves with a quilt so we wouldn't be cut by flying glass. The stench stayed for months. A few bottles survived, and Mother reported that the beer was quite good, but she never again tried to make it.

She next turned to winemaking, filling a five-gallon glass jug with cans of Welch's grape juice concentrate, sugar, yeast and water, then fitting a balloon over the top. The balloon filled with air as the wine fermented. When the fermentation was complete and the balloon lost its air, the wine was ready to be bottled. Since I was a wine connoisseur by age ten, I determined that Mother's wine was as good as Mogen David, and the bottles didn't explode.

Rituals associated with holy days required hours of preparation. Cooking roasted lamb with bitter herbs for Passover. Cleaning the house to remove all traces of leavened products. Ensuring that we ate Rye-Crisp during the seven Days of Unleavened Bread. Readying everyone in the family over age six for the twenty-four hour food-and-water fast on the Day of Atonement. Buying presents for the Feast of Tabernacles.

The strangest ritual of all was preparing for the adults-only foot-washing service on Passover night. Toenail clippings on the bathroom floor signaled the arrival of Passover to me. I pitied the person who had to wash my Dad's feet. At the service, a curtain separated the men from the women. The person whose feet were to be washed sat on a chair, removed her shoes, and put her feet in a dishpan of water. One woman washed the other's feet and dried them with a clean towel. The positions were then reversed. I never understood why this service was too sacred for children to attend.

What I don't remember from Mother was softness or affection or laughter. She didn't often hug or kiss my brothers or me. We didn't talk about how we felt or what we were thinking. Dad was destroying our world faster than Mother could work to hold it together, but we had no conversations about what we were all going through. Many years later, Mother told me that she was torn apart when Steve and I woke in the night, crying or yelling from nightmares, but I didn't know it then. Now I realize that it took all of her strength to survive. As a child, clueless that she was searching for a way out, I had no hope. The only way I could cope was to put my head down and put one foot in front of the other. Life devolved into a progression of tasks to be accomplished, obstacles to be overcome.

CHAPTER NINETEEN
Meltdown

I drove down Pearl Street, past boarded-up houses, caved-in porches, knee-high weeds. In the place where the Kingdom of God had been promised, junked cars, discarded furniture, and trash littered the yards. Broken-down fences. Hand-lettered For Sale signs. Dirt driveways. Ancient trailers.

The white paint on the house at 310 North Pearl Street looked fresh. Steve had driven by two years earlier and reported that it had partially burned. It had been rebuilt. The awnings were gone. The garage enclosed. Most of the trees and all of the landscaping had disappeared. Only the chain-link fence remained.

I had lived here for eight years, but it didn't feel familiar. Pictures rolled through my head, but they were like clips from a movie telling someone else's story.

By the time I was in the third and fourth grades, I found comfort in the predictable. I knew that the school bus would take me to Imperial School every morning. On Friday afternoons we would prepare food for the Sabbath. On Friday nights and Saturday, we'd go to church. There was a Bible study on Wednesday night. Mother went to choir practice once or twice each week and there were often Ambassador College concerts or lectures. I'd spend the afternoons doing schoolwork and sitting at the piano mastering Hanon's "Sixty Exercises for the Virtuoso Pianist," the "Warsaw Concerto," or Roger Williams' "Autumn Leaves."

After Dan was born, Dad and Mother built a seven-foot-high partition in the bedroom I shared with Steve, so there would be a place for the two boys and a separate area for me. They created a nook with a daybed and built-in bookshelves. Mother made a bedspread, bolster covers and throw pillows in pink. I put a stuffed black-and-white Dalmatian dog on the bed, and, on the desktop a record player for the albums I'd saved to buy. I displayed my ribbons and certificates on a bulletin board above the desk. Mother found an old kidney-shaped dressing table that she painted white; she attached a skirt of pink cotton and netting and put a frilly-shaded white hobnail lamp on top. This half of a room was my haven, my place of safety. Until one night when Dad came home at 2:00 a.m. and ran his fist through my bedroom wall.

I lost my equilibrium during the evenings and weekends. We never knew when

Dad would come home or who he would be when he got there.

One night he'd get home at 5:30, bounce me on his knee and ask about school, drink three or four beers, and eat dinner with us. The next, he'd pull the truck into the driveway going thirty-five and slam on the brakes, throwing gravel into the yard.

"Well, Mary Ann, what delicious offerings do you have for us tonight?" he bellowed at Mother. "Mackerel croquettes? That Chinese crap out of a can? Meatloaf that's half-crackers and oatmeal?"

"Chicken," she said.

Dad pulled the whiskey bottle out of the cabinet and filled a water glass. "Backs and wings in some kind of stew?"

"Fried." Her voice remained even.

"Breasts and drumsticks, too?"

"It'll be ready in about ten minutes."

She set the table and laid out bowls of cream peas and okra that had been warming in the oven. Cold, sliced tomatoes and onions and homemade bread-and-butter pickles completed our feast.

"Wash up, kids, supper's ready," she called.

We scrambled to the table and sat patiently. We didn't dare touch the food before it had been blessed. Dad didn't wait. He helped himself to the chicken, piling on both pieces of split breast, the wishbone, a thigh and a drumstick. We looked at the back, thigh, leg and two wings that remained on the platter.

"Let's say the blessing," Mother said.

Dad kept eating. We bowed our heads and closed our eyes.

"Father in heaven, thank you for this food and for your blessings. We pray that you will take care of the ministers and help them as they preach your Word. Please watch over, protect, and guide us." After Steve and I said "Amen," we opened our eyes.

"Charles, what are you doing?" Mother said, choking on the words.

"I'm hungry," Dad said, spearing the other thigh and leg.

"Leave some food for the rest of us."

"I'm the man of the house and I'll eat what I want. If there's any left, you're welcome to it."

I filled my plate with vegetables. I wasn't about to get into a fight with Dad over a bony piece of chicken. Mother and Steve did the same.

Five minutes later, Dad left the table and drove away. A chicken back and wing remained. My appetite was gone. Mother offered the chicken to Steve, who managed to find a half-dozen bites of meat.

When there was no money for meat, we prepared dinner with the canned and frozen vegetables we had put up the previous summer. Dad taunted Mother.

"Suffering for God's Work, I see." He laughed: a short, bitter sound. "I guess we'll send Armstrong the buck and two bits you saved."

Mother refused to take the bait. "You going to eat?"

"This slop?

"There's nothing wrong with vegetables and cornbread."

"Enjoy it. I'm having something else."

Dad heaved a paper bag onto the counter and pulled out a package wrapped in white butcher paper. He yanked the tape off a thirty-two-ounce slab of beef sirloin. He threw the meat on a plate and added salt, pepper, garlic and Worchestershire sauce, before stomping outside with the plate and a bottle of Seagram's in his hands. A few minutes later we smelled the burning charcoal, and half an hour later, the luscious aroma of grilling steak. After we cleaned up the kitchen and were doing our homework on the kitchen table, he brought in the cooked meat and ate every bite.

There were times when Dad came home in the middle of the night, waking all of us, yelling and throwing furniture. For a while, the morning-after scenes were invariable.

"Toddy," he said, nursing a big cup of coffee, "come here."

I did as I was asked. He hoisted me onto his lap and put his arms around me.

"I'm so sorry for last night. Did I scare you?"

I'd bite my lip to keep it from quivering. "Um-hmmm."

"You know I'd never do anything to hurt you." He squeezed me, and I could hear the emotion in his voice.

"I know, Daddy," I answered, though I didn't believe it. "Did I do something wrong? I'll try to be better."

"I'll never do it again." He looked into my eyes.

"Do you mean it, Daddy?"

"This time will be different. I promise," he said, kissing me on the hair and putting me down. "I love you."

"I love you, too, Daddy."

After the sun went down one Saturday night in early fall 1963, Mother and Dad took their places in the front seat of the Buick with a bottle of pre-mixed screwdrivers and a six-pack of beer. Steve and I piled into the backseat with pillows, blankets and a grocery bag full of greasy popcorn. We were excited, bouncing up and down in our seats at the prospect of going to see a movie. We didn't own a TV, and I'd never seen a movie, other than *Ben Hur*, which the church had shown on a wall at the old tabernacle. Tonight we were going to the River Road Drive-In in Longview.

Dad found a spot he liked and parked the car next to the speaker pole. He rolled his window down halfway and clipped the speaker over the top.

When the sky was pitch-black, the cartoons started. Steve and I sat up straight, craning our necks to see over the front seats and around Mother and Dad's heads. We laughed as we watched the manic animals.

When the cartoons were over, the car filled with strains of familiar music. Dad had bought an Andre Kostelanetz record album called "The Wonderland of Golden Hits" that contained an orchestral version of the movie's title song. It was haunting music that made me sad. The two people on the screen drank and kissed and fought and drank some more. I watched until my tears made the screen a blurry mess. Then I hid my face in my pillow. I didn't want to watch. I couldn't watch *The Days of Wine and Roses*. It reminded me too much of home.

After Dan was born in November 1964, Dad behaved for several months, but he couldn't sustain it. By mid-1965, he dropped the pretense of wanting to change. I never again saw the gentle Dad I had known as a child. There were no more apologies or acts of contrition. We got calls that he had been picked up by the police for sundry breaches of the peace, like walking barefoot down the middle stripe of Highway 80 at night. He brawled, set fires, drove incoherently drunk, and generally made life miserable for everyone who came into contact with him.

The phone rang after midnight, awakening me. It was a school night, and I was in the fifth grade. Mother dragged herself out of bed and went to the phone nook in the hall near my bedroom to answer it. "Mary, it's Bill Sawyer."

"Yes, sir?" Mr. Sawyer was a family friend, but it was too late at night for a social call.

"Charles's been arrested," he said.

"What?" Mother answered.

"Charles is on his way to jail."

"Why?"

"Tried to burn the plane."

"Mr. Sawyer, I was half-asleep and must not have heard you right."

"Charles tried to burn the Armstrongs' King Air."

"How?"

"Piled up brush and started a fire under the gas tanks." Mother was silent, and Mr. Sawyer added, "Someone saw the fire. We got it put out before the tanks blew."

"Drunk?" she asked in a small voice.

"Oh, yeah. Taking punches at everybody. Took four of us to get him down."

"Is the church going to press charges?"

"He needs to cool off in the pokey for a few days, then we'll decide."

I crept into the bedroom after Mother hung up. "Everything okay?"

"Sure, honey. Nothing to worry about."

Everyone at school the next day was abuzz about what Daddy had done. None of my friends and classmates made jokes about my crazy father. It had begun to dawn on them that he was a dangerous man.

Saturdays were the worst. Whatever the weather, Saturdays were gray and dingy. The house, with its yellowed wall paint and low-wattage overhead fixtures, became a prison. In that dark house of my childhood, sometimes Dad would disappear when it was time for us to go to church; other times, he would lie on the bed in his Tee-shirt and boxers, hurling insults.

You're stupid sheep.

Still waiting for the Tribulation? How many more times will Armstrong's prophecies fail before you figure it out?

Your Mother is Armstrong's whore.

Your Mother's ignorant.

The dread of being humiliated at church because of Dad's increasingly visible conduct wasn't as bad as the fear of what Dad would do when we came home.

CHAPTER TWENTY

Breaking Point

The more Dad drank, the more he ranted about the church. This was the unpardonable sin, as explained by Mr. Armstrong:

"...If and when you criticize or accuse or condemn THE WORK, THEN YOU ARE SPEAKING AGAINST THE HOLY SPIRIT — and if and when you do that, YOU SHALL NOT BE FORGIVEN!"[17]

Dad's words doomed him to the Lake of Fire.

"God," I'd pray, "please forgive Daddy. Make him change. Don't send him to the Lake of Fire." At night, I lay in my bed and cried about the loss of his eternal soul.

"Mother, do you think Daddy will go with us to the Place of Safety?"

"Only God knows."

"What will happen if he has to stay here? Will we have to stay here with him?"

"God takes His people, even if it means splitting up families. Whatever happens will be His will."

"If I'm better, will that help Daddy?"

"He has to change."

"I'll try even harder."

Mother kept taking the abuse. She didn't complain about having no money for groceries, clothing, or gas because that would be an affront to his dignity. She didn't let him know that her odd jobs were putting food on our table. That would suggest he wasn't a good provider and he would order her to stop. She didn't lay down the law and kick him out when he was drunk — it wouldn't have done any good. She tried to be reasonable and submissive and non-threatening, just as the church taught women to behave. It made him worse.

Music was my lifeline. I dreamed of the evening gowns I would wear when I addressed the Steinway concert grand in Pasadena's Ambassador Auditorium. I imagined that hall filled with people delivering an exuberant ovation when I finished. At the piano, I wasn't Carla Powers, the daughter of Charles Powers, the drunk. But there was a price to be paid. If, in a thirty-minute program, I made one mistake, I'd leave the stage in tears. I wasn't perfect! I had failed. No amount of congratulations for the good things I'd done could compensate for the error. I'd lie awake, replaying the failure over and over.

I was able to tune down the ever-critical voice in my head by reading. My nose was perpetually buried in a book. Every week I checked out as many books as they would allow at the Gladewater Public Library. *Nancy Drew*, the *Hardy Boys*, and biographies were my staples. When I read, the fear, abandonment, and imperfection that consumed me were replaced by mystery, excitement, and achievement.

Another refuge was the kitchen. When I was six, I stood on a stool and made cookies from a recipe in Imperial Sugar's *My First Cookbook*. I loved cooking and felt safe when I was up to my elbows in flour. After we got a used Emerson black-and-white television in late 1963, just before President Kennedy was assassinated, most Saturday nights, Mother, Steve and I would watch the old set in the little den next to the kitchen. I'd make gingerbread or popcorn balls while we watched Lawrence Welk and Hollywood Palace. The smells and tastes provided comfort.

To my teachers, the ministers, and the parents of my classmates, I was a paragon of perfection, the kind of kid all the others despise. I labored over my schoolwork so my marks would be all A's, except for penmanship, which still bedevils me. I ran ten miles a week so I could be in shape to win the most blue ribbons on Field Day. Nothing kept me from practicing the piano. I obeyed my elders. My clothes were ironed and matched from hair bow to socks. I babysat for three different teachers' families when I was nine. The worse Dad acted, the more I labored to achieve perfection.

Dad's obsession with fire grew. He burned trash in barrels at home and behind the shop at all hours. He lit a frozen turkey on the barbeque grill and advanced to tire fires in the backyard at two or three in the morning. The red glow and acrid smoke would wake me up. One night our house caught on fire. When smoke started pouring from the attic, the volunteer fire department showed up. I grabbed schoolbooks from my room and my bike from the garage and took off down the street. I stopped in a driveway two doors down, watching the red lights and listening to the shouts of the men. Mother told me that the motor on the attic fan had overheated, but I wondered.

Two families grew close to us. One was the Prociws; the other, the McIntyres. Mr. McIntyre taught speech at Ambassador and visited our house when Dad was gone. He became a friend and father figure. He gave me racy paperbacks by Ian Fleming and Rafael Sabatini and rubbed linament on my calves when I got charley horses from running. He told me I had scoliosis and manipulated my neck and back, yielding loud cracks. Mother helped deliver his daughter, Caitlin, whom we called Katie. In the fifth grade, I babysat for them for fifty cents an hour. These were people with whom I felt safe, protected.

One night the McIntyres were late getting back to their home. After their older daughter Vicky and Katie went to sleep, I stretched out on the couch to watch *The Tonight Show*. I was sound asleep when they arrived and wasn't entirely awake when I dragged myself to their car for the short drive home. When Mr. McIntyre came to the intersection of Highway 155 and Pearl Street, he didn't turn right onto my street. Instead, he continued down the pitch-black, heavily forested highway.

"Where are you going?" I asked, still groggy.

"Nowhere," he replied nonchalantly and kept driving in the opposite direction from my house.

"I'm sleepy." I couldn't imagine what was going on.

About two miles out of Big Sandy in the hamlet of Shady Grove, he turned onto a dirt road and drove a half-mile into the woods. He shut off the lights and the ignition.

Before I knew what was happening, Mr. McIntyre was kissing me. I felt his tongue in my mouth. He ran his hand over my chest. "Before long you're going to need a bra."

It took a couple of seconds to register that this was really happening. I felt bile rise up in my stomach as panic overwhelmed me.

"Stop it!" I shouted and flailed my arms at him.

He took my wrists and calmly placed them on the car seat.

Mr. McIntyre's face didn't register concern as he turned the key in the ignition and put the car into gear. I stared out the window during the drive home, trying to stop shaking. Neither of us said anything. I felt like I needed a bath.

I'd never tell anyone about tonight, and Mr. McIntyre knew it. Who would believe me, a child, accusing a teacher at Ambassador College? If I told Mother, would she think I had done something to make it happen? Armstrong had taught us that when men were unable to control themselves sexually, it was because a woman had fueled his lust. While I wasn't a woman and didn't know what one did to fuel lust, I was sure I'd be blamed. I couldn't tell Dad — he couldn't stand Mr. McIntyre and would enjoy the excuse to beat the hell out of him. So, I lay awake on my virginal pink bed and wondered if I had sinned so badly that I'd be denied entrance to the Place of Safety and to the Kingdom of God. I prayed as I had never prayed before, asking God to forgive me for my terrible sin.

For Mr. McIntyre, nothing changed. He was still viewed as a trusted family friend who came over whenever he liked. For me, everything changed. That blow, and Dad's ever-increasing violence, started to undermine my mental health.

Sleep was fitful, nightmare-filled. I started hallucinating. Every time I closed my eyes, the images came. A stick figure whose legs went out and back together over and over again as it struggled to stand on the back of a racing mechanical horse. I didn't tell anyone. I was afraid that the ministers would conclude that I was demon-possessed and exorcise me.

Dad, *1949*

Dad's army photo, *1952*

Charles Powers in Verdun, France, *1952*

**Mary Ann Holloway Powers, working at Sterling's,
Conway, Arkansas,** *1953*

Charles and Mary Powers in Arkansas, *1950*

Dad's Shar-pei pose in front of the travel trailer, *1968*

Grandaddy Powers (Charley) in front of his home, *late 1960s*

**Mother with me in Big Sandy, Texas at the
Feast of Tabernacles,** *1955*

Feast of Tabernacles, Big Sandy, Texas, *1956*

Dad and me beside our house in Little Rock, *1958*

Steve and me dressed for Passover, *1960*

In Arkansas, *1962*

Steve and me with Mr. Fox in Wisconsin, *July, 1962*

Carla Powers, *1960*

First grade at Imperial Schools, Big Sandy, Texas, *1961*

Third grade, *1963*

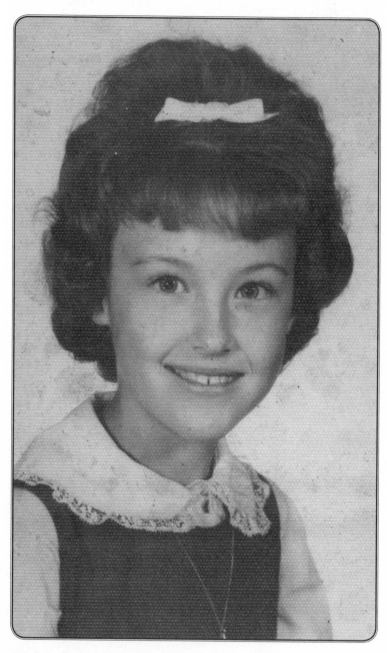

My fourth-grade picture, *1964*

At the Prociw's house, the night Dan was born, *November 30, 1964*

Mrs. Scudder's piano students pictured outside her home in Big Sandy after a recital — I'm on the front row in the white dress with red cummerbund; *around 1964*

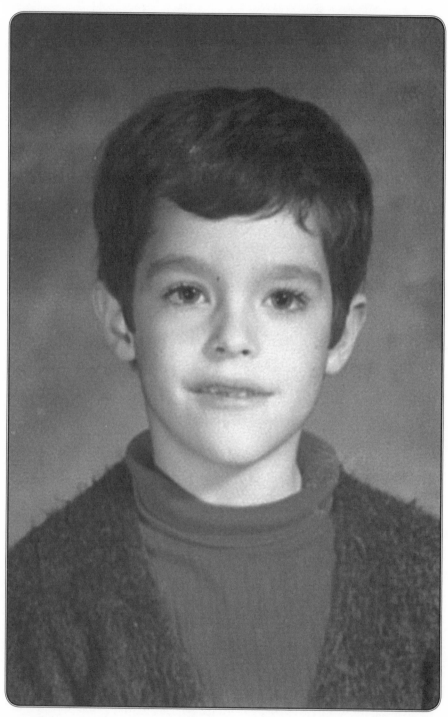

Dan Powers, seven years old, *1970–71*

Steve Powers, third grade picture

Steve, Dan, and me on the front step of our house on Pearl Street, *1965*

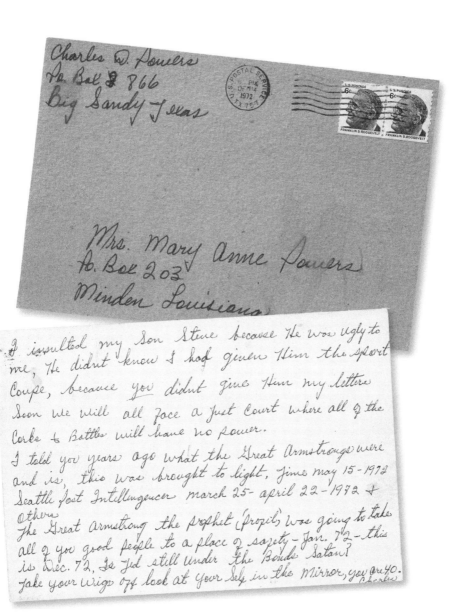

A card cut from a box sent by Dad to Mother, *December 1972*

The old Holloway house, Wooster, Arkansas, *1968*

Summer Educational Program, Orr, Minnesota, *1968*

Canadian canoe trip, *Summer 1968*

Powers Family — Dr. J.T. Powers is at far left; *circa 1900*

Aunt Dortha Hightower   **Uncle Shelby Hightower**

Uncle Jake and Aunt Hattie Sims, *1998*

ONE OF THE Y-TEEN—Banner Clubs at the Y-Teen Banquet held at the YWCA recently is from Peeples Junior High School. Representing their school. Representing their school and accepting the award are Carla Powers and Joyce Crane. Mrs. Wanda Price is the Banner Club's teacher-sponsor.

Joyce Crane and I representing our school and accepting the award.

Mrs. Lewis and six debaters, Chuck Shaffer, Kay Mc Kinney, Randy Rentz, Mike Haney, Carla Powers, and Debra Benedict were involved in an accident enroute to Minden from Lake Charles on October 15, returning from the McNeese. Tournament. Their car was struck from behind by a car going nearly 90 m.p.h. because the driver had gone to sleep at the wheel. Fortunately there were no injuries except soreness and bruises.

The accident enroute to Minden from Lake Charles.

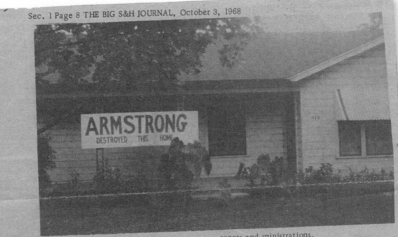

Sec. 1 Page 8 THE BIG S&H JOURNAL, October 3, 1968

The Big Sandy home of Charles Powers at 310 N. Pearl Street had this sign tacked across the front on Friday night, September 27 by its owner Powers and a co-worker in the Auto Body Business.

Mrs. Powers and their three children, the oldest a girl 13 left without notice and no forwarding address on that date.

Powers alleges her alienation through church tenets and ministrations.

The couple had been members from the mid fifties.

His name was stricken from the rolls as a communicant more than three years ago and subsequently, while his wife remained a co-worker and their children attended Imperial School, he was ex-communicated and his business, he maintains, was boycotted by his former "Co-workers."

Article and picture from the *Big S&H Journal,* *October 3, 1968*

Charles Powers, a Big Sandy business man since 1955, put a sign on the front of his residence, at 310 N. Pearl Street in Big Sandy on the anniversary of the un-announced departure of his wife Mary and children to parts unknown to Mr. Powers.

Accompanying the original sign erected in 1968 was one which added some detail of his efforts to locate his family.

From a recounting of his tactics in locating the family it was apparent that he'd used means not unlike those employed by detective agencies.

The sign came down Tuesday night after his attorney, Ernest Martin of Gladewater, had elicited a willingness of the attorneys for the Worldwide Church of God and its Big Sandy Business Manager Mr. Neff to meet with Powers in company with Martin in Gilmer Wednesday morning.

FASTED

Powers had recently gone on a five day fast in which he declared that no morsel passed his lips. Asked how it seemed to affect him he retorted "The hunger I felt in my stomach was not one bit worse than the hunger in my heart for a year now."

Wednesday afternoon Mr. Neff, contacted at his office at Ambassador College, was asked if he could assure Mr. Powers an audience with Mr. Herbert W. Armstrong during his attendance at the Big Sandy Feast of Tabernacles. Mr. Neff demurred that Mr. Armstrong would probably be too busy to see Mr. Powers or even himself.

Mr. Neff declared that the organization had nothing to do with the decision of Mrs. Powers to leave home.

From Page 3 This section your sins be as scarlet, they shall be as white as snow. Though they be red like crimson, they shall be as wo——

There is a very proper in the program of the c for the expression of comp sion and care for the poor a neglected. This should not, ho ever, take the place of spiritual ministry of the ch but should complement it

If We Began to Pray

There is no place in tural program of the the funding of the a those who would stroy the nation have freedom o placing it with those who ha ened to dest they do demand Wh hap no

Article and picture of original sign and its additions
in *Big S&H Journal,* September 1969

310 North Pearl Street, Big Sandy, Texas, *1970*

The moment after being crowned Miss Minden, *1973*

Performing "The Cremation of Sam McGee" in the Miss Minden Pageant, *1973*

My official pageant picture, *1974*

**High school
graduation picture,
taken before
make-up!** *1972*

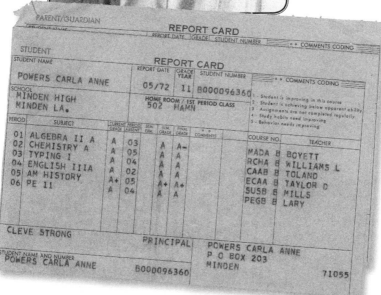

Final report card for my junior year at Minden High School

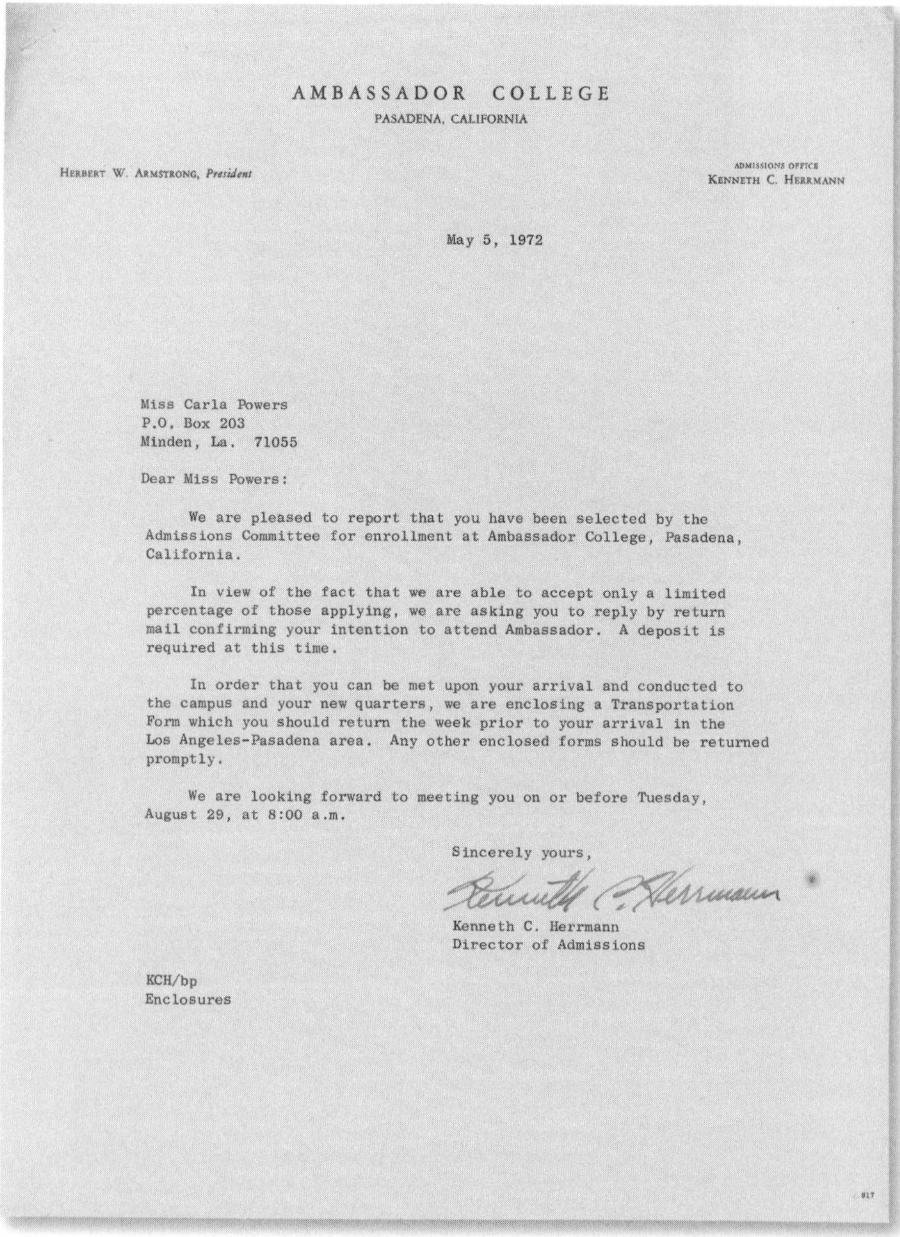

AMBASSADOR COLLEGE
PASADENA, CALIFORNIA

HERBERT W. ARMSTRONG, *President*

ADMISSIONS OFFICE
KENNETH C. HERRMANN

May 5, 1972

Miss Carla Powers
P.O. Box 203
Minden, La. 71055

Dear Miss Powers:

We are pleased to report that you have been selected by the Admissions Committee for enrollment at Ambassador College, Pasadena, California.

In view of the fact that we are able to accept only a limited percentage of those applying, we are asking you to reply by return mail confirming your intention to attend Ambassador. A deposit is required at this time.

In order that you can be met upon your arrival and conducted to the campus and your new quarters, we are enclosing a Transportation Form which you should return the week prior to your arrival in the Los Angeles-Pasadena area. Any other enclosed forms should be returned promptly.

We are looking forward to meeting you on or before Tuesday, August 29, at 8:00 a.m.

Sincerely yours,

Kenneth C. Herrmann
Director of Admissions

KCH/bp
Enclosures

Admission letter from Ambassador College at the end of my junior year of high school. I hadn't even applied!

Mother, Steve, Dan and me at the house on Myrtlewood Drive in Jackson, Mississippi, *1968*

Dan, Steve, and me in Minden, Louisiana, *1974*

Steve, Mother, Dan and me in Arkansas, *1989*

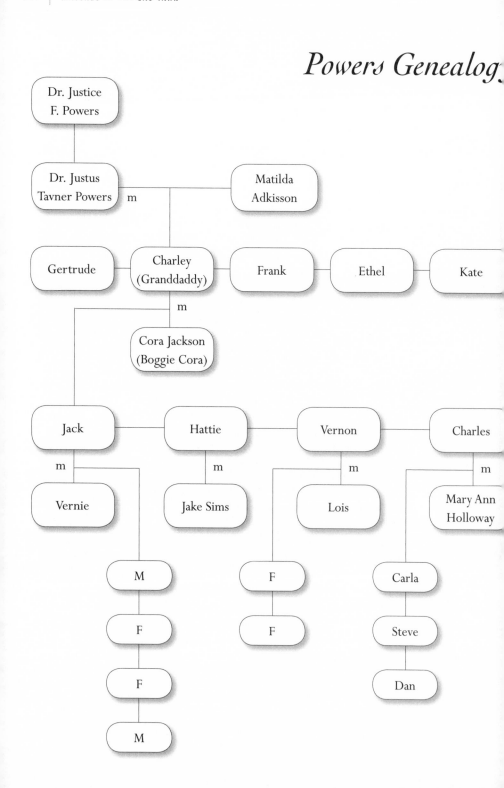

Powers Genealogy

Holloway Genealogy

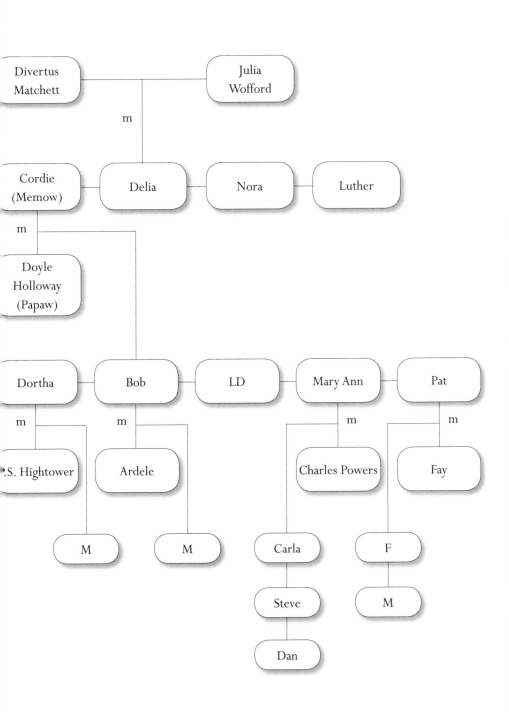

CHAPTER TWENTY-ONE

Sins of the Flesh

The mid-sixties were times of change in the Radio Church of God. Congregations were established in cities across the U.S. and England. Ministers were posted to these locations, but no church buildings were constructed. Services were held in hotel ballrooms or VFW halls. As God's Word began to be communicated through television, Garner Ted Armstrong became the face and voice of the church. In 1968, the church was renamed the Worldwide Church of God.

Herbert W. Armstrong largely abandoned the airwaves to become a self-described statesman. Back in Big Sandy, we heard stories of his travels on the church's jets to meet with world leaders. Herbert W. pontificated about how he lavished Steuben glass upon King Hussein of Jordan and the Philippines' prime minister. Rank-and-file members gossiped with approval about his three homes on the forty-eight-acre Pasadena campus, his chauffeured Rolls Royce, his personal collection of Steuben glass, his tableware that had belonged to the Czar of Russia.

It took money to support this lifestyle, and Armstrong wasn't about to let even the widow's mite escape. In the mid-sixties, he sent this letter to members:

> Many professing to be Church MEMBERS say, when a Co-worker letter arrives, in a grumbling, complaining disgust: 'Oh, that's another of Mr. Armstrong's REQUESTS for MONEY,' and many don't even read the letter!

> Are YOU one of those? If so, LET ME BURN YOUR EARS before the Almighty GOD burns YOU in the Lake of FIRE! ...You are some of the ROTTEN, PUTRID, spiritual WASTE that has been PLUGGED UP INSIDE OF THE SPIRITUAL BODY OF CHRIST'S WIFE, just as physical waste is plugged up in my dear wife's body! And the living Jesus is just as able to EXPEL YOU from the spiritual Body of HIS WIFE as He is to expel this physical waste from my wife's body![18]

Garner Ted's popularity quickly eclipsed that of his father. Movie-star handsome with a rich baritone voice, his charisma jumped off the screen. Where Herbert

W. came across as regal and authoritative, Garner Ted was warm, seductive. He confessed to youthful drunkenness, smoking, and womanizing before finding the truth. When Garner Ted — sometimes called GTA by church members — preached about giving up a life of sin to follow God's way, members figured he knew what he was talking about. By the end of the sixties, Garner Ted had wide public recognition and was perhaps the first internationally known televangelist.

I liked Garner Ted and was thrilled when he greeted me by name. His three boys and an army of nieces and nephews went to Imperial; his middle son and I were in the same class. As first- and second-graders, we held hands in the playground. He was a dear, cute little boy. Sadly, two of GTA's three sons were born profoundly deaf. That didn't keep me from becoming friends with the one my age. Despite the fact that they were church royalty, people avoided the boys. I had heard from the pulpit that having a child born with a defect was a message from God that the parents had committed some horrifying sin. I could relate to the idea of being ostracized for something over which I had no control. Another reason I was able to become friends with Garner Ted's son was my being comfortable with deafness. Dad learned to sign when he taught at the Arkansas School for the Deaf and developed the habit of reflexively signing in all conversations. He helped me not to fear people who were different from me.

Herbert W. and Garner Ted both spent a great deal of time preaching about the evils of sex outside of a marriage recognized by God. What they did was apparently a far cry from what they told others to do. Much has been written about the old man's alleged incestuous relationship with his youngest daughter, which purportedly began when she was thirteen years old and continued for a decade. Accounts say that she told Garner Ted about the abuse, which included rape, bondage, and hush money. Garner Ted's tastes were more pedestrian. He had a penchant for chasing women, lots of them. It has been widely reported that he had sex with more than two hundred women.

Herbert W. turned a blind eye to Garner Ted's womanizing. I suspect Herbert W. ignored whatever Garner Ted did because Garner Ted was now recognized as the face of the church. If he were run off, the money would dry up. His father, other ministers, church members and his beautiful, long-suffering wife, Shirley, all looked the other way. Garner Ted was in heaven. He had money, power, fame, and scores of college girls and churchwomen to choose from, with no rules to constrain him.

Dad became convinced that Mother was sleeping with Garner Ted. "I'm living with Bathsheba," he said, his forehead knotted and his voice getting louder and louder. I was ten and knew what he meant. King David lusted after Bathsheba, the wife of Uriah, the Hittite. After she became the king's lover, David dispatched Uriah to the battlefront where he was killed. "I'm like Uriah," Dad raved. "Garner Ted wants me out of the picture. He'd like to see me dead. They both would. Whore!"

I never saw Mother interact with Garner Ted, other than to exchange casual greetings. But with his well-known reputation and Mother's good looks, Dad seized upon an imagined betrayal as the reason for his downfall.

Tension between them escalated to the point that whenever Dad was home, I felt the need to become invisible. "Whore!" he'd shout at her again, or "Been with him today?" Then he'd kiss Mother or put his arms around her. She didn't push him away. I suspected that she didn't feel that she could. Had she rejected him, Dad would have taken it as proof of his accusations.

One night in 1965, I was awakened by Dad's moans. The sound came from my parent's bedroom. At first it scared me; I almost rushed in to see what was wrong. Then I heard Mother's voice. "Charles, ssshhhh. You're going to wake up the kids." I didn't fully understand what was happening, but I realized Mother wasn't in danger. I couldn't comprehend how Mother could lie in the same bed with a man who cursed at her, called her names, and deprived her of the money needed to care for us.

Early in 1967, Mrs. Herbert W. Armstrong — Loma — became ill. She refused medical treatment, though many writers said that her husband regularly sought treatment from physicians and took medicine. The church required members to observe days of prayer and fasting to facilitate her recovery. It didn't work, and Loma died.

Mrs. Armstrong had been a moderating influence on Herbert W. After her death, he further tightened the rules under which church members lived. The harshest involved divorce and remarriage. In the early days of the church, people who had been divorced and remarried were allowed to live with their new spouses, like everyone else in America. But after Loma died, Armstrong claimed to receive new orders from God. He decreed that once married, always married; so, if a former partner were still alive, you were still married to him, even if the court had granted you a divorce and you had legally remarried. "God will not forgive any form of adultery," Herbert W. decreed, so these relationships had to cease.

At first, divorced people living with new spouses could remain together — as long as they were celibate. Later, things got worse.

Steve, Dan, and I occasionally stayed with the Woods family, who lived in a beautifully maintained, old-fashioned frame house that faced the street parallel to Big Sandy's railroad tracks. We had gotten to know them when we lived behind the Texaco station and yearned for a real home with a yard. The Woodses had a big shaded lot without fences, filled with trees, flowers and comfortable places to sit. Grandpa Woods was a thin, bright-eyed man with round glasses who wore light brown work clothes around the house. Grandma Woods was also thin, with gray hair twisted into a bun, always wearing an apron. They were healthy and active. She made gingerbread men for us; the inside of her house smelled of cinnamon. There was no clutter, no mustiness.

Even as a child, I knew that those two dear old people loved each other. They contrasted sharply with other older couples I had observed, like Memow and Papaw, who only tolerated each other. The Woodses sat side by side on the porch swing and held hands. But as a teenager, Mr. Woods had been briefly married to someone else. The church piously explained that he was now an adulterer and that he must move out. Separating people like the Woodses, Herbert Armstrong said, was the mandate of a loving God. The old couple was separated; apart, both withered away.

Such separations were not uncommon. Men were forced to leave their wives and children. Children of adulterous liaisons were deemed bastards. Yet, when Herbert W. Armstrong decided he wanted to marry a divorcee after Loma died, all of the wrecked lives were forgotten and scripture was once again reinterpreted.

My understanding of sex came from the pulpit and the first edition of HWA's book *God Speaks Out on the New Morality*. It was required reading, even for preteens like me. The original, which came out around 1965, contained graphic drawings of genitalia and instructions about how to have sex — in the missionary position. Armstrong drew parallels between humans and farm animals. Most of it didn't make sense to me and was too creepy to try to understand. There were emphatic condemnations of sexual sins, such as oral sex, masturbation, and premartial coitus.

What haunted me most was a story about a girl who had gotten pregnant without intercourse. She and her boyfriend were petting (the term wasn't explained, although I certainly wish it had been) and somehow his sperm hopped into her vagina and fertilized an egg. I lay at night on my bed feeling the pulse in my stomach. Was that a baby moving around? Had I sat too close to someone? Maybe a sperm had jumped on me!

By the time I began having a period, most of the other girls had already experienced "the curse" and prepared me for it. Mother explained nothing. Tampons were forbidden; you would lose your virginity. An intact hymen was essential so your husband could be sure you were a virgin on your wedding night. *God Speaks Out on the New Morality* provided instructions about how to break the hymen. The whole idea all sounded disgusting to me, and I wondered why people made such a big fuss about it.

The church forbade young people of the opposite sex to touch each other in any way. No hugs, no pecks on the cheek, no hand-holding. That could lead to lust, and thinking about anything sexual was as bad as doing it.

The church's control over people's lives extended to their choice of spouses. If the ministers decided that young people who weren't old enough to marry were getting too serious, they were ordered to stop seeing each other. Marriages needed the minister's approval; the ministers suggested mates for promising students at Ambassador. If a die-hard romantic declined to marry the person the church selected, she or he would be kicked out of college for being rebellious. As Mr. Armstrong explained: you don't fall in love, you fall in lust. That thing the world calls love — and writes songs about — is lust. The elders knew what it took to make a successful marriage and had the wisdom to see in people the characteristics that would make them love each other. With time. Who needed sparks and excitement?

Nothing that related to sex and marriage mattered to me anyway. Armstrong had become emphatic that Christ was going to return on the Feast of Trumpets in 1975. That meant that we would flee to Petra in 1972. I wasn't going to get married at seventeen before we left, and I doubted that anyone would hook me up while we were sequestered in the rocks of Jordan. And, Armstrong had been clear that during the Kingdom of God, which would begin after Christ's return in 1975, there would be no earthly marriages and no sex. That would leave me out of the whole nasty mess.

CHAPTER TWENTY-TWO
....
Disfellowshipped

It was 1965 and I was in the fifth grade. As we did every week, Mother, Steve, Dan, and I went to the Saturday afternoon service. Dad hadn't gone with us in over a year. In our world, attendance wasn't voluntary. You had to be there or else. We knew that Dad was on the edge of "or else."

We passed the new guard station gates and the Ambassador College sign with the church's seal of the lion, the lamb and a little child huddled together peacefully in the Kingdom of God. It was a regular Sabbath day, and attendance was brisk. On the field, the cars of people who'd arrived before us were lined up in neat rows a quarter-mile wide and deep. A deacon waving an orange flashlight directed us into a parking space. Worshippers who chose not to walk rode past in open trailers pulled by tractors.

When the tabernacle had been built a few years before, no one believed there would ever be enough members to fill it. But with the growth of the church and the expansion of Ambassador College, the auditorium was seated to capacity most of the time. The ministers didn't just have a pulpit from which to preach; they had a full stage with a Steinway grand, risers for the choir, and massive bouquets of flowers.

At one-thirty on the dot everyone in the room was seated. The song leader instructed us to rise and open our songbooks. We sang two short hymns and listened to an interminable, rambling prayer. I always thought ministers competed with each other to see who could pray the longest. No one given center stage on a Sabbath missed the opportunity to dazzle the congregation with a prolix supplication tying together world events, scripture, and the Work of the One True Church. After standing with a deeply bowed head for four or five minutes, I wondered if the "Amen" that echoed from the throng was an affirmation of the prayer or a celebration that it was finally over.

We took our seats for the sermonette. A minister of lesser importance spoke for twenty minutes, punctuating his message with arm-waving and podium-pounding. When he wrapped up, the congregation rose for another hymn so circulation could be restored to our bodies before the long sermon began. We sang, we sat down, we waited for routine announcements.

But this day was different.

"My friends," the minister said with feigned sadness, "I regret to advise you that Charles Powers —" hearing the name, I felt like I had been jolted with a live power line "— Charles Powers is no longer a member of our congregation." 700 people were silent, listening for the rest. "He has been marked from our church for failing to follow God's laws."

I knew that the eyes of everyone around us were boring into Dan, Steve, Mother, and me. My skin flushed; I felt heat creep up my chest and my neck. I couldn't breathe. "Please continue to love and have fellowship with his wife and children, who remain members of our congregation. But you may not go to their home or socialize with Mr. Powers, and you may not do business with him."

I wondered if I was going to faint.

I wanted to look at Mother, but I had to keep my eyes glued to the stage. I couldn't let the rubberneckers know that I was upset. A brave front was the only way to survive. I was Carla Powers. My father's disgrace didn't change who I was. But there were not enough blue ribbons or A-pluses or well-played renditions of "Malagueña" in the world to cover the brand I now wore.

"He is no longer fit to be a member of God's church."

There was nowhere to hide. I had to pretend to listen to the sermon that followed. I didn't hear a word.

When it finally ended, Mother, Steve, Dan and I ducked out of a side door and made a beeline for our car.

We didn't dare speak until we were on Highway 80.

"Mother, what'll happen now?"

"Nothing. Life'll go on like always."

I didn't argue, but it wasn't true. When I stepped on the yellow Imperial School bus on Monday morning, all eyes would be on me. The air would be heavy with my classmates' unasked question: What did your Dad do that was so bad? Even my friends would avoid me because they wouldn't know what to say. They wouldn't be allowed to come to our house. Those who didn't like me would whisper and point when I walked by.

More than before, I had to prove that I wasn't my Dad.

CHAPTER TWENTY-THREE

The Walking Wounded

From late 1965 until Father's Day 1968, I don't remember much. Those three years — the worst years — have mostly slipped into a black hole. All that's left are a handful of mental snapshots.

I lived on autopilot, mastering more complex piano pieces and giving recitals to larger and larger audiences at the college. I set school records as a sprinter. I cleaned Mrs. Starley's and the Prociws' homes until they could have eaten off the floors. I babysat for neighbors. My grades never faltered. I was told that I would likely be granted early admission to Ambassador College. Members remarked that I was going to make an excellent minister's wife. Miss Perfect. Or, as Ernie Prociw said, Miss Goody Two-shoes.

I buried myself in books and music, trying to shut out the thoughts that were swirling in my head. I played the Beach Boys' *Surfin' USA* album so many times that the needle wore grooves in the tracks. My friends loved the same music, but we didn't listen to records together because they couldn't come to my house, and I rarely spent nights at theirs because of what might be happening at home.

I began to realize that there were deeper doctrines taught by Armstrong than those I was able to readily comprehend as a child. I heard about the pagan doctrine of the Trinity and learned that the Holy Spirit is not God but rather is "divine sperm" that impregnates the believer. This occurred simultaneously with baptism. But this miracle was reserved only for adults eighteen and older. Holy Spirit was also given in degrees, so that Armstrong received much more than a lowly member like Mother. There was also a doctrine that never clicked with me — the United States and Great Britain are the ten lost tribes of Israel and became the substitutes for the Israelites in the Bible. Apparently this made it possible for prophesies in Revelation to be fulfilled without having to deal with the pesky problems in the Middle East. Herbert W. taught that he was an Elijah and John the Baptist type whose appearance precedes the return of Jesus Christ. We were provided with precise dates 6,000 years earlier when man was created by God in His image.[19]

Dad's patterns became more difficult to predict. Despite the fact that church members could no longer do business with him, he bought a piece of property on the west side of Big Sandy, at the intersection of Highway 80 and the Tyler Highway, and built his own shop from cement blocks. Every penny he got was poured into construction of his building. We had no money for food or clothes or the house payment. The house was repeatedly posted for foreclosure.

More often than not, Dad spent nights in the travel trailer parked behind the shop. Sometimes we didn't see him for days. When he was away, we fell into a weeknight routine: homework, piano practice, supper and shelling peas or mending while watching TV. But we were always on edge, listening for the truck to pull in.

My adrenal glands never rested: my body was perpetually fighting or fleeing. Psychosomatic illness — migraines, tonsillitis and stomach spasms — became as familiar as fear. Since we couldn't take medicine — not even aspirin — I'd lie in my dark room with a cold washcloth on my forehead. Sometimes I'd tie a rag around my forehead to relieve the pressure. When Mother told me that Boggie Cora used to do the same thing, it made me feel worse.

Then there were my "attacks." My abdomen heaved from the expansion and contraction of muscles, stomach acid etched its way up my esophagus into my mouth. I'd retch for forty-eight nonstop hours.

I was lying on the bathroom floor. "Mommy, can you do something?" I whispered. My mouth was dry as powder and tasted of bile. My overworked muscles refused my body's command to move.

"I wish I could." She tried to get me to accept a spoonful of crushed ice. "The ministers'll be here before long."

"Can you boil the grapefruit rind like you did last time?"

"I'm sorry, honey, but we don't have any." She wiped my face for the tenth time. "I'm going to get you some clean pj's."

When Mother returned, there were two ministers with her.

"Same as before?" Mr. Fisher asked.

"Yes, sir," Mother answered.

"You need to get her up." His voice had an exasperated edge. It was clear that he wasn't pleased to be visiting the Powers home. "We can't anoint her in the bathroom."

Mother hoisted me up while they watched. We staggered the few steps to my bed. The ministers and Mother knelt beside me.

Mr. Fisher placed his hands around my head. "Father in Heaven, thank you for all of our many blessings. We know that You and You alone have the power to heal. Grant us the faith to trust you...."

He took a miserly vial of olive oil from his pocket and placed a drop on his index finger. He then transferred the oil to my forehead. "I anoint you with healing oil. In Jesus' name, Amen."

After sealing the bottle of olive oil, the minister looked down at me and said, "God's will be done. If you believe in Him and have faith, you will be healed."

"Thank you," I mumbled.

After forty-eight hours, the spasms stopped just like they had all the times before.

CHAPTER TWENTY-FOUR
Matches in the Gas Tank

June 1968. Dad had been arrested in Hope, Arkansas, for doing bad things while drunk. Nobody ever told us exactly what the bad things were. He didn't call home, but after sitting in jail for a few days, he worked up the courage to ask his sister Hattie's husband for money. Being a decent fellow, Uncle Jake took him the cash.

We didn't know where Dad was, and it didn't occur to our relatives to spend the money on a long-distance call to tell us. Even given his bizarre patterns, four days without any word from Dad was unusual. I stewed about what had happened to him and wondered if he would ever come home again. A part of me was afraid he wouldn't. Another part was terrified he would.

It was Father's Day. Steve and I had labored to make cards for Dad. I folded a piece of blue construction paper into the shape of a store-bought card and pasted a red cutout flower on the front. I carefully printed "Happy Father's Day" in crayon and signed, "Love, Carla." Steve drew pictures of a truck and a car on yellow paper and wrote in scrawling cursive, "Love, Steve." We stood the cards on the dining room table with a bottle of Old Spice wrapped in bright foil and tied with a piece of ribbon.

It was dark when I heard Dad's wrecker pull into the driveway, and I peered out the kitchen window to see if I could judge what kind of mood he was in. Sometimes he would come home drunk and ignore us. Sometimes he would come home drunk and rage through the house, cursing; sometimes he'd build a fire in the back yard. Other times he would be less drunk and would only mock Armstrong or call Mother "whore." That day it didn't take long to figure which it was.

He slammed the door of the truck. There was a pose Dad struck when he wanted us to know that he was really, really angry: He would narrow his eyes into slits, crinkle his nose and furrow his brow so that the lines were as visible as the folds on a Shar-Pei dog. His face would turn red and the veins on his forehead would pop out. He would cross his arms across his chest and stand with his feet planted about fifteen inches apart. That was the way he looked tonight. He stomped toward the house, his feet crunching the gravel.

I ran to the bedroom next to the kitchen and cowered, my bowels threatening diarrhea. The screen door squeaked as he yanked it open, then the wood cracked as Dad ripped the frame from its hinges.

"Damn it!" he shouted, as he stepped into the kitchen. "Get your asses in here *now!*" He threw an empty bottle of Seagram's 7 against the kitchen wall, smashing the rooster Mother had made by gluing beans onto a board. Shards of glass and beans bounced against the kitchen table.

Since we weren't moving fast enough, he tore the wooden doors off the cabinets. One after the other, four cabinet doors skittered across the linoleum, clanging as they collided with the metal kitchen chairs.

"I said NOW!"

He jerked the oven door from its frame and threw it to the floor where it landed with a thirty-pound thud. I felt the pier and beam foundation shake. The burner grates and a cast-iron skillet clattered to a halt near me. I caught my breath and held it. My brain told me to keep moving or things would get worse, but my feet were rooted.

Dad was a half-inch under six feet tall and weighed a rock-solid 240 pounds. He was an auto body repairman who worked six days a week swinging an iron sledgehammer. He looked like an NFL linebacker.

Mother eased through the doorway between the kitchen and the boys' bedroom. Dad hit the side of her head with his forearm. She fell to the floor, blood trickling down her neck. Glass from the broken whiskey bottle cut her hands. Steve rushed forward, pummeling Dad's chest with his fists. I screamed, "Stop it, Daddy! Please stop it, Daddy!" He ignored me and pushed Steve away.

"This is my house, and I'm the master. I'm sick and tired of your lack of respect. You're to obey me, not some god-damned minister. I'm going to show you who's boss." He lifted Mother, dazed, from the floor and dragged her by the arms through the family room adjoining the kitchen. She staggered to her feet as they passed the Father's Day cards and gift.

Dad looked back at Steve, Dan and me who were still cowering in the kitchen. "Come on," he said, "or you'll get the same thing." We followed.

Dad pushed Mother out the front door onto the porch and down one step to the yard. He shoved Steve, Dan, and me through the yard to the driveway in front of the garage and planted us a foot away from the wrecker. "Stand there! Don't move!" I stayed exactly where he'd put me, because there was no telling what he'd do if one of us defied him.

My daddy unscrewed the truck's gas cap and threw it on the ground. He took a box from his pants pocket, pulled out a match, and struck it. After he was sure that the stick was burning, he dropped it in the open gas tank.

"You're going to kill us all!" Mother cried, encircling us with her arms.

Dan, who was almost four, broke away and grabbed Dad's leg. Dad cackled with psychotic laughter and threw another burning match into the tank. Then another. And another.

"I and I alone have the power over whether you live or die," he said.

He lit and threw more of the matches.

When the box was empty, he moved to the driver's door of the truck, opened it and sat behind the wheel. He put the key in the ignition, turned it and pushed both the accelerator and the clutch to the floor. The big truck's engine revved higher and higher; the pistons groaned and the valves began to rattle. My ears rang from the roar.

After five minutes of abuse, the engine began to burn oil. Acrid black smoke billowed into the night sky. It was so thick that I couldn't see the neighbors' houses. Oil spewed from the tailpipe, spattering the ground. The engine threw its rods, each sounding like a rifle shot. The truck shook for a final time when the engine died. Then, all was quiet. We stood, transfixed, wondering what was going to happen next. None of our neighbors came out to check on us. No police or constables arrived. They were afraid of Charles Powers, too.

Dad got in Mother's Olds 98 and floor-boarded it. He pushed the engine for a minute, put the car into drive, and peeled out, burning rubber.

After he drove away, we didn't move. We were like actors waiting for the director to tell us what to do next. I looked up and down the street to see if anyone was watching. I couldn't see through the smoke, but I knew people were shaking their heads, talking about that crazy Powers family. This was why none of my friends could come over to play. This was why we'd never be as good as other people. This was why I had to work so hard every day to be perfect. But I knew there was nothing I could do to erase the stigma of being my father's daughter.

CHAPTER TWENTY-FIVE
The Respite

During this time, my Dad died. Not in the sense that Charles D. Powers ceased to draw breath. But I became as much an orphan as the McMillan children whose father had died in a car wreck. I'd lost the man who had tossed me into the air and caught me. I lost the big Teddy Bear who'd held me close to his chest and protected me from the world. He had broken all of his promises, implicit and explicit. I knew he wouldn't be there for my future, whether climbing the rocks in Petra or welcoming Christ to earth at the start of the Kingdom of God. While the words never entered my consciousness, I wanted him out of our lives. I perfected the skill of building a wall against pain. I blocked the past, wiped it away. I lived only for today and the future. Gradually, like the rain that washes away the springtime pollen haze, my father's indifference to us erased his place in my heart. By the time I was twelve, when I looked at him, I felt as cold as the bags of vegetables piled in our freezer.

But it had taken a toll. In the summer of 1968, I was a wreck. Even though I put on a brave front, an anonymous donor — I suspected the Prociws — was sufficiently concerned about my well-being to pay for transportation and tuition to the church's Summer Educational Program — SEP — in Orr, Minnesota. A few weeks after Dad threw the matches in the gas tank, I left Big Sandy on the yellow Imperial School bus.

Sending me to camp was the kindest thing anyone in the church ever did for me. Before we hit the Oklahoma border, the knot in my stomach relaxed. Surrounded by laughing, singing schoolmates, listening to music — "I Love You" by the People and "Pictures of Matchstick Men" by Status Quo — and trying to dance in the aisle of the bus, I felt like the kid I was supposed to be. Kansas and Nebraska sailed by in a sea of corn. We held our noses passing Iowa's hog farms, and, finally, on the third day we reached Minnesota.

The church did camp the way it approached every other development project — with lots of money. Set along the banks of Pelican Lake near the Canadian border, there were ten rough cedar dormitories for boys and ten for girls. There were bathhouses — one for boys, one for girls. The showers were communal and the first few times I stood stark naked in front of other girls, I thought I'd melt from shame; but by the end of the summer some of us regularly soaped the shower floor and slid on it in our birthday suits. The dining room/meeting hall was the focal point, with its vaulted ceiling, rock face and a wall of windows that looked into a birch forest. Boathouses protected the spanking new ski boats from the elements; sailboats were moored.

Despite the fact that the water never got above fifty-five degrees, there was a swimming area with lane markers in the lake. Once a week, the camp's counselors required us to make a racing dive into the frigid water and compete with our cabin mates in the breaststroke and backstroke. It built character, they said. There were ranges for archery and riflery, piers for fishing, hiking trails, horses, and canoes. Away from the campers' area were accommodations for adult staff, offices and a garage.

We wore uniforms at all times. The blue camp logo of an eagle in flight was ever on our nightshirts. The campers in each dorm sang marching songs while walking together in perfect alignment, step and cadence. We lived military-style: clothes rolled and organized in cubbies according to precise regulations; daily inspection to ensure that sheets had knife-edged corners and were tight enough to bounce a quarter; white-glove tests for dust. We were issued demerits for violations. The boys' and girls' dorms with the fewest demerits received weekly awards. When campers got too many demerits or engaged in bad behavior, they were spanked.

My dorm counselor — an Ambassador College student — was the daughter of old family friends. Becky was kind and wise enough to give me something I'd never known: a happy childhood experience. She kept me busy so I didn't have time to think about home and picked me for two of the summer's best events. The first was a three-day horseback trip into the wilds. A small group led by one of my Imperial School teachers rode horses all day, made camp at night and cooked our food over a campfire. As part of our survival training, we trapped grasshoppers.

"Mr. Hamm," I asked our leader, "don't you think these are unclean?"

"No," he answered confidently, "the Israelites ate them when they were wandering in the desert for forty years."

"I can't imagine that it's okay to eat bugs."

"We know that these are," he said, as he placed a skillet over the open fire. "They're plentiful in Petra. Better get used to them."

I watched as he pulled the heads off a handful and tossed them into the hot pan. "You cook them until they are crunchy."

Two minutes later, Mr. Hamm emptied our appetizer into a plate. "Everyone has to try at least one."

I popped the insect into my mouth and swallowed it whole.

"Tasty, isn't it?" the teacher asked.

"Yes, sir," I answered without conviction.

Canoeing for eight days in Canadian border waters was more fun. We were far away from civilization, or at least thought we were; and when we made camp every night, we dug latrines, built fires and pitched tents. My ego bloomed when I was selected as the partner for an evangelist's daughter named Joy, a short petite girl my age. She was strong for her size, and we portaged our bright-yellow canoe and muscled our way through swirling eddies that seemed impossible to escape. Joy was friendly and treated me as her equal. Toward the end of the trip we stopped at a trading post and tied our canoes to the dock so we could shop. I still remember the plaid wrapper on the English toffee.

Garner Ted Armstrong liked camp and often came for visits. He had a fine singing voice and led sing-alongs under the stars, accompanying himself on the guitar. We sang folk songs like "If I Had a Hammer" and inspirational ones like "How Great Thou Art" that had been vetted for compliance with God's message. Garner Ted and other ministers lectured us about music, particularly how to tell good from evil. The Beatles were a constant source of conversation, and they were held up as role models for a satanic lifestyle. Garner Ted was particularly incensed about the lyrics to "Louie, Louie." And there was the usual preaching about the evils of sex. To make sure we didn't get any sinful ideas, the boys and girls were allowed to mix only for a short time after Sabbath services.

Maggie Murphy was a petite blonde dynamo two years my senior. Her dad, a former furniture salesman, was pastor of the church in Jackson, Mississippi. We were assigned to the same dorm, and she became my closest friend. When Maggie laughed, she threw back her head and let go. There was something a little dangerous about her, as though she was skating on the edge. Whenever pranks were pulled or we had an idea about something fun to do, Maggie was invariably the instigator. I had never known anyone with such joy for life.

"Powers," Maggie said, "you worry too much."

"I know."

"Let loose," she said. "Laugh. Do something wrong. You take this rule stuff way too seriously."

"I want to go to Petra."

"I think half of what they tell us is a load of crap."

"Maggie Murphy!"

I drew in a sharp breath. "It's a sin to say that."

Maggie rolled her eyes.

"Do you really believe God is sitting on His big throne writing down on a notepad whether I put on mascara when I get to school? Doesn't that seem pretty silly to you?"

"I never thought about it."

"Girl," she said, shaking her head, "you need help. We're going to find a way for you to get the attention of big, blond and handsome."

"Surfer boy?" My heart jumped in my chest.

"And," she said, "it won't be by following the rules."

Maggie and I sat on her bunk, scheming.

"You'll chicken out." Maggie looked at me disapprovingly.

"No, I won't," I replied.

"We're not taking any chances. I'm going to handle this." And she did. Surreptitiously dropping a note beside his plate at breakfast.

After services the next Sabbath, Maggie grabbed my arm and dragged me through the throng of kids to the northeast corner of the meeting area.

"He'll be here."

"I don't see him. Let's go."

She faced me but didn't let go.

"Hi, Mike," she said. I whirled around to see a six-foot-tall boy of fifteen with sun-bleached-blond hair and broad shoulders walking toward us.

"Bye, kids," she said and disappeared into the crowd.

It took a few seconds for my vocal cords to work, but I finally summoned the courage to speak. "Hi, Mike. I'm Carla."

"I know," he said, grinning.

I promptly fell in love. From southern California and two years older than me, Mike was miserable because the church had separated his parents, enforcing the new policy on divorce and remarriage. He was too cool for the church and had a way of looking bored at everything that was going on. Knowing that it was a sin, I lusted after him and didn't feel guilty. I dreamed of holding his hand or maybe, if I was really, really brave, sharing a kiss. My heart did flips on the last day of camp when he signed my hat.

The kids who went to SEP were, with some notable exceptions like me, at the top of the church pecking order. While I can't remember the total number of campers in 1968, I doubt if there were more than 300. Only a handful of kids from Imperial School went. Many were the children of ministers and teachers at Ambassador College. Those who weren't offspring of the elite attended because their parents still had enough money left for camp tuition after paying more than their share of tithes and offerings. A few, like me, received scholarships. Being selected for camp and performing admirably while there put you on the path to being accepted into Ambassador College.

Given the church's rigid hierarchy and the fact that my Dad was a notorious nut case, I'm not sure why it embraced me by letting me perform in the big church auditorium or telling me that I would probably get into Ambassador early or by talking about my prospects for becoming a minister's wife. Other kids, even bright hardworking ones, were ostracized for carrying a lot less baggage than I bore. My classmate, Natalie Jefferson, who was smart, great at track, a good pianist, and an excellent singer, never got the same breaks. It's one of those questions I'll never be able to answer.

CHAPTER TWENTY-SIX

Our Place of Safety

My last indelible memory of Big Sandy came on a Thursday in September 1968. I'd been home from camp for six weeks. Dad was gone again. Mr. and Mrs. Prociw had invited Mother, Steve, Dan, and me to dinner at a cafeteria in Tyler. By this time, my family was down to its last dollar, and we couldn't afford to eat in, much less out. Going to Luby's was very special. I dressed in my best outfit — a homemade black-and-white full skirt with lacy white blouse, ate all I could hold, and watched my brothers do the same. We were able to forget, at least for a little while, the violence and fear that waited for us at home.

Drowsy after eating too much, the boys and I nodded off in the backseat of the Prociws' big Chrysler. As we drove down Pearl Street, Mother roused me. I rubbed my eyes and, as we neared our house, saw Dad's red wrecker parked across the driveway, facing Highway 80.

"This is the sign I've been waiting for," Mother said, her voice flat. "Mr. Prociw, will you please take us to your house?"

"Why?" I interrupted.

"We're leaving."

"Leaving?"

"Honey, I fasted for three days and three nights and asked God to help me know what to do. He's telling us to leave."

I struggled to get my head around the idea.

"Don't we need to get our clothes?"

"We can't."

"Why not?"

"Wouldn't be safe."

Steve leaned toward Mother. "How long are we going away?"

"Don't know. Depends on Daddy."

We drove about a mile farther and turned down a street where rich people lived. The Prociws' new house stood in a row of single-story brick houses.

Mr. Prociw pulled in the driveway. "As soon as I stop," he said, "run inside. Go!"

We dashed to the unlocked door, pulled it open and ducked inside.

"We don't have much time," Mother said. She wrung her hands and paced the floor. "Charles is going to start looking for us. This'll be the first place he goes."

"Mary, he doesn't know you're here. Your car is at home. I know you've put up with Charles and his violence for way too long. Everyone in the church knows that. No one questions that it's time for you to go, but we can't panic." Mr. Prociw put his hand on her shoulder. "Let's think this through."

"He'll be violent."

"I'll deal with that when it happens. Let's just think about what you and the children should do."

"Where do you want to go?" Mary Prociw put coffee in the top of her percolator and plugged it in.

"I have no idea. It can't be anywhere he would think to look."

"Your sister…"

"No. We have to hide." Mother paced around the small den.

"Charles'll be a crazy man," Mary said.

I had been standing by the window watching for Dad. "I have an idea," I piped up. Since one of the church's tenets was that children were to be seen and not heard, the adults looked surprised. "We can go to Jackson, Mississippi."

"Why on earth?" Mother asked.

"Maggie, my best friend from camp, is from Jackson. Her dad's a minister. They could take care of us."

"Anybody have a better idea?" Mr. Prociw looked at Mother.

"No." She thought for a second. "Jackson it is. Mr. Prociw, can you please drive us as far as Dortha's house in Louisiana? She and Shelby can take us from there."

"Why not take your car? We'll wait till Charles is gone and I'll run into the yard and get it for you."

"I don't want anything that's his. If I could, I'd strip off every piece of clothes paid for with his money and leave those, too." She spoke with such vehemence that the room was still for a moment.

I'd never heard Mother talk like that. I knew now that she was going to go through with it. We were really going away.

"We'll drive you," said Mr. Prociw.

Mrs. Prociw weighed in. "Tomorrow'll be a long day. I want y'all to stay here tonight and get some sleep. We'll leave before sunup in the morning."

I was in the Prociws' back bedroom with the boys thinking about how much fun it would be to see Maggie again when I heard a commotion. I held my breath. Mother hurried in and pulled the door behind her, leaving a small crack so she could hear.

"Where are they?" Dad yelled from the front yard.

"Who?" answered Mr. Prociw.

"Don't be a smart-ass. You know who."

"No." Mr. Prociw's voice was calm.

"Where are Mary and the kids?"

"Aren't they home?"

"Cut the crap." I imagined that the blood vessels on Dad's forehead were pulsating and that he was shaking his index finger in Mr. Prociw's face. "I know they're here."

"Charles, your family isn't here. I won't have you making a scene at my home. Leave."

"I'll leave when I get good and damn ready."

"Let go of my door. Now." Mr. Prociw's voice was calm but menacing. "Get off my property."

"I'll bet she's with one of the ministers. Whore!" I heard the door slam.

From outside came a muted final salvo. "I'm going to get you, Steve Prociw. You just wait."

During the night, Mr. Prociw worked through ministerial channels to get word to Mr. Murphy that we were coming to Jackson and to make certain that he was willing to accept responsibility for us. Before sunrise the next morning, Mother shooed us out the front door. "Run to the car and lay down in the backseat."

Hearts pounding, Steve, Dan and I jumped in the back. When he was sure the coast was clear, Mr. Prociw motioned for Mother to come out. She scooted Dan across the seat to make room and crawled in. Steve Prociw drove; his wife Mary sat beside him.

Mother insisted upon leaving the keys to her car, so we slowly drove down Pearl Street. As we neared the house, Mother craned her neck to see if Dad's truck was there. It was gone.

We halted in front of our house. Mother jumped out, sprinted for the back door, tossed the keys on the kitchen table, and ran back to the Prociws' car.

I could hardly breathe as we drove through Upshur and Gregg counties. By the time we got to Marshall, I stopped shaking and tried to rest my head on the doorframe. It didn't feel like we were leaving for good. I thought about all we were leaving behind — my piano, records and record player, the Field Day ribbons on my bulletin board, the stuffed dog on my bed, my clothes. It would be weeks or maybe months before we would be back home. But this would make Dad change. It would be okay. I dozed, then awoke with a start.

"Mommy, what about Tiny? We forgot Tiny."

"Daddy will feed her."

How could she think that Dad would take care of the dog when he wouldn't even take care of us? "But what if he doesn't? She'll die." Tears started to run down my face, as I thought about my little spotted dog.

"The Prociws will make sure she's taken care of."

There was nothing I could do about it.

CHAPTER TWENTY-SEVEN

Home, Anything but Sweet

It was still early morning when we arrived at the Baptist parsonage in Dubberly, Louisiana. We had a sense of urgency because Dad could show up any minute.

Mrs. Prociw hugged each of us good-bye.

"Mary, Mr. Prociw," Mother said, "I can't thank you enough for all you've done.

The stoic man opened his wallet, pulled out some bills and shoved them into Mother's hand. "You're like family." She shook his hand and thanked him again.

When their car pulled out of the driveway, our umbilical cord with Big Sandy was cut.

I was a jumble of emotions. Fear that Dad was going to find and hurt us. Sadness at leaving all I'd ever known. Exhilaration at being free from Dad. Anxiety tinged with a little excitement about the unknown.

I'd loved the few times I'd visited Aunt Dortha and Uncle Shelby. I had good memories of going to Lake Bistineau and fishing in the murky water with cane poles and worms dug from the garden. We threw back the catfish because they were unclean. But we kept perch and bream that anyone else would have found too little to eat and deep-fried them with potatoes and hush puppies in a big cast-iron pot.

Aunt Dortha, who showed me how to plunk out scales on her out-of-tune upright, was the person who piqued my interest in the piano. She taught me to make chicken and dumplings and doughnuts and chocolate mayonnaise cake. Always respectful of our dietary practices when we were there, she replaced the white sugar with brown and didn't cook anything with pork in it. I watched my first television at Aunt Dortha's, laughing at Lucy's antics and pretending that Cara Williams' first name was really Carla.

Uncle Shelby — known to most as Brother Hightower — was a packrat who dabbled in electronics. Their garage was crammed floor to rafters with junk that he was going to repair and sell but never got around to. His vocation was tending to a flock of fewer than one hundred souls at the Fellowship Baptist church next door. Uncle Shelby preached twice a week — Wednesday nights and Sunday mornings — in the small sanctuary. Aunt Dortha accompanied on the piano as he led the singing. He spent the week taking care of people in the church — visiting the sick, making small home repairs for the widow-women, delivering food to people in need. I had heard him preach once and was scornful that he didn't sound like the ministers from the One True Church. But he could quote the Bible. He spoke with few notes, tying scriptures together to paint a picture of how Jesus — not Jesus Christ or Christ Jesus — expected us to live.

But we couldn't linger in Dubberly. It was the second place where Dad would look for us, and we expected him to appear at any moment.

The trip to Jackson was slow. Uncle took his time and, every hour, stopped for belly wash — his name for ice cream and soda. When we reached the restaurant in Jackson where we were to meet, Maggie and her family were waiting in the parking lot. I saw Maggie get out of the car, and I dashed toward her. We hugged like we hadn't seen each other in years, even though it had been only six weeks. Maggie opened the backdoor of the car, grabbed a stuffed dog from the seat, and handed it to me.

"Thank you so much," I gushed. "I had to leave all of my stuffed animals in Big Sandy."

"That's what I heard," she said. "Now you have a new friend."

"What kind of dog is it? I've never seen one like this."

"It's called a Lhasa Apso." I decided then that I would eventually have a real one.

During my first days in Jackson, I felt like flotsam floating on the sea, clueless about where I was going and out of control. For the first couple of days, we bunked with the Gradys, a well-to-do church family, in a sprawling ranch-style house that seemed to go on forever. Then, the church came up with a dribble of money so Mother could rent a house. She found one place that fit her budget of $45 per month — 926 Myrtlewood Drive. It was a real prize, furnished with castoffs and dark, dark. A single bulb in an overhead fixture illuminated each room. The backyard was treeless, low and wet. The garage sagged in the middle. Mother and I shared one bedroom and the boys took the other. She was given enough extra money for us to buy toiletries, underwear, a clock, a radio and a little food. For transportation, we relied on Hilda Grady to drive us in her new Cadillac.

I had never thought of myself as poor until we moved to Jackson. Poverty meant using other people's cast-off sheets, towels, and clothes. Preparing meals from canned goods that church members didn't want, delivered with an embarrassed "Here's a little something to help." Money was so tight that Mother handwashed all of our small items at home and made us reuse towels and washcloths for days. Mrs. Grady took Mother to a Laundromat once a week to wash the pieces that couldn't be effectively cleaned in the kitchen sink. Scraping together enough change for the washing machine required a sacrifice. There was no money left for the dryer, so Mother took the clothes and linens back home wet. For months we couldn't afford clothespins, so Mother draped the items over the clothesline in the backyard. "I feel so embarrassed," Mother said, pointing to the mess strung out in view of the neighbors. "It looks like I'm too lazy to hang the wash properly."

Poverty tasted like soup made from vegetables in unlabeled cans. It felt like scratchy muslin sheets. It sounded like a tinny AM radio. It smelled like mildew. It looked like the same clothes worn day after day until the color faded away.

We had left Big Sandy a week before Mother's thirty-sixth birthday. She had dropped out of high school before finishing the tenth grade and had no marketable job skills. She wasn't licensed as a midwife or a beautician and had no tools to work as a seamstress. Even if she'd been able to make a living, the church wouldn't have allowed it because real jobs would have required her to work outside the home, which was prohibited. Mother had no friends outside the church, and her family — other than Aunt Dortha and Uncle Shelby — didn't offer moral or financial support. Memow and Papaw — he was so troubled that he had locked himself inside his bedroom with a gun threatening suicide — couldn't make ends meet. Uncle Dee made their house payment. Her younger brother Pat was just getting started and, with a wife and two young children to care for, was struggling. Her eldest brother Bob and his wife were financially stable but were too tight to part with a penny.

The Powers family was oblivious to our circumstances. Granddaddy Powers lived in a falling-down rental in Heber Springs, Arkansas, which should have been condemned when the highway was built ten yards from the front porch. When I was six, Granddaddy Powers called me "cotton-top" and gave me a zircon necklace. When I was a teen, he didn't know I existed.

We hardly knew Uncle Jack and his family, who had put down permanent roots in Michigan. After the trip to Michigan in 1962, we'd seen them only once more — at Aunt Hattie and Uncle Jake's. Margie's folks had neither the money nor the inclination to help. I could imagine Uncle Vernon saying, "Blood's thicker'n water. I don't care what my brother did. He's still my brother." Aunt Hattie remained convinced that Mother was the cause of all of our problems. Uncle Jake slipped us a few dollars now and then without Aunt Hattie's knowledge.

The Worldwide Church of God was Mother's only port in the storm. But, as the old Eagles song goes, "every form of refuge has its price."[20] Faced with the mandate that a mother with children should stay home with them and without the ability to work from home, Mother's economic prospects were limited to getting $200 a month on the church dole. The church didn't allow us to take anything from the government, even food stamps. She had no hope of improving her situation by finding another husband. In the eyes of the church, she was forever married to Dad. In what should have been the prime of her life, Mother was locked inside an eight-hundred-square-foot coffin.

When we lived on Myrtlewood Drive, Mother became a shell of her old self. She lay awake at night, quietly sobbing into her pillow. She went through the motions of creating a life for us, but lacked the emotional strength or the money to give us anything beyond subsistence. As the consequences of our runaway began to sink in, Mother and I became afraid that if Dad found us, he would kill us. Mother warned us not to use the Powers name, except at school where it was legally required. She rented the house and signed for the phone and utilities as M. A. Powell. We watched for Dad like sentries. The thought of him made me shake. Now that we had gotten away, I let myself fully acknowledge my feelings: I hated my father and never wanted to see him again. As bad as life was in Jackson, it would be worse with him.

Mary Prociw told us a story that heightened our fears. Dad appeared in the Prociws' front yard one night shortly after we left and yelled for Mr. Prociw to come out. Dad stood with his hands behind him and took an in-your-face position with Mr. Prociw.

"Steve, I have a question for you. Did you help my family leave me?"

"Charles, I'm not going to lie. I helped Mary and the kids."

Dad pulled out the club that he had been holding behind his back. "Since you told me the truth, I'm going to let you live."

We knew that Dad could show up any time and beat the daylights out of one or all of us. We also knew that no one would do anything until after he'd drawn blood.

After we moved to Jackson, Mother told me that after Dad beat her up and threw the matches in the gas tank, she became concerned enough about our safety to try to get help from the law. While I was away at camp in the summer of 1968, she had consulted a lawyer and the district attorney in Gilmer, the Upshur County seat, asking for help and protection. Mother said that they'd told her that they couldn't do anything until Dad committed a crime or violated a court order. But in Big Sandy, we did have one safe place: behind the fences that surrounded the church and college grounds. The guards would never let Dad through the gates.

In Jackson, the situation was more tenuous. Mother hadn't filed for divorce, so she and Dad had equal visitation rights. If he showed up at school or the house and wanted to see us, Mother couldn't stop him. I played out in my head what I would do if he came for us. I imagined being a heroine, ready to sacrifice my safety to save Mother and my brothers.

We had been living on Myrtlewood Drive for a month when Mother got a phone call.

"Mrs. Powers?"

It wasn't a voice she recognized, and the phone was listed in the name M. A. Powell. She was immediately on guard. "Who's calling?"

"Agent Ferguson. FBI."

"FBI?"

"Ma'am, we understand from your husband that you and your three children have been kidnapped by the Worldwide Church of God. We need to talk."

"That's not true."

"Your husband seems to think so, and you've run off with his children."

"He's a violent man. We ran away because we were afraid he would kill us."

"He's filed a complaint. You can either come down here and talk to us or we'll go to your home."

"I'll come down there." Then something occurred to her. "Have you told him where we are?"

"No, ma'am. Not yet."

"Please, please don't do that. I'll explain everything to you."

"You need to come today."

"Mr. Ferguson, have you talked to the police in Texas about Charles?"

"We have the information we need."

"I don't think so, if you believe the church kidnapped us. Check with the authorities in Upshur and Gregg counties in Texas. In Hope, Arkansas. Call Steve Prociw in Big Sandy and ask him what we went through."

"I'll be in my office all afternoon. I'll expect to see you."

Mother called Mr. Grady and asked him to go with her. He owned a manufacturing plant and was sufficiently prominent to give her credibility. They convinced the agent that Dad was dangerous, and the FBI agreed not to tell Dad our whereabouts.

A lot of lawyers from my generation say that they were inspired to enter the practice from watching *Perry Mason*. Not me. I was driven by indignation. I made the decision to become a lawyer after Mother's meeting with the FBI. I was furious that the law seemed to protect the abuser, not the abused. That a woman was less likely to be believed than a man. I was, by damn, going to represent women and children who were battered and hurt. No one should have to go through what we did. I was going to give them the help and protection the laws were supposed to provide. Why I thought I could pull it off is beyond me. At that time in many parts of the South, the idea that any woman — much less someone in my circumstances — could become a lawyer was nothing short of fantasy. No one in my immediate family had finished high school. I had no money to fund an education and no prospects for getting any. And, the idea violated two of the church's rules — that a woman's place is at home, and that it is dishonorable to practice law because it places man's law above God's law.

I told Mother of my decision, but no one else. She told me, "You can do anything if you want it badly enough. You need to be able to take care of yourself and your family. Don't put yourself in a position where you have to rely on a man to put food on your table and clothes on your back." Those words became my mantra.

Not long after we moved to Jackson, Mrs. Prociw sent Mother a clipping from the October 3, 1968, *Big S and H Journal (Big Sandy and Hawkins Journal)*. The paper ran a photo of the ten-foot-wide, five-foot-deep billboard that Dad had attached to the front of our house.

ARMSTRONG Destroyed This Home

The Big Sandy home of Charles Powers at 310 N. Pearl Street had this sign tacked across the front on Friday night, September 27, by its owner Powers and a coworker in the Auto Body Business.

Mrs. Powers and their three children, the oldest a girl 13 [sic] left without notice and no forwarding address on that date. Powers alleges her alienation through church tenets and ministrations. The couple had been members from the mid-50s.

His name was stricken from the rolls as a communicant more than three years ago and subsequently, while his wife remained a coworker and their children attended Imperial School, he was ex-communicated and his business, he maintains, was boycotted by his former "Co-workers."[21]

CHAPTER TWENTY-EIGHT
In an Alien World

After spending the first thirteen years of my life in the Worldwide Church of God bubble, starting public school was a rude entry into the real world. It was the last week of September 1968 — one of the most tumultuous times in U.S. history. I was oblivious to the assassinations of Bobby Kennedy and Martin Luther King, Jr., antiwar protests at the Chicago Democratic National Convention, the My Lai massacre, and race riots from Wisconsin to North Carolina. I didn't know about hippies, free love, drugs, black power, miniskirts, or acid rock. Current events were unimportant other than to support Armstrong's prophesy that the Tribulation would begin in less than four years.

The day I climbed the steps to the front door of Peeples Junior High in Jackson, Mississippi, to attend the eighth grade, I felt like a child left behind when her family went to Petra. Peeples was gritty and rough around the edges — like the neighborhood where we lived. The students were predominantly white, though there were some African-Americans attending through the "Freedom of Choice" program that would be replaced with forced integration the following school year.

For an eighth-grader, survival is about blending in. You must look, dress, act, eat, and play like everyone else. You don't want to do anything that draws attention. I was a walking billboard. The old graffiti-marred building teemed with hundreds of pubescent kids dressed in slacks and miniskirts. Day after day I wore the same mid-calf black-and-white checked skirt with my frilly white blouse. My classmates wore heavy eyeliner, white lipstick and blue eye shadow; my face was scrubbed. I listened to The Vogues, The Lettermen, and the Everly Brothers. Normal kids preferred the Beatles, the Doors, and the Rolling Stones. On Friday nights they watched Wingfield High play football. I went to church. I heard whispers about joints and grass. I'd never taken so much as an aspirin. When they giggled about making out, I wondered what it was. The girls passed notes in class and carved "Becky loves Randy" in the desktops. They cut class and smoked cigarettes in the bathroom. They ate hot dogs and hamburgers with fries. I ate fried liver and peas.

Members of the Worldwide Church of God didn't make their own decisions.

Rules governed all of life's choices. In Big Sandy, it was easy to follow those dictates. Everyone lived the same way and members "helped" each other color within the narrow lines imposed by the church. In my new life outside the cult enclave, I faced decisions about situations I'd never been aware existed.

I instinctively knew that I shouldn't share our beliefs with people outside the church. It would have been social suicide to announce that I went to church on Saturday or couldn't go to a doctor or didn't keep Christian holidays. I made compromises. In the lunch line, I stopped asking if food contained traces of pork products. I rationalized that if I didn't know something was unclean, I couldn't lust after it. When Maggie's sister Melinda, who was in the ninth grade, told me, "As soon as you get out of the car, roll up your skirt," I rolled it up. When Maggie, a worldly-wise sophomore at Wingfield High, instructed me to put Vaseline on my eyelashes and lips and to use an eyelash curler, I did it.

Friendship was problematic. I had been taught from infancy that friendships with nonchurch people could jeopardize my eternal life, but I couldn't function in Jackson without allies. Since there was only one other church member going to Peeples — Melinda — I decided that I had to be friendly with people and make acquaintances. I'd draw the line by refusing invitations to slumber parties and visits to my classmates' homes.

I walked out of the house on Myrtlewood Drive and into the cool fall air. The butterflies in my stomach were making their daily flight. I ignored them and crossed the street, schoolbooks tucked firmly under my arm. I pulled open the screen and rapped my knuckles on the dirty front door of the house across the street.

Arlene, the girl who answered, was tall — five-foot nine. A burning cigarette dangled loosely from the left side of her mouth.

"Hey," she said, taking electric curlers out of her bobbed, streaked hair, "gimme a minute."

I took a seat on the couch situated perpendicular to a console color TV. The radio blared from a room in the back of the house, "Young girl get out of my mind. My love for you is way out of line."[22]

"Damn." Through the thin wall that separated her bedroom from the living room, I heard Arlene mutter as she tossed shoes out of her closet. "Where are those fucking brown boots?"

While I had seen "fuck" written on a bathroom stall and figured it was something nasty, I had no idea what it meant.

Two minutes later, the Wingfield High junior emerged, dressed in a short skirt, turtleneck and the errant boots.

"Want one?" she asked, grabbing two powdered sugar doughnuts from a box on the kitchen counter.

"No, thanks," I answered, though I really did. I knew most brands contained lard, and I didn't want to take the chance.

Arlene took one last slurp from her coffee cup, grabbed the car keys, and motioned toward the door. I followed and got into the front seat of the Corvair. When she turned the key in the ignition, the engine and the radio came on simultaneously. B. J. Thomas was crooning about being hooked on a feelin'.

"Nice of you to take me to school," I said.

"No big deal. It's on my way." She fiddled with her turtleneck. "God, I hate this thing."

"Scratchy?"

"Yeah, but I have to wear it."

I looked at her, waiting for an explanation. When none came, I had to ask, "Why?"

"Hickey."

"Oh," I answered knowingly, pleased that I had figured out what it was from classmates' conversations.

"Wayne told me that he wants me to do it to him, just in a different place," she laughed and rolled her eyes.

My face colored and I stared out the window, willing the car to get me to school before she said anything else.

Not long after I arrived at Peeples, I joined the Y-Teen Club, a service organization affiliated with the YWCA. At the first meeting I attended, I took a seat apart from the thirty girls clumped together in their cliques. A pretty red-haired girl sat down beside me. "I'm Joyce," she said, a smile creasing her freckled face.

"I'm Carla. Carla Powers." I spoke quietly and forced myself to make eye contact.

"You must be new."

"Uh-huh. We've only been here two weeks."

"Where'd you come from?"

"Texas."

"Miss it?"

"Yeah," I answered. "It's hard to start over in a new place."

"You'll be fine," she answered, as the club's president called the meeting to order.

Fifteen minutes later, the president said, "It's time to elect officers." I wished I hadn't come. I didn't know a soul. "The floor is open for nominations for our new president."

Joyce raised her hand and stood.

"I nominate Carla Powers."

I turned to Joyce, my face felt like I'd been sunbathing for an hour too long. I mouthed, "Why?"

Joyce shrugged and whispered, "It's a good way to meet people."

I wanted to disappear between the cracks in the wood floor. The last thing I wanted was for everyone in the room to look at me, dressed in my old-fashioned homemade clothes. Under the high-necked blouse, I felt heat on my neck and chest. The three of us who had been nominated were asked to make a short statement. My first impulse was to say, *"Never mind. I don't know why I was nominated."* But, I didn't.

"I want to be in Y-Teens to help people who are less fortunate. I think we can make a difference."

When it was time to vote, I turned in a blank piece of paper. The church taught that it was a sin to vote because it places the laws of men before the laws of God. I figured that rule applied here.

"It'll take a few minutes," said the president.

I made small talk with Joyce and two others sitting nearby, wishing the miserable experience would end.

"Girls," the president said after a five-minute break, "please say hi to your new president, Carla Powers."

No way. That couldn't be right. These girls didn't know me. I was too much of a nerd to be elected to anything. But when I turned to Joyce, she nodded affirmatively.

Joyce became the program chair for the Y-Teens and my first non-church friend. At the end of the school year, she and I were pictured together in the Jackson newspaper when our club won a service award.

My other lifeline was athletics. Years of running and exercise at Imperial School had made me strong and fast. I played softball and basketball, and was the only girl from the eighth grade to make the President's All-American Team. At the end of the year I won the school's Outstanding Athlete Award. I started a scrapbook and still have the clippings pasted in the first of many books that record the tumultuous years after leaving Big Sandy.

Steve, who was ten, had the most difficult time adjusting to our new life. He was sullen and erupted into violent temper tantrums. I couldn't bear being around him because he reminded me of Dad. The only way Mother knew to respond was by spanking him with a wooden paddle until her arm gave out. Steve would yell at Mother and fight with her. It felt like he was trying to become Dad.

Dan turned four that year, but I have no memories of him as a little boy. I was too focused on my own survival to pay much attention to anyone or anything else. I fantasized about getting my stuff from Big Sandy and started making lists of all I had left behind. I inventoried my records and identified in order the songs on the albums sitting on my desk in Big Sandy. I tried to remember all of my ribbons and stuffed animals and clothes. When I was sure that I would never have a piano again, I let the music go. Just as I did with people and things lost to me, I severed it from my consciousness. I refused to listen to classical or piano music because it made me cry. I thought of Tiny and hoped she was still alive.

Aunt Dortha and Uncle Shelby were our angels. Despite the fact that they were almost as broke as we were, they helped out.

"You said they'd be here an hour ago," Steve pouted, as he pulled apart slats in the blinds and peered through the window into our empty driveway.

"It's a long trip," Mother said, looking up from the carrots she was slicing for

CHAPTER 28 — In an Alien World | *191*

the salad. "Be patient."

I stirred a pot of spaghetti sauce flavored with a half- pound of hamburger meat. It smelled so good.

"Do I have to ride with Arlene after you get the car?" I asked.

"No, I'll take you and Steve to school."

Before I could respond, Steve yelled, "They're here!" He yanked open the door and ran outside, Dan on his heels.

I wasn't far behind.

Uncle Shelby steered a 1961 powder-blue Rambler into the dirt rut beside the house. Aunt Dortha, who was following behind in their Pontiac, pulled off the street in front of the house.

After hugs all around, Uncle Shelby handed Mother the keys to the Rambler. "It's the best I could do."

"Thanks so much," Mother said, tearing up. "I promise I'll pay you back."

"Take it for a spin around the block," responded Uncle Shelby.

"It'll take time to save $150."

"Stop worrying," Aunt Dortha said.

"Seat belts?" Mother asked.

"No," said Uncle.

"Can I get them?"

"It'll set you back a good $50."

"Doesn't matter. I have to keep the kids safe."

"Hey, what's all this?" said Steve, looking into the car.

Aunt Dortha opened the back door of the Rambler and handed Mother a pole lamp. "A few things for the house. There's more in the other car."

I checked out the Pontiac and let out a whoop. "A TV! Hey, everyone, they brought us a TV!"

Uncle Shelby smiled. "Got an old one to work. Don't know how long it'll last."

The living room was soon cluttered with paper bags and boxes of linens, pots and pans, dishes, lamps, and plaster of paris wall hangings. There was an ice chest filled with bags of frozen vegetables harvested from Aunt Dortha's garden and a box of home-canned goods.

We kids weren't interested in anything but the TV. It took all three adults to drag the heavy box into the house and place it on top of a sturdy table. When Steve plugged it in, the picture was snowy and the voices were barely audible.

"I left the rabbit ears in the trunk of the Rambler," Uncle Shelby said, reaching into his pockets. "Where are those keys?"

We combed through the stuff on the floor. We looked in the bathroom and kitchen. Mother and Aunt Dortha checked their purses. No keys.

"Maybe they're in the trunk," Steve offered.

"Trunk's locked," said Uncle Shelby. "I can't get in there without the keys."

"Oops."

"Did you lock them in the trunk?"

"Yes, sir." Steve couldn't make eye contact and cowered in the corner.

"Come on. I'll show you what to do."

Dinner cooled on the stove for thirty minutes while Uncle took out the backseat and retrieved the keys. He didn't say a cross word to Steve.

There is a picture of the four of us taken by Aunt Dortha on the day when they brought us the car. We are posed around a metal-framed chair, in front of the pole lamp, teeth clenched in unnatural grins. I don't know those people. They bear no resemblance to my family.

CHAPTER TWENTY-NINE
Lifeline

There was no building in Jackson for our Worldwide Church of God congregation: no physical presence for the church. Services were held in a rented hall. Garner Ted and Herbert W. preached that persecution of the church and its members was imminent. They prophesied that someone who had been a member and who knew the inner workings of the church would align with the Devil to shame and ridicule God's Work. God's chosen people would be less of a target if we didn't gather together in a place that was visibly associated with the church. What they didn't say was that if they didn't spend money on infrastructure, there would be lots more available for silk suits, mansions, fine wine, Steuben glass, and jets.

The Mississippi congregation was small. The only people I remember are the Murphy family, the Gradys and the Williamses. The beautiful Mrs. Williams was a young wife with a baby who invited Maggie, Melinda, and me over for slumber parties. She giggled with us about boys and let us curl up in blankets in front of the TV until the wee hours of the morning. We wondered what she saw in Mr. Williams, a perpetually smiling man with spiky blond hair and extraordinary ears. Mr. Murphy — a round man with a balding pate — wasn't a dynamic speaker and was too nice to be a successful minister. Mrs. Murphy, who had long salt-and-pepper hair worn in an eighteen-inch-tall beehive, always looked unhappy and was a strict disciplinarian. I tried to keep my distance from her.

"Religious tolerance" and "Deep South" were not words you would have put together in the sixties and seventies. Baptists and Methodists could barely stand each other, but they did agree that Jews and Catholics were on a slippery slope to eternal damnation. Episcopalians and Presbyterians and Church of Christ melded into the Protestant world, but the more fundamentalist churches knew they didn't obey Jesus. Drinking, dancing, and card-playing were repugnant to God-fearing people. If, heaven forbid, you were a member of one of those strange churches, like the Nazarenes or Latter-day Saints, you didn't tell anyone. Those who insisted on proselytizing their off-the-beaten-track views — like the Pentecostals and Seventh-Day-Adventists — were ostracized. But all decent people belonged to some kind of religion.

Having no religion at all was worse than being a part of something strange. When people were getting to know you, asking church affiliation was as ordinary as asking about siblings. I confessed to being in the Church of God. Not the Worldwide Church of God, mind you — just Church of God. I remember thinking about the Apostle Peter who denied Christ three times before the cock crowed and wondered if I had committed a terrible sin by not saying the complete name of the church. But I was unwilling to profess the whole truth to my new friends. It was like the first loose thread in my Worldwide Church of God uniform. A tiny, innocuous flaw that becomes bigger and bigger every time it is pulled until the garment eventually unravels.

Every October kids from the Worldwide Church of God had to come up with an explanation for missing a week of school for a trip to Squaw Valley, California, or Big Sandy or Jekyll Island, Georgia, for the Feast of Tabernacles. Before moving to Jackson, I couldn't imagine a world in which everyone didn't celebrate the Feast. It was as ordinary as Thanksgiving. In Jackson, I knew I couldn't tell people the real story or I'd be sitting by myself in the lunchroom every day. I followed the church's party line and said that we were going to a church convention.

The ministers directed members to the Feast at a place chosen for their region. Our location was Jekyll Island. Staying home wasn't an option: anyone who cared about ruling in the Kingdom of God made it to the Feast. All, except for widows and women supporting families by themselves, were expected to have saved enough to cover their expenses. The church made arrangements for people like us. They found people we could ride with and provided housing and food for eight days. Mother and the boys were to ride with the Gradys; the old Rambler wasn't in good enough shape for us to take it, and we couldn't afford the gas. The Murphys asked me to travel with them. We stopped to play in the sugar sand beaches at Destin, Florida, and, on the way to Georgia, spent the night at the most beautiful place I'd ever seen — the Thunderbird Motor Hotel in Jacksonville. The soft nighttime illumination made the two pools and tropical landscaping look like paradise. We swam until the pool closed. I kept a postcard from the hotel and pasted it in my scrapbook.

When Mother arrived in Jekyll Island, she checked in with the housing office. There the church told attendees where they were to stay, even the ones who had money to pay for their own rooms. The more prominent a person, the nicer and closer the accommodations were to the tent where services were to be held. Since we were nobodies, we didn't even get to stay on the same island. We were put in a comfortable beach house on Sea Island, half an hour away. Each day someone would pick us up at 9:00 a.m. and return us after services were over at 5:00 or 6:00 p.m. While those with cars and money went to evening social events and dined at restaurants, we went back to the cottage and prepared our own meals.

The services at Jekyll Island were held in a tent on a deserted stretch of beach. It was windy, cold, and gray the whole time we were there. Wind whipped through the open flaps of the tent, and the folding metal chairs were harder and more miserable than usual. For eight days we gathered at least twice a day to drink in God's Word. Herbert W. Armstrong flew in on his private jet to be with us on one of the days.

"God would have never called someone with a name like Peabody to be his apostle," he said, jowls quivering as he vigorously shook his head. "Armstrong is a powerful name. My family's lineage has been traced back to King David. This is another sign that I have been called by the Almighty God to do His special work." I was glad I didn't have a weak last name.

The Feast was a time for romance among the kids — a "Feast fling." The kids hung out in packs, segregated by gender. Groups of us sat together in church, under the careful scrutiny of parents and deacons, shuffling seats at the last minute so the people who liked each other could sit together and ever-so-discreetly pass notes during the service. At the catered lunches the church sold to members, we were usually allowed to leave our families and eat with our friends. Two boys were vying for my attention: Harold from Mississippi, who was stocky and had a crew cut, and a dark-haired, dark-eyed smaller-built guy named Terry from Alabama. You could tell that someone liked you if his group of boys joined your group of girls so he could talk to you. My most daring act of the Feast of 1968 was taking a fifteen-minute walk with Terry down the beach away from the tent. His bravery in walking with me and avoiding the deacons won my heart. We kept in touch for a short time after the Feast by exchanging a few letters.

Our beach house was pretty and restful. The only excitement was finding a lifeless sea turtle that had washed ashore. I had seen the ocean on our trips to the West Coast in 1958 and 1962, but didn't remember it. Walking in cold, salty ocean water and listening to its music gave me a sense of awe I'd never before experienced. I sat outside on the beach, wrapped in a blanket, listening to the crescendos and decrescendos. I looked at the stars and the fearsome beauty of the sea, thinking it strange that God was going to destroy such a magnificent creation in a few short years.

Maggie and Melinda were friends with a trio of boys who attended the New Orleans church — Paul Richter and his younger brother, Ralf, and Paul Weston. When the New Orleans and Jackson churches got together in New Orleans to celebrate the 1969 Days of Unleavened Bread, I met them. Ralf was a sophomore at East Jefferson High School in New Orleans and, being more than six feet tall, played basketball. With a mop of straight hair that was extraordinarily long by church standards, cut like Ringo Starr's, and brown, puppy-dog eyes, he was *über* cool. Sometimes I'd look at him and think he was very cute; other times I'd decide his nose was too big or his neck too long. The boys listened to forbidden groups — like the Beatles — and their rock band played songs that the church said would lead us into the arms of the Devil.

The New Orleans church was much more *laissez faire* than the one in Big Sandy. Parents didn't seem to think it was a problem to leave a group of kids to their own devices or to let them listen to anything they wanted. They even let three girls pile in a car with three boys. Mother didn't mind as long as the minister's daughters were with me.

Ralf became my first male friend. His real world was outside the church. Mine was the opposite. Sometimes when we'd ride in Paul's car, we'd sit close together, legs touching legs or he'd surreptitiously brush my fingertips. I felt a stirring of feeling for him. It was different from the childish crush on surfer boy. Ralf and I talked about things that mattered. I told him about my fears and how it felt to leave everything behind. I'd never shared these thoughts with anyone else. He listened and didn't make me feel worthless because I was my father's daughter.

In an intelligent and edgy way, he made fun of the rules. "We need to carefully listen to the words of the songs on this Beatles album. It's important for us to understand what they're saying so we'll recognize sin and avoid it next time we hear it." He and his brother mocked the petty Napoleons whom we heard preach and developed elaborate plans to circumvent chaperones.

Ralf told me that life is to be enjoyed, not endured. We laughed. We wrote letters. Ideas began to germinate. I began to wonder about things. "Why?" became a part of my vocabulary. Another thread began to unravel.

CHAPTER THIRTY

The Tide Begins to Turn

After a year in Jackson, Mother told us that we'd been away long enough for Dad to have cooled off some and that we were moving to Louisiana. I don't know whether she believed it or was motivated by isolation, loneliness, poverty, and depression to return to something more familiar. Moving to Louisiana near Aunt Dortha and Uncle Shelby would let her start to build some semblance of a life.

We found a three-bedroom, one-bath farmhouse in the country, three miles outside of Minden and five miles from Aunt Dortha and Uncle Shelby's house in Dubberly. A church family named Farley lived next door, and it was through them that we'd learned about the property. Rent was $35 per month. The place had no heat or air conditioning except for an ancient green Fedders air conditioner in Mother's bedroom that kept that room just short of stifling in the summer. The rest of the house relied on an attic fan to pull air through big, screened windows.

On cold mornings Mother would get up early to turn on the oven and burners so the kitchen would be reasonably comfortable when we dashed in. There were lots of openings that let critters crawl into the house. We had mice, squirrels and roaches. The worst were the snakes. After I found a nasty black one curled up with the towels in the bathroom, I was careful to approach the linen closet with adequate light and much caution. One night an evil-looking thing slithered around the kitchen floor. Steve ran out of the room shouting that he was going to get his gun.

Mother yelled back, "You can't shoot him. You'll put a hole in the floor."

"Mom," he said, returning to the kitchen with a shotgun, "I'm not stupid."

"What're you going to do with the gun?" she asked.

"Use the barrel to shoo him back down the drain pipe."

"Wouldn't a broom be easier?"

The gun barrel worked, and Steve chased the snake until it crawled out the way it had come in.

The driveway was dirt, and there was a rickety lean-to on the side of the house next to the backdoor that served as a carport for our Rambler. The land across the road was pasture. The Farleys' house was a block away. A murky pond stocked with fish was a quarter of a mile behind the house. The snakes that invaded the house lived around the pond in the tall weeds. Mother used a boat paddle to kill the water moccasins that curled under the little aluminum boat that lay overturned on the bank. She refused to let snakes keep her from a pastime that also provided us with food. To the north were dense woods. We heard coyotes wail. In a clearing deep in the forest, Steve watched a pack of wolves devour a calf and heard the screaming wail of a panther. Mother and Steve hunted duck in the boat on the pond.

The church rule that we were to separate ourselves from nonmembers was impossibly inconvenient, so we ignored it. Aunt Dortha and Uncle Shelby were vital to our survival. Aunt Dortha shared with us the vegetables she grew in her garden and the pickles and preserves she canned. Uncle Shelby changed the tires and oil on the car, fixed our TV when it went on the blink, and did home repairs. He got us a calf for the fenced pasture behind the house, taught us to feed and care for it, then took it to be butchered when it was fat enough to eat.

Because Aunt Dortha and Uncle Shelby could be at our home in five minutes if I called, Mother decided that it was time to leave me in charge of the house and my brothers while she went to night school. It was my responsibility each day after school to watch the boys, clean the house, wash the clothes, and get dinner on the table.

In 1969, Minden was home to fewer than 15,000 people. A billboard on the edge of town announced, "Welcome to Minden. Friendliest City in the South." It had wide boulevards and tree-lined esplanades and a thriving central business district. Residential streets near downtown contained vestiges of the Old South — grand houses with columns, big windows and deep porches, gazebos, knee-high wrought-iron fences, magnolia trees. Unlike their Catholic cousins in the southern part of the state, most residents in north Louisiana were Protestant. The Baptist and Methodist churches on Main Street were in open competition with each other, but Dr. Prince, pastor of the First Baptist Church, regularly drew the larger crowd.

There was big money from forest products and oil and gas in the hands of a few, and comfortable money in the hands of many. Whites, that is. African-Americans were expected to toe the line and keep to themselves, which was mainly on the south side of town. Segregation extended to the schools. Minden High was white, though it began token integration in 1969, and Webster High — across town — was black. The wealthy didn't flash what they had, but everyone knew who they were and treated them with deference and respect. Family lineage mattered. People cared about who your daddy and granddaddy were. It helped establish the pecking order.

Lower-class whites — meaning poor people — were expected to stay with their kind, too. In a world where school standing was judged by the number of pictures of you in *The Grig* — the MHS yearbook — or the *Tide Talk* newspaper, kids whose parents scratched out a meager living usually had their pictures only in the year-book's alphabetical class listing. There was no expectation that they would excel or be elected to anything meaningful or serve as the public face of the school or the town. In that world, I felt like the poster-girl for "white trash."

Shortly after I entered Minden High School as a freshman, we were reminded that Dad was still on the warpath. Mary Prociw sent another clipping from the *Big S & H Journal*. It was a picture of our house in Big Sandy with a revised billboard on the front:

I SEARCHED 7 MONTHS — 23,000 MILES
TO FIND
MY FAMILY IN JACKSON MISS
SUPPORTED BY THE WORLDWIDE CHURCH OF GOD

It was the same size as the original, nailed directly under it. Again, the local newspaper brought readers up-to-date on the status of the town's most sensational marital breakup:

> Charles Powers, a Big Sandy business man (sic) since 1955, put a sign on the front of his residence, at 310 N. Pearl Street in Big Sandy on the anniversary of the un-announced (sic) departure of his wife Mary and children to parts unknown to Mr. Powers.

Accompanying the original sign erected in 1968 was one which added some detail of his efforts to locate his family. From the recounting of his tactics in locating the family it was apparent that he'd used means not unlike those employed by detective agencies.

The sign came down Tuesday night after his attorney, Ernest Martin of Gladewater, had elicited a willingness of the attorneys for the Worldwide Church of God and its Big Sandy Business Manager Mr. Neff to meet with Powers in company with Martin in Gilmer Wednesday morning.

Powers had recently gone on a five-day fast in which he declared that no morsel passed his lips. Asked how it seemed to affect him he retorted "The hunger I felt in my stomach was not one bit worse than the hunger in my heart for a year now." Wednesday afternoon Mr. Neff, contacted at his office at Ambassador College, was asked if he could assure Mr. Powers an audience with Mr. Herbert W. Armstrong during his attendance at the Big Sandy Feast of Tabernacles. Mr. Neff demurred that Mr. Armstrong would probably be too busy to see Mr. Powers or even himself.

Mr. Neff declared that the organization had nothing to do with the decision of Mrs. Powers to leave home.[23]

I was frightened all over again because I didn't know he had learned that we were living in Jackson. If he were that determined and resourceful, it was only a matter of time before he found us in Minden.

The closest Worldwide Church of God for us to attend was twenty-five miles to the west in Shreveport. Services were held in a day care center. That church was just as oppressive as Big Sandy — the easy-going ways of the New Orleans church didn't extend to the northern part of the state. I thought our new minister, Ron Rogers, was cold and dictatorial. He expected to-the-letter adherence to every rule of the church and, in my mind, delighted in humiliating people.

When members moved from one location to another, the old and new ministers would talk about their character, history, and financial standing. There was no such thing as a fresh start. From the moment we started attending Rogers's church, I was in his crosshairs. I couldn't understand why he seemed to take an instant dislike to me. I'd never been in trouble, and he had enough information about my academic achievements and good behavior at camp to know that I had some redeeming qualities. Having spent my young life trying to be perfect and adhere to the letter of all of God's laws, it was puzzling and painful to be viewed as a problem child.

I later found out that Toni and Priscilla Farley, who lived next door, apparently decided that it was to their advantage to tell Mr. Rogers fanciful stories about my escapades with Ralf. The truth was a lot more boring. In Minden High where girls my age were beginning to date, it was easy to avoid the issue by professing to have a steady boyfriend in New Orleans. While Ralf and I had affection for each other, our relationship wouldn't have been viewed by anyone outside the church as boyfriend and girlfriend. We communicated by writing letters and saw each other at the Feast. We didn't kiss or hold hands or go on dates. In my church-molded mind, it was daring to brush against him or slip off to talk without someone watching. I was still a good Worldwide Church of God girl through and through, and wasn't about to jeopardize my eternal life by doing something wrong with Ralf.

Mrs. McConathy was one of the most popular teachers at Minden High School. Petite, with salt-and-pepper hair, black cat-eyed glasses and a quick smile, she was nice to everyone, even though she was a magnet for her popular son's crowd. I was assigned to her Spanish I class. During the Christmas season, Mrs. Mac decreed that all of her Spanish classes would go caroling — singing the songs in Spanish — then come back to her home for refreshments. It was part of our class requirement. If I'd behaved as the church required, I would have told her that I wasn't allowed to participate in such heathen activities — but I didn't. I wanted to avoid standing out. Problem was, I had never heard a Christmas carol. Since I could read music, I picked up the tunes and learned the words in Spanish. I couldn't have sung them in English if my life had depended on it. Even now when I hear "Jingle Bells," I think "*Cascabeles, cascabeles, Tra-la-la-la-la. Qué alegria, Todo el dia y…*"

Dan was a Christmas bell in his school's Christmas pageant. The program included his name and role. Toni and Priscilla's brother went to school with Dan and shared the information with his family. They felt duty-bound to report the violation to Mr. Rogers, along with proof of our lack of piety — the mimeographed program. Mother was corrected for allowing Dan to participate in pagan activity.

In the spring of 1970 as I was finishing my freshman year of high school, the half-dozen high school kids who lived within walking distance of our house congregated in a neighbors' yard. We listened to music, gossiped about our friends, and played basketball. When the evening broke up, Nate, who was a year older than me, kissed me on the cheek. No boy had ever kissed me. Mr. McIntyre didn't count — that was something entirely different. I ran home and washed my face. In a state of panic, I retreated to my room, closed the door, and fell to my knees. I prayed and cried for hours, asking for forgiveness for the terrible sin I had committed.

My first year of high school passed unremarkably. In my memories, I was part of the nameless, faceless underclass that walked head-down, avoiding eye contact. With my fresh-scrubbed face and long skirts, I didn't think I looked like the girls who dated and had friends. Since my neighbors Toni and Priscilla didn't roll up their skirts, I knew that if I did, they'd tell the minister. I resembled the Pentecostal girls, but since I wasn't Pentecostal, I didn't fit with them. There were several girls who tried to make friends with me — Janet, Debbie, DeeDee, Terri. But I wouldn't let myself get close because I had too many secrets. I was sure they wouldn't have wanted anything to do with me had they known about Dad and the church. On Friday nights, they invited me to see the MHS Crimson Tide play football and to slumber parties, but I always declined because of the Sabbath-keeping rules. They encouraged me to join the Tidettes pep squad with them, and I made up stories to explain why I couldn't join them. They must have thought that I was a miserable snob; in reality, I was a mass of humiliation and fear.

CHAPTER THIRTY-ONE
Auld Lang Syne

In the fundamentalist culture in which I grew up, marriage was forever. Divorce was taboo. A woman who endured physical and emotional abuse, infidelity, alcoholism, or poverty to stay married was more valued than one who severed a bad relationship to save herself and her children. According to the Worldwide Church of God, every marriage was salvageable if the couple worked hard enough. They meant that wives were supposed to take whatever their husbands dished out and stifle their anger, frustrations, and unfulfilled needs. The more a woman put up with to stay married, the more honorable she was in God's eyes. Divorce might keep the person who left the marriage from going to Petra and getting into the Kingdom of God.

Dad called Uncle Shelby in the spring of 1970.

"I've changed, Shelby. I want my family back."

Uncle Shelby didn't answer.

"I've given up the booze," he said, waiting for a reply. When Uncle Shelby continued to keep his silence, Dad went on, "I really have. I didn't know I scared Mary and the kids. You know I'd never do anything to hurt them. I was just trying to get through Mary's thick skull that Armstrong's wrong."

After thirty years in the ministry, Uncle Shelby knew a lot about human nature. It was sustained behavior that mattered. Not words. Not being good for a week or a month. But he couldn't ignore his Christian duty to attempt to bring about reconciliation between Mother and Dad.

"All I want is her phone number," Dad pleaded.

"Can't do that, Charles."

"Why not?" Dad asked, trying to keep his voice calm.

"I promised Mary."

"How can I convince her that I've changed if I can't talk to her?"

"I'll have to think about it."

"What if I come over to your house and see them there?"

"No."

"They still in Mississippi?"

"You know I won't talk about that."

"Are you going to help me see them, or do I have to get the law involved?"

"I'll think about it."

A few weeks later, Uncle Shelby, Aunt Dortha, Mother, Steve, Dan, and I sat in Stuckey's restaurant on I-20 near Dubberly, waiting. I figured that if all went well, we'd go back to Big Sandy. But I didn't expect that to happen. I couldn't square Dad's new rant against the church in the revised billboard on our house with a change in behavior. As much as I yearned to have a father and live in my home, I couldn't handle the prospect of more violence and fear.

When Dad's truck pulled up, Steve ran outside and enveloped him. When Dad walked inside, Uncle Shelby stood, extended his hand and said, "Hello, Charles." Aunt Dortha nodded a curt hello. Mother didn't move.

"Carla, aren't you going to give me a hug?" he asked. His voice sounded taunting. I didn't like it.

I put my arms around him halfheartedly. He squeezed me, but it wasn't like the bear hugs he used to give when I was little. There was no emotion. I got the sense that he doing what he felt was expected.

Dad turned to Dan, who was five. "Danny, do you remember me?"

Dan shook his head no and stayed in his seat.

"Mary, how are you?" he asked, without making an effort to move toward her.

"Good," she answered, looking him straight in the eyes. "Got my high school diploma, and I finish secretarial school in May." There was defiance in her words.

"Church going to let you work?" Again, I felt that he was mocking us.

"What do you want?" she asked.

"Come home," he said.

"Why?" Mother asked.

"I've changed," he answered. "I've stopped drinking."

"How long?" Mother asked. Skepticism tinged her voice.

"A month," Dad responded, earnestly.

"You can't expect me to believe you're different after all the broken promises."

"You'll see."

Uncle Shelby spoke up. "Charles, after all that's happened, it'll take time."

Over the next three months, Dad called and came to Louisiana to see us, but Mother wouldn't let him come to the house. When she relented, he showed up in a gold 1967 Ford Fairlane pulling a ski boat the same color. The boat was meant to win me over. I didn't believe he'd really changed, but I loved to ski and wasn't about to turn down a chance to spend the day on the water. On Lake Claiborne, he towed me until my arms got too tired to hold the ropes and the muscles in my legs quaked. I smeared baby oil mixed with iodine on my skin and poured lemon juice on my hair, then baked until well-done. Out on the water, I saw glimpses of the Dad I had once loved, but the ice chest packed with cold Bud made me wonder if the monster would reappear.

Dad's visits were short and infrequent, but they gave me hope that we would move back to Big Sandy. Not that I wanted to be with Dad. I wanted my old life back, but without the craziness and fear. I still thought of life in Big Sandy as my reality. Living in Minden was passing time. I told Terri, Janet, DeeDee, and Debbie that I might not be back for my sophomore year, and some wrote farewell wishes in my yearbook.

During the summer of 1970, Dad told Steve and me that we could go to Big Sandy and take whatever we wanted from the house on Pearl Street. Uncle Shelby borrowed a truck and drove us. Mother stayed home. I was excited about the trip and made mental notes about what I wanted. It would feel good to be home again, even if only for a couple of hours. How wonderful to lie on the bed in my room with my head resting on the stuffed Dalmatian I'd left behind almost two years ago!

The yard was ankle-deep with weeds; the grass brown. All that remained of the shrubs at the front of the house were dead sticks. The "Armstrong Destroyed This Home" signs had come down, but nail holes outlined where they'd hung. Inside, a foul wave of air choked me. It smelled of dirty clothes, oil, and rotten food. The piano hadn't been dusted in two years; the keys were covered in dust and sticky to the touch. The tabletops were covered with papers, keys, and grimy dishes. The filth...

This wasn't my home. I didn't want anything from this place except the piano, and I wasn't too sure about it. I had to fight the urge to bolt out the front door and plant myself in the truck. I felt stupid that I had been excited about getting my things back. I should have stayed in Louisiana. There was no point in taking clothes because they no longer fit. At fifteen, I'd outgrown my childish pink ruffled room. Mother didn't want the furniture or her clothes. Tiny was gone.

In addition to the piano, I took a green pixie doll that Mother made before I was born, my music, metronome, and records. Nothing else. It didn't occur to me to retrieve Dr. Justice's old dictionary and saddlebags or family pictures.

Now I knew that we'd never go back. I had lived between two worlds for two years. It was time to let go of the old life and make a new one.

Steve stayed with Dad for a week. It was two months before his twelfth birthday. Steve still idolized Dad. In Steve's eyes, Dad could do no wrong. He was angry with Mother and blamed her for separating him from his dad. Mother was wise enough to know that Steve could now handle a dose of reality. As painful as it was likely to be, he needed to get to know Dad. When Steve got home, he didn't say anything about the visit, other than that Dad was giving him a car. A blue 1952 Ford.

Years later, Steve described that time with Dad, drinking Bullfrogs — limeade and gin — together. Riding in Dad's white Chevy Nova to Gladewater to buy thick steaks that they cooked on the grill. Listening to Dad talk into the morning hours, his already-thundering voice becoming louder and more powerful as his blood-alcohol level rose. Playing old reel-to-reel tapes of Herbert W.'s and Garner Ted's sermons, mocking the prophecies that had failed to materialize. Being treated like an equal — not like a child. To Steve, they are precious memories.

Before school started in the fall of 1970, Dad's façade fell away. On a final trip to the lake, he started drinking beer in the morning. As the hours passed, he became drunker and drunker, driving the boat faster and more recklessly. I refused to ski and was afraid that we were going to have an accident with the boat or the car on the way home.

Back at the house in Minden, vitriol poured out. "I knew you're a whore, Mary. Nothing has changed. You love Armstrong more than me." Again, I cowered from my Dad and thought about how to protect my brothers. I worried about him striking Mother. The matches in the gas tank feeling was back. And I hated it.

When Dad left that night, we knew it was for good.

Our well-honed survival instincts kicked in. Now that Dad had given up the pretense of change, there was danger.

"Mother, when are we going to move?" I asked.

"We're not," she said, slowly and emphatically.

"He'll come to the house and hurt us."

"I'm not running anymore."

Uncle Shelby wired a panic button inside the back door that sounded a horn outside if we pressed it. Mr. Farley had agreed to call the police if he heard the horn go off. Uncle Shelby also installed bright outdoor lighting so Dad couldn't hide in the shadows and surprise us. He built brackets along the back doorframe so we could place an iron pipe across the door when we went to bed.

It was eight o'clock on a Sunday night in September 1970. We'd been at a church softball game in Shreveport. About a mile from the house, a police car was parked beside the road. A uniformed man outstretched a hand, indicating that we should stop. Mother rolled down the window on our new silver 1966 Ford LTD.

"What's happening?" Mother asked.

"Do you live on this road?" asked the policeman.

"Yes, sir. The house where the road curves," she answered.

"Mrs. Powers?"

My heart skipped a beat. Whatever was going on had something to do with us, or he wouldn't know Mother's name.

"Yes, what's wrong?" Mother asked, her words clipped with concern.

"Mr. Powers broke into your home. He smashed the back door and ransacked the house. Your neighbor called us, but when we got there, your husband took off into the woods. His car is still parked in your yard."

Mother gaped at the cop. "What did he do to the house?"

"Ripped the sheets off the bed." He gave Mother a knowing look and nodded toward us, indicating that she needed to read between the lines because the explanation was inappropriate for tender ears. "Appeared to have been looking for something in the bed. Tore out some electrical equipment. Broke a couple of windows. Smashed the back door."

I was shaking with fury. I was sick and tired of being afraid. *Why won't he leave us alone? What does he want? Do I have to endure another town talking about my dad's crazy behavior?*

Mother just shook her head.

"You need to stay somewhere safe tonight," the officer continued.

"Can you go in with us to get school clothes and books for tomorrow?" she asked.

"Sure," he said. "Follow me."

One policeman stood with our car and another escorted us inside while we gathered our things. That night, while we fitfully slept at Aunt Dortha and Uncle Shelby's, Dad emerged from the woods. The police had gotten tired of waiting and had gone. Mr. Farley watched him go and stayed quiet.

CHAPTER THIRTY-TWO
Changes

Six weeks after Dad broke into our home, the church sent us to Big Sandy for the Feast. Ministers in Shreveport and Big Sandy knew about Dad's latest violent episode and that they were taking a chance with our safety. But we were required to go to the Feast and our chosen location was Big Sandy. We had no option but to go where we were told. When Mother pressed her case with Mr. Rogers, he said that if we had faith, then, like Daniel, we should be willing to walk into the lions' den. It wouldn't have surprised me if he'd suggested that we ask Dad if we could bunk with him while we were there.

The church could have assigned us quarters in Gladewater, Longview or Gilmer. Instead, they put us in a rooming house on Highway 155, three blocks from our old house. We drove the LTD into town after dark, checking every vehicle that passed to make sure it wasn't Dad. We pulled deep into the yard of our Feast residence and turned the car so that the Louisiana tags weren't exposed. We rode back and forth to the campus with friends so Dad wouldn't spot our car.

During my sophomore year of high school, Mother started working as a secretary for the most prominent lawyers in Minden. The wages were too low for us to live comfortably, but she was on her way to self-sufficiency. It was also helpful that her employers could use the law to protect us from Dad. One of the attorneys invested small sums of Mother's money to give us a little more financial stability. How the money was invested was a little fuzzy, and the returns were well above market rates.

Mother's employment gave me a wonderful, and unexpected, benefit. The wife of one of the lawyers wore beautiful, expensive clothes that she retired after light wear. She and I were the same size, and she routinely gifted me with her castoffs. The skirts were very short, even by Minden High School standards: abhorrent by Worldwide Church of God standards. I wore them anyway, with Mother's blessing. I kept a selection of long dresses to wear to church. I cared more about looking nice than I feared being ratted out by Priscilla and Toni. Another thread unraveled.

I don't know why the church permitted Mother to work: the $200 a month savings to the widows' and orphans' fund must have been determinative. From that point forward, our relationship with the church changed. I was scrupulous about keeping the Sabbath, holy days, and dietary laws. I avoided physical contact with boys. We didn't go to doctors. But, I ignored the rules prohibiting association with nonmembers. After getting a 1963 baby-blue Ford Fairlane to drive with a hardship license, I spent time with kids from school doing service work, participating in extracurricular activities, and generally hanging out. I'd go to Debbie's house and listen to records or to the Dixie Cream with Janet, Terri and DeeDee. Chuck, my confidant and running buddy, hung out at the house, trying unsuccessfully to convince Mother to let me go with him to concerts and movies in Shreveport.

Notions of the Tribulation, Petra, and the Kingdom of God became more abstract. They didn't fit with the world in which I was living. I couldn't believe that things were so terrible that we were going to flee to the Place of Safety in another year and that the world was going to erupt into cataclysm. At Imperial School, we were told what to think and how to behave in minute detail. When state-mandated science and history books spoke about our ancestors being here for millions of years, our Imperial School teachers explained the fallacies and told us the truth: that we hadn't evolved and that humans had been on earth for only 6,000 years. We were told that only books written by Mr. Armstrong or an ordained minister could be taken at face value. Books inconsistent with Mr. Armstrong's views on history or politics were not included in the library. Teachers and ministers watched over our every move to help us maintain compliance with God's laws. Away from those constraints, I was free to read, think, and act for myself.

I got involved in speech and drama. There was something liberating about being onstage. I could become someone else or let loose the real me that I'd kept in check my whole life. I won awards at speech and debate tournaments, was elected to statewide leadership positions, was inducted into the National Honor Society, and was picked to be an officer in two clubs. Mrs. Mac selected me as the school's best Spanish-language student when I was a sophomore, and my picture appeared in the Who's Who section of *The Grig.*

While I was no longer a part of the nameless, faceless crowd, I still had my place in Minden: a poor kid from the wrong side of town. My friends weren't from the higher echelon of society. None of us would ever be there because it was a birthright, dependent on the pedigrees of daddies and granddaddies.

Ralf and I had been corresponding for more than a year and in the spring of 1970 he drove from New Orleans to Minden to see me. He had just gotten his new senior ring and asked me to wear it. I wore the oversize blue-stone ring, wrapped with a rubber band to hold it in place, everywhere but church functions. This was another sign to Priscilla and Toni, as well as Mr. Rogers, that we were doing something wrong. But nothing had changed. We were still totally chaste, though I did hold his hand. I knew it was wrong in the eyes of the church, but I didn't feel that I was doing anything wrong. Mother tolerated my relationship with Ralf. And why not? It was long-distance, chaperoned, safe. And it kept me away from the worldly boys at school.

I started to see changes in Mother by the end of 1970. There were times when she didn't come straight home from work. Her clothes began to look more stylish, and she wore her skirts shorter. There was a man whose name came up from time to time. "Just a friend," she said. While I didn't understand then, there are women who can live without sex and those who can't. Mother wasn't meant to be an ascetic. I don't know when she took a lover, but over time she put the rules she couldn't live with in one compartment and everything else in another. She read her Bible daily, went to every church service, tithed, and kept the Sabbath. But I had a vague sense that something was different. She expected me to follow the rules and would have whipped me had I necked with Ralf or worn makeup or gone to a football game on Friday night. I started to feel, though, that Mother didn't expect me to follow the church's more onerous restrictions.

Mr. Rogers became increasingly apoplectic about my relationship with Ralf. It didn't make sense that seeing Ralf twice a year — mainly at church - could create such a ruckus. I didn't know that my neighbors were watching my every move.

I was talking with a group of teenagers after church. "I need to see you," Mr. Rogers said to me. Everyone stared. My face and neck immediately became a blotched red. I was both embarrassed and puzzled. Being called in to speak with Mr. Rogers was not a good thing.

I followed him into a small room in the Southland Park Day Care Center — our church building. He motioned me to a chair and closed the door. Then he took a seat across from me, so close that our knees were almost touching. I felt a little like I had when Mr. McIntyre kissed me. This man was too close and it didn't feel right.

"I understand you've been seeing a boy from New Orleans."

"Yes, sir," I answered. "There's someone I've talked to at church."

"Where else have you seen him?" he quizzed, his brows furrowed.

"When I lived in Jackson, I saw him in a group with the Murphy girls and some other teenagers from New Orleans. We see each other at the Feast, and he came to visit at my home."

"Have you ever been alone with him?" asked Mr. Rogers, leaning in so close to my face that I could feel his hot breath.

"Not really, sir," I answered, wondering where this was going.

"What is that supposed to mean?" he asked, derisively.

"The only time we've been alone is at my house with Mother in the next room." I met his gaze and didn't waiver because it was true.

"That's not what I've heard," he bored into me with his eyes, trying to shake my resolve.

"That's not right." I had heard that he'd grilled other people, but I never thought it would happen to me.

"I've also heard that you wear his school ring."

"Yes, sir."

"So you're going steady?"

"I guess you might call it that, but having the ring keeps people from asking me out. It just makes things easier."

"Not acceptable. Give the ring back," he said, his thin lips starting to break into a smile.

"Yes, sir," I answered softly, hoping the discussion was over.

"Has anyone ever touched your breasts?" he asked, gesturing within inches of my chest.

I was horrified. *Why is he asking me this stuff? I'm not like that and he knows it.* "No, sir," I managed to squeak.

"Has anyone ever touched your vagina?"

I was stunned and looked at him with a puzzled frown, mouth agape. "No, sir."

"Make sure you keep it that way."

"Yes, sir."

"You may go now."

I slipped out a side door and went to the car. I didn't want to see anyone. My face was red; my throat burned from reflux. I felt dirty. It didn't feel right for anyone, even a minister, to ask me those questions. When I told Mother, she was furious, but there was nothing she could do or say. His words and conduct were sanctified. To question him was to commit the unpardonable sin.

My doubts about the church were becoming more pronounced. I didn't care that Mr. Rogers was a minister; what he had done was sick. There was something wrong with a church that says that anything a minister does is right, even when it is filthy and degrading. How could he castigate Ralf when he didn't even know him? Why did his long hair make him a bad person? What was the harm in me wearing his ring?

Passover was the time to honor the Crucifixion. When Mr. Rogers started his Passover sermon in 1971, he walked around the front of the hall waving a whip with metal tips. He said it was a cat o' nine tails. Just like the one that had been used to scourge Christ. He put the weapon down on the pulpit and walked out for a moment. When he returned, his arms were full of cabbages. He laid one of the cabbages on a table that had been placed beside the pulpit.

"I'm going to show you what happened to Christ's back when he was scourged." He picked up the cat o' nine tails and began furiously beating the cabbage. Pieces flew into the air; vegetable matter sprayed the audience. When one cruciferous head was reduced to pulp, he lined up the other cabbages on the table and asked another minister to join him. He, too, had a whip. Together they flailed away at those cabbages for a good five minutes.

I knew that if I laughed, I would be in the biggest trouble of my life. I bit the insides of my cheeks until they hurt. A cabbage as Christ! Oh, man.

In the car on the way home, I couldn't help myself.

"Mother, don't you think that was weird?"

"It was different," she answered noncommittally.

Steve piped up. "I thought it was funny."

Now that I had support, I pressed on. "I got cabbage on me. What about those poor people on the front row? They smell like coleslaw."

"Good thing we sat in back," Mother said, trying to keep from laughing.

"Honestly, don't you think Mr. Rogers's lost it?"

"He does appear to have some issues," she said, turning serious again.

"He's a nut," I pressed.

"We still have to show him respect. He's God's minister."

Sure, I thought. Sure thing.

I attended camp for the third and last time in the summer of 1971 as a worker. It was odd that I kept my status as an exemplary Worldwide Church of God girl in view of Mr. Rogers's dislike for me. I suspect it was a last-ditch effort to save me from the clutches of sin. Before I left, Rogers decreed that Ralf and I could no longer communicate. Despite my questions about the church, I played the game at camp. I didn't share my doubts with anyone. I attended services, read my Bible, stayed in the prayer closet for thirty minutes a day, participated in Garner Ted's sing-alongs, kept my cubby perfect. But my heart wasn't in it.

CHAPTER THIRTY-THREE

Betwixt and Between

DeeDee wrote in my yearbook: "You've really made a hit this year." The rest was more telling: "Keep it up if that's what you really want." It was what I wanted. More than anything in the world, I wanted to be popular and smart and a leader. To be so perfect that everyone would forget that I was white trash. That I lived in a dump outside of town. That I didn't have a dad. That I went to a strange church in Shreveport instead of being Baptist or Methodist.

By the end of my junior year of high school, I'd lost my unconditional belief in Armstrong's teachings. We'd been taught that our flight to Petra was going to take place in 1972. When 1971 arrived, all mention of our departure the next year and Christ's return in 1975 stopped. It was as though these prophetic pronouncements had never been made. I thought about how impossible the whole notion had been. If God wanted to divinely transport his people to Petra, why would He fly two hundred of them at a time on an airplane that wasn't airworthy? He'd just snap His fingers and — poof! — they'd be there. Why would the Jordanian government accept thousands of refugees without food, clothing, or the basics to sustain life? If the purpose of the exercise was to hide in a Place of Safety until Christ's return, how would the exodus of thousands of people go unnoticed?

I concluded that Armstrong wasn't a prophet and that his apocalyptic ravings hadn't come from God. But I wrestled with which of the rules were right and which were wrong. Some were easy to reject because they didn't have anything to do with morality, like clothes, makeup, food, relationships with outsiders. I accepted doctors and medicine after concluding that God expected us to do all we could to help ourselves in addition to asking for His help. Others were more difficult. Was Saturday the Sabbath? How strictly was it to be observed? Weren't Christmas and Easter pagan celebrations and the holy days ordained in the Bible? Was it a sin to have sexual feelings before marriage?

Stan was my companion while I lived between the world of the church and the world outside without feeling comfortable in either. He was cute and popu-lar and did everything well: quarterback of the football team, fifth in our class academically, president of the student council, and a class officer every year. But he was driven by his own demons, some real, some imagined. He was ethnic in a town that didn't readily accept people who were different, belonged to the Greek Orthodox Church, and felt that he was an outsider.

We started dating when I was a sophomore. Over time I shared with him the church's teachings and my issues with Dad. He was kind and patient. Stan and his family sent Christmas presents to my family, knowing we couldn't reciprocate and weren't supposed to keep them, though we did. He put up with my clumsy social skills, my prudishness, and Friday night restrictions. Because he honored the tight restraints Mother kept on my social life, he eventually won her confidence.

By my junior year, we were steadies. I watched him play football on Friday nights, then went to after-game dances. We parked on dark country roads and necked. He took me to dinner in Shreveport where I ate my first shrimp cocktail. We rode in his blue Cutlass, powered by a propane tank in the trunk that came from his father's gas business. I went to the Easter service at his church. Together we worked on charity projects and the school newspaper and were inducted into the National Honor Society.

I didn't feel any guilt about the choices I'd made, though I was confused about sexual issues. I was confident that kissing above the shoulders wasn't a problem. I felt a little queasy and uncertain about Stan putting his hand on my clothed chest. Any touching under the clothes was definitely off-base.

On Saturdays I became someone else. I put on my long skirted dresses, scrubbed my face, and grabbed my Bible for church services. Down the road, Priscilla and Toni were doing the same thing. They, too, had changed. Like me, they wore short dresses and makeup to school, dated, and went out on Friday nights. They'd stopped running to Mr. Rogers about my transgressions because theirs were equally odious.

Shortly before the end of our junior year, I showed Stan a letter I received from Ambassador College. The piece of white bond paper dated May 5, 1972, said:

Dear Miss Powers:
We are pleased to report that you have been selected by the Admissions Committee for enrollment at Ambassador College, Pasadena, California.

In view of the fact that we are able to accept only a limited percentage of those applying, we are asking you to reply by return mail, confirming your intention to attend Ambassador. A deposit is required at this time.

We are looking forward to meeting you on or before Tuesday, August 29, at 8:00 a.m.

Sincerely yours,
Kenneth C. Herrmann
Director of Admissions

At that time the church professed to have a membership nearing 75,000. Many teenagers were vying for the 200 slots at Ambassador College. I hadn't applied and found it strange that the church wanted me to forego my senior year of high school. Ministerial recommendations were as important as good grades. I couldn't believe that Mr. Rogers had recommended me for early admission. There was no greater honor for a young person in the church than to be admitted to Ambassador; it was an even greater one to be asked to attend a year early.

"What are you going to do?" Stan asked.

"It's complicated," I answered.

"You want to go?"

"No," I hastily replied, "I'm not going to accept, but I have to handle it right."

"Why? You'll be seventeen this summer. That's old enough to make your own decisions. Just tell them no." Stan sounded perplexed at my dilemma.

"It's Mother," I answered. "I'm afraid that if I tell her how I feel, she'll make me follow all the rules again."

"She doesn't do everything they say," he replied, "so why would she make you?"

I paused, searching for words. "If I do what I feel is right and don't ask Mother, she doesn't question me. If we talk about where to draw the line with things having to do with the church, she has to tell me to follow the rules."

"I still don't get it."

"Like with wearing makeup. I just started doing it, and she didn't say anything. If I'd asked if I could wear mascara, she would have to tell me 'no' because that's the rule. Then, if I slipped around and did it, she'd have to punish me."

He threw up his hands in a gesture of frustration.

"Look," I said, "Mother's like me. She doesn't know what to believe and what not to believe. She's worried about drawing the line in the wrong place. If I tell her that I'm not going to Ambassador, I'm afraid she'll tell me that I have to go. Don't worry, I'll figure it out."

And I did. It was easy to tell Mother that I wanted to finish my senior year before attending college. I wrote to Ambassador College, asking them to defer my admission until August 1973.

At the beginning of my senior year, we moved from the house in the country to a new brick house in Minden next to a factory that made plastic fishing worms. Mother purchased the house through a government assistance program for low-income earners. It was the size of a postage stamp but had three bedrooms and a living room that she decorated in black and red faux Spanish furniture, accessorized with figurines of bulls. Here, without the neighbors watching our every move, Mother openly dated men outside the church. More and more went into the compartment of beliefs we couldn't live with.

Dad resurfaced, mailing filthy messages written on pieces of cardboard that had been cut from boxes. Mother's boss — a lawyer named Corky Marvin who later became District Attorney and a Court of Appeals justice — received several of them. Dad accused Mr. Marvin, whom he referred to as "Corky-Screw," of sleeping with Mother. It was a preposterous allegation.

When Steve had spent a week with Dad in the summer of 1970, Dad had promised to give him an old Ford when he was older. Steve sent Dad a letter two years later, asking him to make good on his promise. Mother kept one of Dad's cardboard notes about the car, dated December 14, 1972. There is no salutation.

"I insulted my son Steve because he was ugly to me, he didn't know I had given him the sport coupe, because you didn't give him my letters Soon we will all face a just court where all of the corks and bottles will have no power. I told you years ago what the Great Armstrongs were and is, this was brought to light, Time May 15 – 1972 Seattle Post Intelligencer March 25 – April 22 – 1972 and others The Great Armstrong the prophet (profit) was going to take all of you good people to a place of safety – Jan. 72 – this is Dec. 72, Is Ted still under the bonds Satan? Take your wigs off look at your self in the mirror, you are forty. Charles"

In my senior year of high school, I received a letter from the Minden Young Women's Service Club inviting me to compete with fourteen other girls in the Miss Minden pageant, a Miss America preliminary. I was shocked to receive the letter because I'd never been chosen for anything having to do with appearance. Once I got the letter, though, I knew I wanted to win. I would win. I had to acquire social graces in order to succeed. I didn't know the difference between a salad fork and a cocktail fork. I didn't know how to handle myself in a private club. I was clueless about the nuances of dressing for different occasions. I'd never been in an airplane. The ways of the wealthy and powerful were foreign. If I were to win a pageant, I might learn some of these things.

Mother had taken a different job as secretary for the Webster Parish School Board. One of her colleagues, Iris Baucom, knew about pageants because, a decade earlier, her daughters had been stars in the pageant world. I became Iris' project. As she instructed, I walked with a book on my head up and down the hall at home for hours each week. She drilled me in swiveling my ankle and striking a pose. I learned to stand so that when I put my legs together, I had three visible diamonds — ankles, knees and thighs. Iris showed me how to apply makeup for interviews and the stage. She took me to Shreveport to pick out a white Benét formal for the evening-gown competition. She approved the powder-blue pantsuit I bought at Goldring's for the judges' interview. She told me that I had to catch the attention of the judges the first time I met them, so we decorated a white hat with flowers that matched the pantsuit. She picked out a classic white Catalina swimsuit with matching white pumps for the swimsuit competition.

I had saved money from working as a secretary at Carey's Real Estate and as a helper for Mr. Prothro, the high school guidance counselor, but I didn't have enough to cover all of the costs associated with the pageant. Mother dipped into her meager reserves to fund the balance. To save money, she made the light blue palazzo pantsuit that I was to wear for the opening number. My participation in this pageant was a huge investment for us — the equivalent of one month of Mother's salary.

The show's opening was a production number in which all of the contestants danced. I was hopelessly uncoordinated and had no rhythm. Iris came to rehearsal to see the steps. She worked with me until I could dance the opening number. "Tilt your head." "Smile." "Look at the judges." "Relax those shoulders."

For talent I wanted to play the piano, but I was too rusty. I chose to do a dramatic interpretation of the Robert Service poem, "The Cremation of Sam McGee." It's a funny story about Sam McGee, a prospector in the Alaska Gold Rush who, before he dies of cold, extracts a promise from his buddy to cremate him. His friend carries the body all over the Yukon until he finds the shell of an old boat — the *Alice May* — and sets it afire to fulfill his promise. When the fire blazes, Sam comes back to life and announces, "Since I left Plumtree down in Tennessee, it's the first time I've been warm." Mother made gold lame hot pants and a gold satin blouse with dolman sleeves for me to wear. We spray-painted matching boots and a billed cap to complete the ensemble. Mr. Kinsey, an African-American art teacher at the black high school whom Mother knew from her school board job, made a papier-machè version of the *Alice May.*" It was big and difficult to work around backstage. Worse was getting it onstage so I could stand in the hull, in a dry-ice fog, to recite most of the poem. But it was an amazing prop.

The evening was a blur of quick changes, hairspray, and nerves. We were all reassembled on stage in our evening gowns for the decision. "The first name I read will be that of the second runner-up. The next name will be that of the first runner-up; and it is important to remember that, if for any reason, the new Miss Minden should be unable to fulfill her duties, her title would be assumed by the first runner-up. The second runner-up is Contestant number 11, Miss Debra Thomas."

I hoped it was down to Cindy and me. She'd won the talent preliminary; I'd won swimsuit — but talent was worth more points than swimsuit. I held my breath. "The first runner-up is Contestant number 12, Miss Cindy Dowell." Now I couldn't breathe, even though I needed air. "And now for the big announcement, Miss Minden 1973 is Contestant number 1, Carla Powers." I'd thought I was prepared, but when my name was called, I felt an icy-hot jolt course through me. This shock was different, though, than what I felt when I heard from the pulpit in Big Sandy that Dad had been disfellowshipped. I was stunned by the realization that hard work and effort could make dreams come true. That I could be whoever I wanted to be. I could overcome my past.

Blinded by the footlights, I couldn't see the audience. I heard applause and made the obligatory walk down the runway to "Will She Be Miss America?"

At the reception following the pageant, Mother, Steve, Dan, Stan, and I went to the receiving room where I was supposed to greet Young Women's Service Club members and local dignitaries. The five of us stood together in an empty room waiting for people to appear. I wore my new crown and the white rabbit wrap that came with the title. Instead of coming to congratulate me, the club members retreated to the kitchen with their families. My family, Stan, and I stood alone while they had a party in the next room. After fifteen minutes, Mother, enraged at the snub, told us to get our coats. We walked out. Nobody noticed.

Someone gave me a snapshot of my stroll down the runway. It captures the faces of the people sitting in the audience. They are dumbstruck. Poor girls from the wrong side of town weren't supposed to win. I wasn't particularly bothered by the slights. I had what I wanted and intended to wring everything I could from it.

CHAPTER THIRTY-FOUR
Moment of Truth

As high school came to a close, I was chosen to attend a speech tournament in south Louisiana.

"Mother, there's a big tournament in Lake Charles in two weeks. It starts on Thursday and runs through Saturday. I have to go."

"You'd miss the Sabbath?"

"Yes, ma'am."

"I don't feel good about you going."

At least she hadn't said no. "Mother, please."

"I have a feeling that something bad is going to happen."

"Oh, Mother," I groaned. "You sound like Memow with her premonitions."

"I know it's silly to you."

"I'll be in Mrs. Lewis' new Buick. We'll be fine," I answered.

"I need to think about it."

Returning from Lake Charles, we were about an hour from home at midnight on Saturday. Fifteen of us were divided among three cars. I was resting in the backseat of Mrs. Lewis' car, with my head on the shoulder of a teammate named Mike. My friend Chuck was driving. The Eagles' "Witchy Woman" was playing on the eight-track.

"There's a guy coming behind us really fast," Chuck shouted.

I turned to look out the back window and saw headlights bearing down on us. "Get down!" Chuck yelled.

Mike grabbed my shoulders and pushed me towards the floor. Chuck hit the accelerator at the moment of impact. I felt the jolt, heard the crunching of metal. Broken glass rained around me.

The momentum propelled our car forward, but Chuck was able to keep us on the right side of the road. We finally stopped. We climbed out and tried to stand on the shoulder of the highway. My legs were too weak, and I had to sit on the grass. The car that had hit us had run off the road and lay at the bottom of a deep embankment.

Our friends in the other cars went for help. Chuck and another boy hiked down to the other vehicle to see if they could help the driver. They soon returned.

"The guy's unconscious. I can't tell how bad he's hurt," Chuck announced. "We need to wait till the ambulance gets here."

At the sheriff's, I called home.

"Mother, I'm okay. But we've been in a wreck. We're all fine."

"I know. I had the sense a little while ago that it was over and that you were all right. What happened?"

"Looks like a guy went to sleep at the wheel. Hit us going about 90. We took a bad lick, but nobody got hurt."

"Thank goodness."

"We'll be here until Chuck's dad comes for us."

"I'll wait up."

The next day I was bruised and sore. I felt terrible, but lucky to be walking. Around four o'clock, we heard a knock at the door. It was two ministers, Mr. Rogers and his sidekick, Mr. Tennison. Mother showed them into the living room.

"Where's Carla?" Mr. Rogers asked.

I came in, figuring they were there to pray for me because of my injuries from the wreck. Maybe anoint me with a little olive oil.

"Hi," I said, dragging myself to the couch. "I'm grateful to God to be alive."

Mr. Rogers looked at me without smiling. "You have broken the Sabbath. This is not the first time you have violated God's law. You may not come to church anymore."

I looked him squarely in the eyes. "Get the hell out of my house."

Rogers turned to Mother, his lips white with anger. "Control your rebellious child!"

"You heard her," Mother spat. "Get the hell out of our home. If she isn't good enough for the church, then neither am I."

I wasn't too surprised at Mother's reaction. I'd felt it coming for a long time. Maybe she was just looking for the right opportunity. What startled me was the amount of anger in her tone as she spoke those words.

It was over. Finally. Over. We were free.

Later, Mother told Steve. He sat on the porch that evening quietly watching the sunset. Years after, he told me that he thought God was going to strike us dead in the night. He was watching the sun go down on what he thought would be our last day on earth.

CHAPTER THIRTY-FIVE

Just Desserts

I edged my car up to the entrance of the campus of Ambassador College, the Worldwide Church of God, Imperial School. The place was deserted. Ragged around the edges. For sale. Gone were the officious guards, the meticulous landscaping, the seasonal flowers, the hum of vehicles, the people for whom Big Sandy, Texas, was the center of the universe. The gates were bound together with a fat chain and a sturdy lock. I wanted to jump out and rattle the gates and yell at the top of my lungs. You bastards! You sick bastards! You got what you deserved. But I didn't. The Radio Church of God and the Imperial Schools had trained me well. God's people have self-control.

It had taken me thirty years to face this place, and I was going in. I doubled back and found that the unmarked entrance a mile back was accessible. But still—! As I drove through, anxiety replaced bravado. *I'm breaking a rule. I'm driving where I shouldn't be driving.* What if a security person accosted me and demanded that I state my business? Then it occurred to me: When I turned into that property, I had forgotten the last thirty years. I had again become the poor, powerless daughter of the town drunk. I thought of how they would see me now. A stylish woman driving a new Jaguar. If they stopped me at all, no one would do anything more vicious than politely ask me to leave.

The street now called Orange Grove Boulevard was unfamiliar. On the right side was a farm with a silo owned by the church. To the left were vacant prefab buildings and rundown trailers that looked like they hadn't been maintained in a decade. A cluster of booths painted the color of caramel sat off in the distance. The grass was brown. Weeds choked the flowerbeds. Dead limbs defaced the trees. Tractors and maintenance equipment were parked near the front of the campus.

Faculty row was still there, though the entrance was blocked and I didn't try to get in. The homes I saw from the Old Big Sandy Highway were nicer and better maintained than I had remembered. The paving on the runway was in good repair, and the railroad crossing arms that came down whenever a plane was taking off or landing were still in place.

I drove down Acacia Street and found the parking lot in front of the old brown building. At first I wasn't sure it was the same structure, but the color, texture and location gave it away. There was now a peak along the top that looked like the inverted keel of a boat. A wing with top-to-bottom windows had been added to the north end. I parked the car and got out. The place was deserted. Vines covered the entrance, and shapeless shrubs that had become small trees obscured most of the front. Cedar shingles had pulled loose. I walked around the side, past what used to be ministerial offices, to see if the stream was still there. The concrete pathway was broken and I couldn't get to the water, but I could see that a stagnant film lay on its surface. The swiftly moving stream had become a filthy swamp. A tangle of trees, stickery vines, and Johnson grass covered the embankments. The spring's source was nowhere to be found. The air smelled of decay.

I peered in the big windows on the new wing and saw a large dark room that had been a library, its books still on the shelves. Outside, around the corner, the grassy hills I had rolled down as a child were covered with weeds. The stone and concrete bridge across the stream was still intact, but water no longer ran underneath. The banks were choked with wild vegetation that looked inviting only to water moccasins. I stood under a 120-foot pine and surveyed what was left of the place that had played a starring role in so many of my nightmares. In a decade this hellhole would be consumed by the forest from which it had been claimed fifty years earlier.

I got back in the car and drove to the front of the complex. The metal tabernacle, larger than I had remembered, lay to the left of a new administration building. The big trees did a poor job of masking the building's size and ugliness. Farther down the road, plywood had been nailed over the windows of the temporary buildings that had once been Imperial School. All were in desperate need of paint and repair. The oval track remained, but everything else was gone.

This gulag of my childhood was just another broken-down East Texas relic. I had survived. It had not.

CHAPTER THIRTY-SIX
Saying Goodbye

As I stood alone beside Dad's bed, memories came back, unbidden. His breathing was shallow and the monitor made disquieting squeals and beeps. I looked into his face. It had a softness that had disappeared long ago. The angry man was gone.

As the years passed, I concluded that my father was at least partially right. Armstrong did play a role in destroying our home. While Dad's weaknesses alone might have been enough to eventually ruin him and our family, I remembered how he changed after we moved to Big Sandy. My little-girl memories from the Arkansas years were of him as a gentle giant, an affectionate parent dispensing hugs and kisses and bouncing me on his knee. He'd hold my waist and spin me around or throw me up into the air, and I knew he'd always catch me. His stories of faraway places gave me the gift of wanderlust. He taught me to count and to say a few words in French and German. He told me over and over that I could do whatever I put my mind to. He never said I couldn't do something because I was a girl.

Dad introduced me to wheels. Before I was two, he had me driving. My vehicle was a cool pedal car with a red body and a grill that looked like a Tex Avery cartoon animal baring its teeth. I had a tricycle, a wagon, and a bicycle. In Little Rock, he transformed wrecked cars back into works of art made of chrome, fins and bright paint. Dad quizzed me on makes and models of cars and explained the difference between a transmission and a carburetor.

There was always music in our home. Dad loved to hear Ferrante and Teicher, Ronnie Brown, and Roger Williams. Our hi-fi played bossa nova by Joabim and Gilberto and classical pieces by Rachmaninoff, Liszt, and Mozart. Sometimes he'd take Mother in his arms and dance around the living room. He tried to teach me ballroom steps by having me stand on top of his feet, but I had no sense of rhythm. When, in the first grade I convinced him that I was serious about the piano, he bought a cut-down, refurbished old Schafer for me.

Early on, he took pride in my accomplishments, cheering at Field Day, watching me spell "vegetation" in first-grade assembly, beaming with pride over my report cards and listening as cacophony turned to music. I sat in his lap with his arms around me, crying with him over President Kennedy's assassination. I went with him to the stock car races in Mineola where he ran an old white Chevy. We ate enchiladas at the Shamrock, barbeque at Red Brown's, and jalapeno peppers at the kitchen table.

I pulled the curtain around his bed. It occurred to me that if I had a chance to engage in conversation with the father I remembered from my early childhood, he would listen to the things that made my resume look good, and he would tell me that I had done well. He would be proud of the renegade who challenged rules and blazed a trail. But what would make his eyes light up, what he would want to talk about, were my adventures. Going to a tango club in Buenos Aires, walking on glaciers in Alaska, exploring the Greek islands, flying a seaplane across Lake Michigan, walking on the Great Wall of China, visiting the Niger Delta. He would smile at the thought of me following his journey across the English Channel, through France, and into Germany. He would love knowing that I had traced the Powers family genealogy and had walked on the ground trod by my ancestors.

That man would have asked about his grandson. I would show him the picture of a strapping, snaggle-toothed boy whose face and build remind me of how Dad looked sixty-five years earlier. He would see the love in my eyes when I groused about the windows broken from tennis balls hit with a baseball bat. Dad would nod his head approvingly as I talked of beginning his grandson's French-language education and his travels to thirty states and a dozen foreign countries. He would smile at hearing that my boy is a car bug who can name the make and model of every sports car he sees.

Somewhere, somehow that man had been overwhelmed by disappointment, disillusionment, and selfishness. Anger and bitterness were stronger than his love for us. I'd come to understand my dad better by marrying someone a lot like him. Our relationship had followed much the same progression as had Mother's and Dad's, without the crazy religion. As both a child and wife, I knew what it was like to be around someone who was warm and charming when everything was going his way and scarier than the devil when it wasn't. It provided me with context for my dad's life and, for reasons that weren't entirely clear, made it possible to forgive him.

I wanted to touch my dad's hand, hold it in mine. But I couldn't. The old fear, the paralyzing fear, was still there. So I stayed at the foot of his bed and looked at him while I spoke.

"Dad, I forgive you for all that has happened. I know that in many ways you did the best you could with the hand you were dealt. Life wasn't always fair to you. I'm sorry you missed being part of a wonderful family and didn't get to know us as we grew up. I'm sorry you never met your grandchildren. You would've enjoyed them. I hope you finally find peace and a better place than you found on this earth. May God be with you. Good-bye."

The tears finally came as I left Dad's room and headed home. I realized that my journey back to Big Sandy was about more than facing my past. I had to come to grips with tough decisions I needed to make in the present. It was time to go back to Houston.

CHAPTER THIRTY-SEVEN

The Vigil

I was back home on Wednesday night when Steve called. "The doctors have decided that Dad's brain-dead. Tomorrow they're going to discontinue life support."

"What time?" I asked.

"In the morning."

"You going over?"

"I'll be there."

"Any idea what'll happen?"

"Doctor said he doesn't think Dad'll last more than a few minutes."

"I don't think I can get back up there."

"I'll handle it."

"Call me when it's over."

The next morning at 9:00, I began my vigil. I sat in my corner office in a big black leather chair and shuffled the papers on my desk. I couldn't concentrate. I asked my assistant to hold my calls and keep everyone away.

I stared out the forty-eighth-floor windows at the muddy water of Buffalo Bayou and the canopy of trees that is Houston's west side. Would I be here today if not for Dad? If he had been satisfied with his life in central Arkansas and hadn't abandoned the familiar to search for something better, would I have turned out like my aunts, uncles, and cousins? Without adversity, would my cold flint have sparked? Might I not owe my success in the business world to the strength and ambition that were forged in those days in Big Sandy and Jackson and Minden?

But a bigger question haunted me: was I happier? In the midst of a second unhappy marriage, in debt to my eyeballs, living in a huge house that bore little imprint of my personality, working myself to exhaustion every day to avoid facing what awaited at home, I wasn't exactly living the good life. There didn't seem to be much connection between wealth, success, and happiness.

If Dad had ignored Armstrong's call and stayed in Arkansas, would my life have turned out better? I thought of Uncle Jake, who has lived his entire life on Kaney Ridge in Springhill, Arkansas. After returning from World War II, he never again flew in an airplane or ventured more than half a day's drive from the little house on top of the hill. He and Aunt Hattie raised cattle and grew hay and planted a big kitchen garden across the road from the house. They ran a country store, where Uncle Jake — once the chairman of the Faulkner County Democratic Party — chewed the fat with his neighbors and bemoaned how the Republicans were ruining the country.

Aunt Hattie and Uncle Jake were founding members of the Springhill Baptist Church, attending every prayer meeting, Sunday service, Sunday school class, and church social for fifty years. He sang in a gospel quartet, traveling around the state and raising his voice in praise. From the time he was a little boy, Uncle Jake knew that Jesus died for him on Calvary's Cross. When he dies, he knows he's going to Heaven. He has no questions, no ambiguity. "Jesus loves me, this I know, because the Bible tells me so."[24]

While there had been times when I had thought about running to that romanticized pastoral existence, I knew it wasn't for me. Dad had been true to his nature to look for something different. He had just looked in the wrong place. I was grateful that his courage — and craziness — had taken me on a wild roller-coaster ride.

Staring down at the meandering bayou below, I realized that if I turned back now, all of the suffering and sacrifice would be for naught. But I knew that I had to make some changes. I could no longer bury myself in work and share a home with a man who created an atmosphere reminiscent of my childhood. My son deserved to live differently than I had. I deserved more.

I watched the minutes and the hours pass and wondered why I hadn't heard from Steve. I overcame the temptation to dial his cell phone. The call came at 11:30.

"He's gone," he said softly.

"When?"

"A few minutes ago."

"You okay?" For Steve, Dad hadn't died thirty years earlier as he had with me. His death today was real, tangible, and immediate.

"I'm fine. He went easy. I held his hand the whole time. He breathed strong for a couple of hours, then shallow for a little while, then he stopped." I could tell from the way he swallowed his words that Steve was crying.

"I had no idea what to expect. I'm glad you were there. You're a strong person." I wondered if I could hold the hand of someone as he passed from this existence.

"Sis, he's my dad."

Something in his words resonated with me. I realized that Steve had blessed Dad with the ultimate act of love by being with him, holding his hand, as he took his last breath.

CHAPTER THIRTY-EIGHT

Last Respects

It was muggy and the clouds were still gray and low when I left Houston on Saturday morning to meet the family at the funeral home. During the drive, I put a murder mystery into the CD player and tried to tune out the memories that had been accumulating all week. I was tired of thinking, of remembering, of dreaming the recurring nightmare that Dad was chasing me. But the plot didn't hold my attention. I switched it off.

Neither Dad nor the church had ruined my life. Adversity had pushed me to achieve more than the little girl in Big Sandy could have comprehended. It had taken years of therapy to understand how the scars from my childhood wounds still influenced so many decisions. I'd gravitated toward troubled men in an effort to heal my dad. I yearned for love with a man who had a measure of self-actualization. Because I had been dominated and controlled during my formative years by self-centered, power-obsessed people who enforced rigid authority and demanded perfection, I sought similar negative father-working environments. I'd practiced law with predatory senior partners and abusive colleagues while encountering sexism, racism, and outright mental illness. In each of these settings, I'd cast myself in the role of change agent, fighter for the greater good, barrier-breaker. Years of smashing my head against a brick wall disguised as a glass ceiling had left me with a terrible headache. I was suspicious of anything that called itself religion and clueless as to how to connect with a Higher Power. My soul needed nourishment.

Maybe I had reached this place to share my story with the people who had lived as we had — or worse — and didn't believe it was possible to rise above their beginnings. Maybe I could embolden them to jettison the armor. Banish the shame. Believe that anything is possible. Maybe it was to help people understand the insidious evil of cults. Maybe it was to help me understand myself.

But even as I pondered these noble thoughts, I was afraid. It would take courage to stand before a group of my peers and talk about the church and Dad and growing up as I did. Exposing my true self could endanger my social and professional standing. I wondered if I could deal with the nausea that still keeps me awake at night and lingers for days after I conclude that I've embarrassed myself.

Every time I've shared anecdotes with friends, I've agonized afterwards that I have scared them off, but have been buoyed by the fact that most times they seem to like me more. When my friends have heard parts of my story, the edge that sometimes comes across as ruthlessness disappears. I become more a real person. If I started to open up and share my story, perhaps small steps would lead to bigger steps, and I could rid myself of the shame.

The well-kept single-story brick funeral home sprawled on a prominent corner in Gladewater, facing Highway 80. I drove across the parking lot and pulled in beside Steve's Tahoe. A pickup truck bearing Arkansas plates was the only other vehicle in a lot that could have held two hundred cars. A norther was blowing through pushing the clouds to the southeast. A gust hit me as I left the warm car and hustled into the parlor.

Inside, Mother, Steve, and Gloria stood with Margie and her husband making uncomfortable small talk. Steve pulled me to one side.

"I brought some pictures," he said, pulling a small stack of frames out of a bag. "I prefer to have him remembered this way." I looked at each as Steve set them out beside the guest book.

"Is the casket open?" I asked him.

"Unfortunately."

"You know how much I hate that."

"Billy was insistent, and I decided it didn't do any harm. It's in another room, and we can just stay away. It'll be closed for the service."

"What's he dressed in?"

"White shirt, jacket, tie, pants."

"Didn't he tell you years ago that he wanted to be buried in a pine box wearing his work clothes?"

"Yeah, but I decided to dress him up a little more. Billy went to the house and found the clothes."

"Casket?"

"He got what he wanted."

Steve reached into the stack of photos and handed one to me. "Did I give you a copy of this? I had it made from the slide."

It was the picture Dad took of the three of us at the first Feast of Tabernacles in 1955. Mother in her aqua sweater dress, Dad in his slacks and short-sleeved shirt, me swaddled in yellow, lying in a portable bassinet.

"You did. I like the one from 1956 better. It's in my solarium with the family pictures."

"That was the beginning of the end."

"I hate those bastards more now that I ever did." I didn't have to tell Steve who I meant.

"It was all about money."

"And power and control," I added.

The door of the funeral home swung open and Wanda Moore rushed in, words flying. "Oh, lordy, it's getting cold out there. Wind's a-gustin' like nobody's business. Just about blew my coat off. Gee, I wish I'd brought a headscarf. I must look a fright."

It took a moment for the whirlwind to calm.

"Hey, Wanda." I took her arm as she bustled over to envelop me in another of her hugs. "I'd like you to meet my cousin Margie from Arkansas."

"I remember hearing Charles talk about you. I know he'd appreciate you coming all this way," said Wanda, while she removed her coat. She grabbed my arm, and I followed her across the room to the coatrack.

"Tell me. How does he look?" asked Wanda in her matter-of-fact way.

"Sorry?"

"Charles. Did they make him up nice?"

"I haven't been to see. I don't like that kind of thing."

"Oh, come on now. You have to see him with me."

It was a day of compromises. We walked out of the big room and took a left by the front door. Inside an alcove, Dad's body lay in state, his head resting on a satin pillow.

"They did such a good job. Looks so lifelike. Don't you think?"

I thought his face looked grotesque — swollen, puffy. The makeup was caked-on, artificial. If I had come upon this body without being told it was my Dad, I wouldn't have recognized it. But there was no point disagreeing with Wanda. "Looks nice in his dress clothes."

"Steve's been so good to him this week."

"I know. He's a fine man. Dan, too."

When we returned to the room, I passed Wanda off to Steve, looped my arm in Mother's and drew her toward an armchair.

"You okay?"

"You know, Carla, I realized I'm finally over him."

I looked at her and raised my eyebrows. "I mean it," she continued. "After I left the hospital on Tuesday, I went home and cried. I cried for most of the night. It was the first time I had ever grieved over him."

"You cried in Jackson," I reminded her gently.

"That was different. I was alone and scared. I had no idea how I was going to support you kids and me. I missed him, but I was too angry to grieve."

"How do you know it's over?" I was interested in her answer for my sake, too.

"As I cried, I finally saw him for what he was."

"Which is …?"

"I had chosen to remember only the wonderful person I knew in my teens and twenties. But that wasn't the truth."

I remained quiet.

"I thought about him drinking up the money for food and the house, being hit, being cursed, scaring the life out of you kids. Fires in the backyard, holes in the wall, matches in the gas tank. All of it."

"Don't you blame the church?" I asked.

"He turned into a mean, sick man. His pride and his dignity were more important than us. The church pushed him over the edge, but he could have made different choices."

"Would you have left Big Sandy with him if he'd asked?"

"Until '65 or so, in a heartbeat. After he got so violent, I wouldn't have gone with him because I couldn't leave the friends who would help us." She coughed and cleared her throat a couple of times.

"Why don't you sit here for a minute? I'll get you a glass of water." I turned away and walked to the refreshment bar. When I got back to Mother a minute later, she was deep in thought. "You sure you're okay?"

"All my tears are gone. Wednesday morning I stood under a hot shower and felt his spirit wash out of me. I don't feel sad today. I feel free."

She reached for my hand as I patted her on the shoulder. "I think a part of those we've loved always stays with us," I said. "Being free is all we can ask."

CHAPTER THIRTY-NINE
The Pine Box

Our small group gathered at a country cemetery outside of Big Sandy, directly across the road from the tiny frame house in which Dad had lived. Billy told us that Dad had wanted to be buried there. Billy seemed to be calling the shots for our family now, but fighting over turf was the last thing on my mind. Dan and I piled out of my warm car into the cold, persistent wind. The front had blown away the last of the rain and the sky was a brilliant wintery blue. My black suit provided little warmth. I shivered and moved under the funeral canopy in an effort to find some protection from the gusts.

Dad's casket was covered with two sprays of flowers. Ours was made of red and white carnations, as Mother had requested. The other — from Billy and his family — contained a variety of flowers in yellow and purple. It bothered me that the lid on the pine coffin didn't lie flat and at one corner there was a small gap between the bottom of the lid and the box.

A stack of 3 X 5-inch memorial cards was piled nearby. Dad's name was written as Charles D. "Charlie" Powers. It was odd to me that he was called "Charlie" because during my years with him, I had never heard him called anything but Charles.

The service was scheduled for 3:30, but by 3:00 everyone I expected to attend had gathered. I was about to suggest that we go ahead with the service when a car arrived. Then came another and another and another. Before long, the parking lot was filled. People whom we had not seen — nor who had seen Dad — since 1968 came to see us and say their good-byes to him. Some I remembered; others were vaguely familiar, but I couldn't recall their names. I wondered what their lives had been like for the past thirty-five years and whether they were still a part of the church. I wanted to know how my old friends, my contemporaries, had fared, but it was the wrong time and place for such conversations. I wondered why and for whom there was such an outpouring of affection.

The father of one of my classmates from Imperial School greeted me. I knew him immediately and called him by name.

"Hello, Mr. Mansfield. How're you?"

"Fine. Real fine," he answered stiffly, just as he would have when I was a kid.

"Still live around here?" I asked, wanting to know details but not daring to ask.

"Yeah, it's home," he said flatly.

"How's Lynn?" I was curious what had become of his daughter, my former classmate.

"I'm real proud of her. She's a clerk at Wickes — just down the road."

"Family?"

"Sure. Husband. Two kids. They've got a nice trailer not too far from the wife and me."

"I'm glad she's well. Give her my best."

Dan stayed by my side as other people came to greet us. A stern-looking man stopped and gravely shook our hands, saying only "Hello, Carla. I'm sorry about your Dad." He nodded at Dan.

"Who was that last guy?" Dan asked.

"Our fourth-grade teacher at Imperial," I whispered.

"I noticed Leon Moore had been avoiding him."

"Yeah, Leon told me that all he could remember was how Mr. Green used to beat the tar out of him."

"I feel out of place. Like I don't belong," said Dan.

How lucky, I thought. But I just asked, "Why?"

"I don't know this place or these people."

"The whole thing is about as strange as it gets. You have every bit as much right to be here as any of us, I answered."

Tears started to form in Dan's eyes. "I don't know the man in the box and can't feel bad about his death. What hurts is knowing that I'll never know my dad."

"I'm sorry," I said in a barely audible voice.

The group began to congregate under the canopy. My mother and brothers, Margie and her husband, and Billy and his family took the covered chairs in front of the casket. Mother motioned for me to sit. I shook my head. She glared at me, mouthing that I was supposed to sit. This time I refused to budge. It was important for me to stand.

The service was brief. The minister opened with a prayer, read a few scriptures. He led the group in the Lord's Prayer and closed with another prayer. It would have been hypocritical to do more. I didn't shed a tear.

After the service, a tall, lanky man approached me.

"Do you remember me?"

"You look familiar, but I'm sorry, I can't remember your name."

"Jefferson. Natalie's dad."

"Of course. Sorry I didn't recognize you. How're you?"

"Okay."

"How's Natalie?"

"If you'll come with me to my car, I'd like to show you something."

Odd, I thought, but I was curious.

We walked up the dirt path to an old Chevrolet parked under an oak tree. He reached inside the backseat of the unlocked car and pulled out a framed portrait.

"That's Natalie with her husband and kids," he said with pride.

I stared into the face of my old Imperial School rival. She looked good. Natalie, her husband, and children were gathered around a substantial brick fireplace. The photo suggested that she had a prosperous life.

"She looks great. Where's she living?"

"Georgia."

"Working?"

"She's a lawyer now. Been practicing for about five years. Took a long time. She got married and went to college at night. Later, she put herself through law school. She's doing real good."

"Happy?"

"I reckon about as happy as any of us can be." His eyes glistened. I knew he was remembering the days when Natalie and I had been girls; wondering how different our lives would have been had he and my parents not been ensnared by Herbert W. Armstrong.

I started to cry. Words stuck in my throat. The emotions I'd held in check for the past week let loose. I had never let myself celebrate my victory over the Radio Church of God and Charles Powers. It had always felt unseemly to pat myself on the back for succeeding. But now I could celebrate for Natalie. Her success was my success. I put my arms around Mr. Jefferson's skinny chest and squeezed. "I'm so glad."

"Not many of you got through it. But those of you who did are tough. Real tough."

EPILOGUE

The Journey Continues

Much has changed in the seven years since Dad died. My divorce in 2003 dredged up feelings I had as a little girl in Big Sandy, but this time the outcome was different. In the face of fear, I stood my ground, confident in the support and protection from many people and institutions. When my son was torn apart by the changes in his life, I had the knowledge and financial wherewithal to surround both of us with a powerful support structure. While the scars will always be with Andrew, he is learning much earlier than I did how to accept and gain strength from bad experiences.

I didn't date for three years after my divorce. I needed time to get to know myself and my son. When I was ready, a wonderful man came into my life. We're dealing with the chaos of homes 20 miles apart, our collective four children, and two Labrador retrievers. It's joyous, frustrating, exhausting, and comforting.

Work has its place, but it doesn't consume me as it did for so long.

My mother, Dan, Steve, Gloria, my niece, and nephews are well. Mother's siblings are alive and in reasonably good health. At ninety-four, Uncle Jake has the mind of a forty-year-old, and I love to talk politics with him. Dad's brothers and sister, Uncle Shelby, and the Prociws have passed away.

The way in which I feel most different is in my relationship with religion, the spiritual, and the divine. After wiping away everything I'd been taught, I've spent the past decade studying biblical history and translations, the Gnostics, the development of Catholic and Protestant doctrines, Jungian psychology, Buddhism, Sufism, and philosophy. As a result, I've made peace with my inability to connect with institutionalized religion. I know that many people experience the Divine through the symbols and sacred stories of traditional religion. I wish I could. But places of worship, ministers delivering sermons and dogmatic myths are the sources of some of my deepest wounds. What I have found is a deep spirituality. Instead of looking for external authority to tell me how to act and what to believe, I am seeking the truth on my own terms.

I believe that the opposite of love is fear. God, or whatever name you call the Power of the Universe, loves us without condition. Anyone who claims to have a monopoly on the truth doesn't. I don't believe that we must follow a particular religious dogma or adhere to a list of rules or be perfect in order to receive that love; some call this grace. Love — human or divine — doesn't include frightening or bullying another.

I don't profess to have the answers to life's big questions. I'm learning to live in the questions. I ask the Universe for answers and trust that they will come when I'm ready to receive them. Sometimes no answer is an answer. Not all answers are obvious; I also must listen to the voice of my soul. It's easy to overwhelm inner messages with the din of daily life.

I find God in many places. Nature. Love. A special place at home where I play beautiful music, am surrounded by soothing colors, keep a collection of meaning-ful objects, and light fragrant candles. Meditation. Prayer. My lover's embrace.

For me, life is a labyrinth. There is one way in, one way out. I move in circles and spirals, seeing only the path directly in front of me. I don't know when or where the course is going to end. I embrace the journey.

I want to learn, grow, heal, love, live: reach the end that is also the beginning. Revel in the mystery.

ACKNOWLEDGMENTS

Three people are most responsible for my writing this book; I will always be grateful to them. Pittman McGehee is helping me learn who I am and helped me find the courage to share my story. Kerry Blair convinced me to discard the novel I'd begun and write a memoir. He provided encouragement through multiple drafts and rejections. Jackie Simon taught me to write. She gave me confidence that the material was worthy of publication.

My mother Mary Morris and brothers Steve and Dan Powers have supported this project from its inception and have provided invaluable insights. I hope that our many talks have helped us heal. Dan named the book and has provided artistic support. My son Andrew has cheered me on. Chris Skisak has loved and nurtured me. I thank them all.

My editor Lucy Chambers gave me permission to write from the heart. Her input has made the book much better. I am grateful to Nora Shire for tirelessly editing *Matches* and working with me through multiple rounds of changes, and to Al Shire for his thoughtful edits. I am appreciative to Jim Reeder, Sr. for introducing me to Rue Judd, CEO of Bright Sky Press, who is the nicest, best publisher any writer could have.

Many friends have given of their time to read, edit, and provide information, comments, and contacts. A huge thanks to Margaret Shannon, Diana Miller, Steve Krum, Judge Gene Sullivan, Ron Liebman, Bob Owen, Mary Powell, and Sylvia Phillips. I want to particularly acknowledge Ernie Prociw who read the manuscript and verified that I had accurately portrayed Armstrong's doctrines and the church's practices. He asked that his parents' real names be used to honor them.

1   Because of attorney-client privilege concerns, I have created a conversation that is representative of those I routinely have with senior management. It is not a testament of an actual conversation.

2   *History of Hickory County*, (Missouri) by F. Marion Wilson 1907, p. 18

3   Ibid., 65

4   Ibid., 78–79

5   Obituary of Dr. Justice F. Powers, Mt. Vernon, Arkansas, newspaper clipping without additional identifying information

6   Audio introduction to *The World Tomorrow* radio broadcast. See e.g., www.herbert-w-armstrong.org/IndexWTMP3.html

7   Herbert W. Armstrong, *Seven Laws of Success*, 1961, pp. 41–42

8   Herbert W. Armstrong, Bible Correspondence Course, Lesson 1, p. 6

9   Ibid., 5

10 Letter from Herbert W. Armstrong to Radio Church of God Co-Workers (December 18, 1952).

11 Summarized from Herbert W. Armstrong, *Pagan Holidays — Or God's Holy Days*, 1957.

12 Armstrong Co-Workers letter, September 9, 1953

13 Dwight D. Armstrong, Radio Church of God Bible Hymnal (first printing, 1948).

14 Adapted from Armstrong's writings on Christmas.

15 Adapted from Armstrong's writings on Sabbath-keeping.

16 Herbert W. Armstrong, "Is All Animal Flesh Good Food?" 1958.

17 Herbert W. Armstrong, "What Do You Mean the Unpardonable Sin?" 1967.

18 Armstrong Co-Workers letter, March 2, 1967.

19 Walter Martin, *The Kingdom of the Cults*, Updated Anniversary Edition, 1997, pp. 471–494

20 Glenn Frey and Don Henley, "Lyin'Eyes," on The Eagles' *One of These Nights* 1975 album.

21 *Big Sandy and Hawkins Journal*, October 3, 1968.

22 Jerry Fuller, "Young Girl," on *Gary Puckett and the Union Gap's Chronology*, 1968.

23 *Big Sandy and Hawkins Journal*, October 1969.

24 "Jesus Loves Me," Traditional, Words by Anna B. Warner, 1860; Music by William B. Bradley, 1862, © unknown.